# 中国农村留守妇女
# 情况研究

Rural Female Stayers and Their Life
Experience in China

尹诗媛 著

中国出版集团
中译出版社

图书在版编目（CIP）数据

中国农村留守妇女情况研究 = Rural Female Stayers and Their Life Experience in China：英文 / 尹诗嫒著. -- 北京：中译出版社, 2024.10. -- ISBN 978-7-5001-8071-5

I. D669.68

中国国家版本馆CIP数据核字第2024G3T044号

中国农村留守妇女情况研究
ZHONGGUO NONGCUN LIUSHOU FUNÜ QINGKUANG YANJIU

出版发行：中译出版社
地　　址：北京市西城区新街口大街28号普天德胜大厦主楼4层
电　　话：（010）68359827；68359303（发行部）；68359725（编辑部）
传　　真：（010）68357870　　电子邮箱：book@ctph.com.cn
邮　　编：100044
网　　址：http://www.ctph.com.cn

出 版 人：刘永淳
出版统筹：杨光捷
责任编辑：刘瑞莲　王诗同

封面设计：冯　兴
排　　版：中文天地
印　　刷：唐山玺诚印务有限公司
经　　销：新华书店
规　　格：710毫米×1000毫米　1/16
字　　数：324千字
印　　张：19
版　　次：2024年10月第1版
印　　次：2024年10月第1次

ISBN 978-7-5001-8071-5　　　　定价：59.00元

版权所有　侵权必究
中译出版社

# Preface

This study aims to explore the everyday experiences of those defined as rural female stayers. Previous research has shown the impact of patriarchy on the gendered division of labour in Chinese society and the disadvantaged position of women in this social context. Research has tended to focus on urban women's experience, but there is a relative dearth of studies exploring the perspectives of rural female stayers. This study addresses this research gap and is based on qualitative, semi-structured interviews with 25 rural female stayers in Northern China.

Conceptually, the project contributes to discussion of gender and agency in China by emphasising both the difficult structural context that women negotiate and their active role in navigating these contexts and making meaning about their lives. It illustrates firstly that rural female stayers actively use their limited resources in an attempt to show how they take agency in their daily lives to be good mothers, wives and daughters. Secondly, rural female stayers protect their *mianzi* (face) by opposing the prejudices of others in order to construct their lives as positive. Thirdly, rural female stayers disrupt previous descriptions of happiness and counteract others' definitions of their lives by demonstrating their understanding of happiness. Across these three areas, women who have urban experience are more active in demonstrating how they exercise their agency, and it also provides them with new perspectives and increased opportunities.

# List of Contents

Chapter 1  Introduction ................................................................. 1
  1.1  Meeting rural female stayers in my daily life ......................... 1
  1.2  Background: The situation of Chinese rural female stayers ........ 5
  1.3  Dominant representations of rural female stayers .................... 8
  1.4  Arguments of the thesis ..................................................... 11
  1.5  Research questions ............................................................ 12
  1.6  Outline of thesis ................................................................ 14

Chapter 2  Literature review ........................................................ 18
  2.1  Introduction ...................................................................... 18
  2.2  The understanding of gender and agency ............................. 19
    2.2.1  What is gender ........................................................ 19
    2.2.2  What is agency ........................................................ 20
  2.3  Research about gender in China .......................................... 22
    2.3.1  Societal background—Characteristics of Patriarchy ........ 22
    2.3.2  The gender situation in China .................................... 27
        2.3.2.1 'Wai'—Outside the home: Women and working ....... 31
        2.3.2.2 'Nei'—Inside the home: Women and family ........... 35
    2.3.3  Research about gender in rural China ......................... 38
  2.4  Research about the rural female stayers ............................... 43

  2.4.1 The reason and result of migration ................................ 46

  2.4.2 Research about rural female stayers in recent years ............... 48

    2.4.2.1 The research about left-behind women ....................... 49

    2.4.2.2 The research about return women ............................ 52

    2.4.2.3 Summary ................................................ 56

 2.5 Conclusion ........................................................ 58

## Chapter 3 Methodology ..................................................... 59

 3.1 Research design and preparation ........................................ 60

  3.1.1 Choosing a research method ........................................ 60

  3.1.2 Ethical approval .................................................. 63

  3.1.3 Interview questions ............................................... 66

  3.1.4 Interviewee recruitment............................................ 70

 3.2. Data preparation .................................................... 75

  3.2.1 Interviewees ..................................................... 75

  3.2.2 The process of gaining informed consent ............................ 77

  3.2.3 Face-to-face interviews ........................................... 80

 3.3 Fieldwork's challenges and reflections ................................. 84

  3.3.1 How to be professional—the relationship

    between me and interviewees ....................................... 84

  3.3.2 Improving interview skills and dealing with

    unexpected problems .............................................. 87

  3.3.3 The difficulties of transcription and translation .................. 89

  3.3.4 The limitations of sample ......................................... 90

 3.4. Data analysis and themes ............................................. 91

  3.4.1 Data analysis .................................................... 91

  3.4.2 Three themes in the project ....................................... 93

 3.5 Conclusion ......................................................... 94

**Chapter 4 Chinese rural female stayers in the family** .................... 96

    4.1   Rural female stayers as mothers ......................................... 97

        4.1.1   The 'child-centred' model in everyday life ..................... 99

        4.1.2   Being a good mother ............................................... 101

        4.1.3   The sacrifice of being a good mother ........................... 108

    4.2   Rural female stayers as wives ........................................... 114

        4.2.1   The household division of work
between husband and wife ......................................... 115

        4.2.2   The right of decision in rural female stayers' families ............ 119

    4.3   Rural women as daughters in the natal family and
daughters-in-law in the husband's family ............................. 124

        4.3.1   Daughter-in-law—living with the husband's family ............ 124

        4.3.2   Daughter in their own family—the married daughter ............ 129

    4.4   Conclusion ..................................................................... 135

**Chapter 5 Rural female stayers and *Mianzi*—their relationships
with the people around them** ........................................ 139

    5.1   **Mianzi** culture in China ................................................... 143

        5.1.1   **Mianzi** and lian ....................................................... 143

        5.1.2   **Mianzi** and Chinese culture ......................................... 144

    5.2   Return women and the maintenance of **mianzi** ....................... 148

    5.3   Stay-behind women and the maintenance of **mianzi** ................. 158

    5.4   Rural female stayers and social support ................................. 165

        5.4.1   Support from family members and other relationships:
money and people .................................................. 167

        5.4.2   Support from government: funding and policy ................. 171

    5.5   Conclusion ..................................................................... 176

**Chapter 6  A 'happy life' for rural female stayers?** ........................... 179

    6.1. Happiness for rural female stayers

        (both stay-behind women and return women) .......................... 181

        6.1.1  What makes a happy life for rural female stayers? .............. 181

        6.1.2  The specific circumstances of return women ..................... 196

    6.2  Rural female stayers and future happiness ............................ 203

        6.2.1  The gap between childhood dreams and reality ................... 204

        6.2.2  **Bentou**—A practical route to a happy future ..................... 208

            6.2.2.1. Dreaming of the future through one's children ............ 209

            6.2.2.2 Other future plans of rural female stayers ................. 213

    6.3  The impossibility of happiness talk ...................................... 215

    6.4  Conclusion ............................................................................. 220

**Chapter 7  Conclusion** ........................................................................ 224

    7.1  Overview ............................................................................... 224

    7.2  Contribution of the research ................................................ 230

    7.3  Limitations of my research .................................................. 235

    7.4  Research themes with potential for the future ........................ 237

        7.4.1  Future plans and back to the urban area ........................ 237

        7.4.2  Rural female stayers and their mothers-in-law .................. 238

        7.4.3  The impact of the relaxation of the one-child

            policy on daughters ................................................... 239

    7.5  Final reflections .................................................................. 240

**Appendices** ........................................................................................ 242

    Appendix 1  Check list for personal information（个人信息检查表）...... 242

    Appendix 2  Outline of interview questions (English Version) ........... 243

    Appendix 3  Outline of interview questions (Chinese Version ) ......... 249

**Reference** .......................................................................................... 255

# Chapter 1  Introduction

## 1.1  Meeting rural female stayers in my daily life

Rural people used to be alien to me, as I had never had the opportunity to reach out to and pay attention to them. As I have lived in the city since I was a child, and none of my classmates were from the countryside, it was difficult for me to interact deeply with rural people in my daily life. However, things changed when I was an undergraduate and I had the opportunity to meet a large number of women from rural areas. Due to my grandmother's advanced age, my family hired a nanny to take care of her daily life, including doing the cooking and cleaning . In fact, as nannies are very mobile, we have to face the situation of having to find a new nanny every year or even every few months. The nannies who take care of my grandmother are from rural areas. Most of them come from the region around my family's city and they usually go home once or twice a month because it is not convenient for them to return more frequently. Consequently, I came into contact with many rural women before coming to the UK. I often went to my grandmother's house for dinner, as often as four or five times a week. So I got to know my grandmother's nannies very well. In their spare time, we would often chat. The topics we talked about mostly revolved around their children or their families. During our conversations, I often found that they were envious of me, usually because of the excellent living conditions my parents could provide for me and the fact that I was able to live together with them. This puzzled me at the time, for in fact, despite living together with my parents, I didn't find it something to envy, and in my opinion, the situation is normal. At the same time, they viewed my mother as a woman who broke the mould. It struck me. My mother is a professional woman who, in my opinion, balances work and family very well. She has a commendable job and is able to be financially independent. At the same time, she takes good care of her family. However, more than one nanny felt that my mother should actually return to her family and become a housewife, for the reason that her family needed her. In their opinion, my grandmother needed care and my mother should have given up her job to look after her. Although my mother did visit my grandmother several times a week and covered the cost of hiring a nanny, it was not enough in the eyes of my grandmother's nannies. However, they envied my father's successful career and praised him when he helped out around the house, even though they often ignored the fact that my mother was doing more of the housework. Although my grandmother's nannies and I often talked, the reality was that we both struggled to understand each other's positions.

When I returned to China from my postgraduate studies in the UK, I met one of the nannies who had worked at my grandmother's house a few years earlier. She was one of the few nannies who still kept in touch with my grandmother, and as she had worked at my grandmother's house for more than a year, I knew her very well. She came into town to send her daughter off to university and therefore took the opportunity to visit my grandmother. At first, she had returned to the countryside because she had to look after her own children. Then, her children no longer needed her, so our family expressed our wish for her to come back as a nanny. Despite the years that have passed, I still remember her reply at the time: 'I have to go back to take care of my mother-in-law, and my husband is not happy with me working outside the home. As you know, a woman has to listen to her husband.' However, her husband still worked in the urban area. At that moment, I suddenly realised that she rarely seemed to express how she felt about herself, and my lack of understanding was probably because I didn't know her in the slightest. This casual chat that caused my thoughts to collide. It became a seed that was buried in my heart. As time goes by, whenever I read articles or watch TV programs about left-behind women, I often wish I could get to know them better. Left-behind women refer to rural women who live alone or with other family members in their domicile after their husbands have left home, usually for six months or more. The seeds planted a few years ago are gradually sprouting. As I resolved to place left-behind women at the centre of my research, I reflected on that conversation I had several years ago and decided to focus my research on the left-behind women themselves, that is, on what they talk about their lives.

The first problem I encountered when starting my research was how to refer to my participants, as I did not want to categorise them as left-behind women in the conventional way. Left-behind women are those whose husbands leave their family and migrate to the urban area for work for more than six months (Zhang and Zhang, 2006; Ye, 2017), and the essential characteristic of a left-behind woman is living apart from her husband (Chen, 2014). In previous studies of left-behind women in rural China, researchers have often used the term to refer to rural women whose husbands are absent for long periods of time (Biao, 2007; Jacka, 2014; Wu et. al, 2016; Wu and Ye, 2016). In academic and policy discourse, the left-behind are portrayed as a 'vulnerable group' composed of passive dependents, abandoned by modernization, and abandoned by the family (Jacka, 2014). In my study, I will replace 'left' with 'stay'. Stay-behind, which in Chinese is called '*liushou*', is a term meaning to stay behind and watch over. This term is not emotionally loaded and is a

3

neutral term in Chinese. 'Left', however, has a passive connotation. In fact, the decision of whether a rural woman stays in the countryside is not entirely out of her hands. So, to avoid unnecessary misunderstandings, I use the word 'stay'. To be clear, I am not characterising women's lives as positive or negative, I am just talking about them. To sum up, I have introduced the concept of 'stay-behind' to describe the situation of rural women whose husbands are living separately from them in urban areas. Then the other group of my participants are return women. Return women are rural women who have had urban experience and have now returned to live in the rural area and do not have any plans to go back to live in the city for a short period of time (e.g. six months).

Furthermore, for the two distinct groups—stay-behind women and return women—I decided to follow Ye (2017) as well as Murphy's (2021) use of the term 'stayer' in their study, which also serves to emphasise that the urban life of these women's husbands is temporary and that the women are staying in the rural area's home waiting for their families. This term allows me to foreground the agency of these women in migration decisions, as opposed to the passivity implied by 'left-behind'. Through my analysis, I will show that by including both return women and stay-behind women as two groups within this category of rural female stayers, it is possible to reflect on both the similarities and differences between their life experiences. In my research, I use the term 'rural female stayers' to encompass 'stay-behind women' and 'return women'. The sixth census in 2010 shows that there were more than 150 million left-behinds[1] and about 47 million were left-behind women (Wang, 2015). Researchers usually use 'migrant' to define rural *hukou* holders who

---

1  The left-behinds here refer to left-behind women, left-behind children and left-behind elderly.

have moved to the city to work (Xu et al., 2022; Chen and Fan, 2018). The main difference between return and stay-behind women is whether or not they have had urban living experience. The term urban living experience refers only to living in the city and includes both rural women who work in the city and those who do not work in the city.

The second point to note is that given that most studies in the past have used left-behind women when referring to *'liushou'* women, I will follow the convention of using left-behind women for clarity when referring to the existing literatures. At the same time, I will use stay-behind women instead of left-behind women in my study.

In this introductory chapter, I will illustrate the rural female stayers' current situation with key demographic data, including the income of rural women and the number of female migrant workers. Afterwards, I will briefly explain how rural female stayers are portrayed and discussed in the media and how they have been studied in existing research. After this, I intend to explain why rural female stayers are worthy of attention. Then, I will move onto the research arguments and questions of this thesis, in order to show why my research is valuable. Finally, I will present the structure of the thesis.

## 1.2 Background: The situation of Chinese rural female stayers

As the level of urbanisation increases, more and more rural people are choosing to work in cities. There is no exact data for the number of migrant workers. The data of migrant workers mainly come from national census, national agricultural census and individual research, which is organised by the National Bureau of Statistics. The data shows that migrant labour is increasing year by year (Bai and Li, 2008). According to the report of the

Statistical Bulletin on National Economic and Social Development, China's population reached 1390.08 million and the population of migrant workers reached 114.67 million, which showed a rising trend (National Bureau of Statistics, 2018). More recently, the number of migrant workers who migrate to urban areas in China reached 290.77 million (National Bureau of Statistics, 2020). In the Migrant Workers Monitoring Investigation Report in 2016, female migrant workers account for 34.5% of all migrant workers; at the same time, married female migrant workers account for about 77.9% of all female migrant workers. The number of married migrant women has increased by 1.5% since 2015 and it shows a rising trend (National Bureau of Statistics, 2017). The large number of rural workers enter the cities. It brings a large amount of labour to the cities, and at the same time, the migrant workers themselves and their families can increase their income. Migrant workers have more job opportunities and higher incomes in urban areas than in rural areas; therefore urbanisation can boost migrant family's income and reduce the urban-rural income gap (Ding and Sun, 2019). China's rural per capita disposable income also more than doubled between 2011 and 2017 (Han, Wang and Liu, 2019). Urbanisation provides more job opportunities for rural residents, while promoting economic development in rural areas, improving infrastructure in rural areas, and stimulating consumption and economic growth (Zhang and He, 2015). On the other hand, urbanisation has also contributed to the creation of rural female stayers.

In China, rural labour migration is mostly based on individuals rather than families, and this can lead to the issue of stay-behinds (Xu, 2010). It is typically men who migrate to the urban area, while their wives remain in the rural home (Chen, 2014). Most rural migration is temporary in light of the *hukou* system[1] and migrants frequently return to their hometown in rural areas (Ye, 2017).

Based on the age structure of the female population in China's villages and towns, it is estimated that there are about 352 million rural women aged 16–70 with the ability to work, of which about 250 million are still living in rural areas (Wang and et al., 2021). There are significant differences in the income of rural women compared to rural men and urban women (see Table 1). At the same time, in the context of urbanisation, rural women have replaced men as the main labour force in agricultural production activities (Wang and et al., 2021).

**Table 1: Annual revenue for 2017**

| Item | Rural women | Urban women | Rural men |
|---|---|---|---|
| Annual Income (Yuan) | 16419 | 46806 | 33080 |

(Source: National Bureau of Statistics, 2017)

In summary, it is easy to see from the above data about the current situation of rural women. As urbanisation progresses, migration gradually tends to increase. This urban migration has its advantages and disadvantages. On the one hand, it provides more income for rural people; but on the other hand, it also leads to the creation of a population left-behind. In particular, while women who remain in rural areas become the main workforce for their families, rural women continue to face incomes lower than their urban counterparts. In addition, among rural women entering urban areas, there is a rising trend of migrant married women. However, most of these migrations

---

[1] The *hukou* system is a national policy of managing the household population on a household basis. The attributes of household registration are divided into agricultural and non-agricultural *hukou* based on geographical and family member relationships.

are temporary.

## 1.3 Dominant representations of rural female stayers

At the beginning of my research, most of the information about rural female stayers came from China's mass media. Since the economic reforms began in the 1980s, there has been large-scale migration from rural to urban areas. Rural-urban migration has resulted in rural women facing different choices: to stay, to migrate or to return. As Reinharz and Chase suggest (2011, p231), 'Social scientists generally agree that a person's social location shapes his or her identity, experiences, and perspectives'. People's lives are influenced by their social and cultural environment. For rural women, their particular social locations can lead them to face particular life experiences. They can make sense of this situation in particular ways. According to the mass media in China, some news shows that women are in a disadvantageous position in China, and the situation for rural women is more difficult because they face more constraints in more traditional environments (Wan and Wei, 2009; Yu, 2014). Rural female stayers are generally portrayed in the media as being at a disadvantaged position in the family, and their choices are limited to those permitted by their husbands and/or the extended family (Xie and Peng, 2008). This negative representation is illustrated in the headline 'The Lives of Left-Behind Women Are in Crisis Under Heavy Pressure', which focused on mental illness (Ye, 2016).

However, in recent years, some media have begun to report on the situation of rural female stayers who have started their own businesses in rural areas. *China Women's News* (2022), for example, reported that 'Women Hold Up Half the Sky', and 'Left-Behind Women in Poor Mountainous Areas Seize the Opportunity to Use the Ecommerce Platform to Embark on the Road to Prosperity', describing how rural female stayers have taken the initiative to improve their lives with the help of government policies (Wu, 2018). Also, *Sohu News* (2022) reports that rural female stayers are employed by working in the seed production base of a specialist ecological planting cooperative. In addition, in recent years, the government measures have been targeted at rural areas, such as 'The Rural Revitalization Strategy' introduced in 2017, and some policies specifically concentrate on rural female stayers. For example, following the release of the China Women's Development Programme (2011-2020) in 2010, emphasis was placed on implementing and improving policies related to ensuring rural women's rights and interests in land issues. It is true that the media has increasingly focused on rural areas and rural women, following the various government policies to assist rural areas. On the one hand, with the help of government policies, the living conditions of rural women have improved; on the other hand, the stereotype that they are in a backward position compared with other women and need help still exists.

Previous studies of rural areas tended to focus more on three rural issues—rural areas, agriculture and farmers—than on rural areas under the influence of urbanisation and other factors. For example, Zhang and He (2015) argued that urbanisation provides more work opportunities for rural residents, and on the other hand, urbanisation promotes economic development and improves infrastructure in the rural area, which in turn stimulates consumption and economic growth. However, as media and researchers began to focus more and more on women themselves, I suddenly realised that discussions on this topic tended to be about urban women, with academics more concerned with the inequalities that urban women face in the workplace (Bi, 2006; Xu, 2012), working mothers (Cooke, 2005) and women and housework (Yu, 2014).

Rural women, as a part of the women's community, are somewhat neglected in academic discussions of topics about women. Although the situation of left-behind women is often discussed in the news, they have not received much attention in the sociological field in recent years. However, with 30% of China's left-behind population being female (Wang, 2015), it is clear that they need more attention. It was some time before the research focus turned to rural women, but one important early study on left-behind women is Ye and Wu's (2008). Their landmark study provided a new direction of research based on women's perspectives and demonstrated the feasibility of this approach. Then, Jacka (2012) wrote a number of articles focusing on left-behind women in China, for example, to focus on the well-being of older left-behind women. In addition, some Western researchers focus on the migration topic. Among them, Murphy's (2021) research showed that the mobility of those left-behind was influenced by family relationships, gender, and economic factors.

Nevertheless, much past research has tended to focus more on the negative aspects of rural female stayers' lives and has attempted to explain the causes of their difficulties and the subsequent effects on their physical health. Reviewing the literature about rural Chinese women, most research concentrates on stay-behind women's difficulties in daily life and mental health issues. For example, research by Zhang et al. (2018) 'Investigation on Sleep Quality of Rural Left-Behind Women and Study on the Correlations Between Sleep Quality and Depression', by Luo et al. (2017) 'Love or Bread? What Determines Subjective Wellbeing Among Left-Behind Women in Rural China?' by Jacka (2012) 'Migration, Householding and the Well-being of Left-behind Women in Rural Ningxia'. Fewer studies have focused on the daily lives of left-behind women and how they use their agency to deal with their daily experiences. My research seeks to move beyond the negative portrayals of rural female stayers in previous studies by showing the positive aspects of rural female stayers' daily lives. I draw on theories of agency to emphasise the possibilities for rural female stayers to make meaning of their own lives (see section 2.2.2. in the literature review chapter for a detailed discussion of my theorisation of agency in this context). Also, as society develops and changes, the environment and living conditions in rural areas cannot remain unchanged; so the current study takes this as a starting point to try to provide up-to-date first-hand information on the living conditions of rural female stayers today. At the same time, it shows the current perspectives of rural female stayers themselves.

## 1.4 Arguments of the thesis

Centring on a concern with gender and agency, this thesis seeks to challenge narrow perceptions about rural female stayers. It argues that rural female stayers often focus their attention on the people around them, like their family. Rural female stayers attempt to demonstrate their understanding of what constitutes a 'good' woman by putting themselves last. To a certain extent, gender shapes the division of household responsibilities in China, and rural female stayers have a variety of roles in everyday life, such as mother, wife and daughter (in law) within the family. However, due to the patriarchal and gendered division of labour, women are expected to take on most of the domestic tasks within the family and are given less recognition. Rural female stayers are aware that they have less space than men to exert their agency in their daily lives. This thesis, nevertheless, argues that rural female stayers' descriptions of their daily lives show us how they exert their agency within the family and in their interactions with others in the neighbourhood. For example, they try to emphasise the efforts and choices they make to be good mothers, yet this may lead them to put their own needs last when resources are scarce, even though they do not feel this is a loss for them. On the other hand, rural female stayers try to protect their own *mianzi* (face) against the prejudices of others, and in doing so, they gain more decision-making power and a higher level of agency, demonstrating their positive attitude towards life. Finally, rural female stayers are active participants in navigating their agency, and they try to express how their lives link with happiness. Their understanding of happiness will demonstrate the rules of being a 'good woman' and may also illuminate the ways in which these rules can be broken. At the same time, their descriptions of a happy life may break down previous stereotypes of them and show them in a different light.

## 1.5   Research questions

There is currently a lack of research that focuses on the daily lives of rural female stayers from their perspective, and most existing studies focus on the negative aspects of their lives and explain the difficulties they encounter. The overall aim of this study is to address these gaps by attempting to show the daily experiences of rural female stayers. It is important to focus on how rural female stayers position themselves as good/moral people because it helps us to understand how they exercise their agency and make sense of their own lives. It is also valuable to focus on their happiness because it helps to counteract other people's definitions of their lives, as social stereotypes make it difficult to associate happiness with rural female stayers. In order to better understand how rural female stayers make sense of their everyday lives, this study sets out research questions from three perspectives: firstly, their lives within the family (their relationship with family members); secondly, the way they get along with the people around them (their relationships with those out

# Chapter 1   Introduction

of home); and thirdly, how they understand happiness and how they describe it. In this study, I explore the following questions:

*1. What are rural female stayers' experiences of daily life?*

The aim of this study is first to understand the daily lives of rural female stayers. It investigates what life is like for rural female stayers and how their everyday experiences affect them. The study of the daily lives of rural female stayers helps us to understand the division of family responsibilities among rural female stayers, and how they talk about their family roles and evaluate themselves. This in turn helps to extend the study of gender in rural China and the gender division of labour in everyday family life in rural China.

*2. How do rural female stayers position themselves as good/moral women in relation to their family and community?*

As well as showing the daily life of rural female stayers, it is also important to see how they get along with people around them. This research question seeks to understand how the women are influenced by people around them and the forms of agency open to rural female stayers in daily life. I therefore propose an analysis of their relationships with those around them in terms of how they talk about and defend their *mianzi*. The study of *mianzi* helps to understand how rural female stayers exercise their agency and through protecting their *mianzi* counteract the bias of others. This extends the research question of understanding how women in rural China demonstrate their awareness of *mianzi* through their relationships with those around them and how they protect their own *mianzi*.

*3. How do rural female stayers understand 'happiness'/a good life, and do they see their lives in these terms?*

Thirdly, many previous studies' descriptions of rural female stayers have tended to emphasise the difficulties and hardships in their lives, but I will explore what a happy life is for the rural female stayers, and how they relate their lives to happiness. This study will focus on the perspectives from which rural female stayers view their lives and how this understanding affects their description of happiness. It is important to focus on rural female stayers' understanding of happiness because it counteracts some of the ways in which others define their lives and it also expresses how they struggle with the difficulties they face.

To answer these three questions, I conducted semi-structured interviews with 25 participants. In the face-to-face interviews with rural female stayers, my participants presented their daily lives and the topics they care about in their own words. The resulting themes are those that concern them and there are different expressions of the same themes by the participants, thus highlighting the complexity of their life experiences.

## 1.6 Outline of thesis

This chapter gives a brief overview of the structure of the whole thesis and the direction of the research. I have already provided an overview of the situation of rural women in China, showing the context and social environment in which rural female stayers live. I have also outlined the scope of the thesis by asking three research questions about rural female stayers, which I will use to present, discuss and analyse the daily experiences of rural female stayers and their living conditions in the community, as well as their descriptions of happiness. I have introduced the thesis's focus on gender and agency, and have begun to reveal how this study bridges the gaps in existing research. The outline for the remaining chapters is as follows.

Chapter 2 focuses on reviewing the existing research through the following areas. Firstly, I introduce the context of patriarchy in China and show the existing research on gender, through which I find that gender factors influence the division of labour between the different genders and their position within the family. Secondly, I critique previous research on rural Chinese stayers by comparing the different life experiences of stay-behind women and return women. The review focuses on the existing literature that has helped me establish my own research knowledge about gender, China's rural female stayers, and the exploration of their agency. I aim to explain how my research is situated in relation to debates about gender, structure and agency. Through the literature review, I identified the gaps in the research. Firstly, there is a paucity of relevant research in recent years on rural women's understanding of their own lives; secondly, there is a lack of relevant research on the impact of urban life experiences on rural women. My research explain in further depth how this study is addressing critical gaps in knowledge within the fields.

Chapter 3 deals with the research methodology. This chapter considers how I designed my research and prepared the fieldwork, how I recruited participants and conducted the survey, and how I collated the data. I also present reflections on this process to explain how I chose my research methods and perceived my position as an interviewer. In this chapter, I show how the interplay between method and data in this phase of my fieldwork became a solid foundation for understanding how rural female stayers perceive their life experience.

This thesis has three data analysis chapters. Chapter 4 focuses on the experiences of rural female stayers in the 'nei', in other words, their daily lives within the family. It documents the daily lives of rural female stayers and their roles in the family. First, how rural female stayers approach their

15

lives as mothers; second, how they make choices as wives; and finally, how they deal with the choices they face as daughters or daughters-in-law. I will discuss how rural female stayers in everyday life and in the home are affected by their different roles, as well as validate, through discussion, whether gender determines the division of responsibilities of women in the home. I will examine how rural female stayers perceive and respond to gender inequality, as well as consider how an understanding of gender shapes their roles.

Chapter 5 focuses on the interactions of rural female stayers in the 'wai', in other words, the interactions with those around them or within their communities, with the discussion focusing on the issue of *mianzi*. *Mianzi* has been called face in many existing studies. As *mianzi* culture permeates all aspects of everyday life, it is important to discuss the issue of *mianzi* in order to better show how rural female stayers live with people around them. This chapter will demonstrate how rural female stayers understand *mianzi* and explore how this understanding leads rural female stayers to exert their agency. In the meantime, the migration experience becomes a point of difference to focus on when discussing the subject of stay-behind and return women maintaining *mianzi*.

Chapter 6 explores the relationship between rural female stayers and happiness, particularly, their understanding of a 'happy life'. When we shift the perspective of studies of rural female stayers from their suffering to their positive emotions, it becomes possible to consider happiness as a dimension of their lived experience. In this chapter, I will look at how they describe happiness in the present, in the future and as children, and how they counteract stereotypes by showing their happiness. In this chapter, I introduce the concept of *bentou*. The possibilities of agency to shape the future of life will be shown through the analysis of it. I also explore how their accounts of happiness demonstrate the confined and normative dimensions of happiness in rural female stayers' lives.

Chapter 7 is the final chapter—the conclusion. In this chapter, I summarise my findings and discuss the limitations of the study. My thesis has provided some substantial insights and reflections on the experiences of rural female stayers, but I also acknowledge that as a qualitative study, this is inevitably a partial account. I acknowledge the limitations of my data and as such, I am aware that this study cannot provide a full picture of rural female stayers' life experience. Finally, I have suggested some possible directions for future research based on my limitations.

# Chapter 2    Literature review

## 2.1    Introduction

In this chapter, I present previous research to establish an academic context in preparation for my own research. This chapter is divided into three main themes, which are identified by three key fields: firstly the conceptualizations of gender; secondly gender in China; thirdly, rural female stayers. Through the exploration of these key themes, I hope to form an effective framework through which I can identify the path I am taking in my approach to my research. I also aim to demonstrate how my research builds on and develops existing empirical literature on gender and rural China. In my selection of literature, I have placed China at the centre, and my focus is on sociology in China.

At the beginning of this chapter, I will review the sociological approaches to conceptualising gender. Then, I will present the current state of research on gender in China, and in this section, I will address an important social context, which is the issue of patriarchy as part of the Chinese societal background. After this, I analyse the existing research about gender issues on '*nei*' (women's life inside the home) and '*wai*' (women's life outside the home), and also the main gender issues in rural areas. Finally, I will review the relevant research on Chinese rural female stayers.

## 2.2 The understanding of gender and agency

### 2.2.1 What is gender

With the promotion of the second-wave feminist movement, and a concern with the social and cultural expressions and suppressions of 'appropriate' gendered conduct, distinctions between the concepts of gender and sex began to be made. In general, sex refers to the physiological characteristics of male and female bodies, while gender tends to refer to social and cultural characteristics (Oakley, 1972). This important decoupling of gender from biology was based on arguments made in Beauvoir's *The Second Sex*, which laid the foundations for a feminist gender analysis that emphasized the social characteristics of women (Beauvoir, 1949, cited in Jackson and Scott, 2002).

Further, if gender is treated as a product of sociality, then the social relations between men and women also become the result of social arrangements (Jackson and Scott, 2002). Gender as a concept of sociality is concerned with masculinity and femininity in the social sphere, rather than in the natural one (Jackson and Scott, 2002). Therefore, some feminists argue that social gender means that women's status is not determined by nature, biological characteristics or natural gender but rather is a socio-political construct (Carole, 1988, cited by Sun, 2020). Through their understanding of gender identity, individuals can make sense of the social world and make decisions based on it. Gender is not just a set of traditional norms that constrain women's behaviour, but also empowers women to legally manage, obtain assets and opportunities (Hopkins, 2007). At the same time, it represents a set of informal 'rules' that stipulate expectations for the appropriate behaviour of men and women, as well as an explanation of male or female behaviour (Hopkins, 2007).

In elaborating how gender works socially, a key strand of theory has emphasised its ongoing accomplishment as a practical activity in social life (West and Zimmerman, 1987). According to West and Zimmerman (1987), gender is not a just personal attribute but also a social practice; that people 'do' gender rather than 'have' gender. This concept of 'doing gender' emphasises the ways people combine their daily behaviour and social interaction with gender symbolic behaviour (West and Zimmerman, 1987). West and Zimmerman argued that doing gender involves both social norms and the more complex process of 'situated conduct' in interaction (1987, p126). According to West and Zimmerman's understanding of gender, it is important to note that doing gender requires gender criteria and that the definition of nature is inseparable from the definition of society; in addition, doing gender requires the interaction of all participants in a particular social context, which cannot be done by a single individual (1987). In West and Zimmerman's opinion, gender relies on interactions in everyday social life, so this process of 'doing' may need further elaboration through an analysis of agency. The 'do' in doing gender refers to action and it has a strong practical orientation (Wang, 2020). Hence, the notion of 'doing gender' is about showing that people are involved in making it, in relation to the structural and social contexts which shape how it can be done. The idea that we 'do' gender is explicitly related to understandings of agency (Grunow, 2019) which I explore further in the following sections.

## 2.2.2 What is agency

The concept of 'agency' is rooted in a tradition that focuses on individual freedom, and places the individual at the centre of social action (Hitlin and Elder, 2007). In other words, agency arises from the interaction of individuals in society. Agency means the ability of an individual to take action (McNay,

2004), and it is described as the basic relative autonomy of a person within a given institutional context (Hitlin and Elder, 2007, cited by Grunow, 2019). Ortner (2001) distinguishes between two categories of 'agency', one closely related to power, which includes both 'domination' and 'resistance'; the other emphasizes intention, which refers to people's life plans and their ability to plan and realise them (Man, 2016).

Like gender, the scope of agentic goals and aspirations is also culturally and socially framed, and 'agency' is often accommodated and enacted within a specific social culture (Man, 2016). In other words, as Ortner notes, the capacity for agency is, to a large extent, unable to escape the basic framework of socio-cultural structures, and hence, 'it is not entirely free agency' (Ortner, 2001). As Karl Marx (1852) argued, people make their own history by making choices in the context of direct encounters, given and passed on from the past, rather than in circumstances chosen by humans themselves (Evans and Strauss, 2010). Feminists such as Whitehead (1979) agree that individuals make choices and have agency within the constraints imposed by their individual circumstances, but they also note the constraints imposed by the structural distribution of rules, norms, resources and identities between different groups; divisions by gender, class, race, caste, etc.; and the resulting inequalities of power and privilege (Folbre, 1994, cited by Kabeer, 2016). Thus, there is a complex interplay between individual decision-making and larger structural constraints in shaping individual agency.

This complicated notion of agency is a helpful lens for us to understand the daily lives of women. For example, Grunow (2019) argues that this nuanced concept of agency may be useful in understanding the unequal burden of domestic work between men and women and the internal and external constraints they face. That is, men may have more agency to resist domestic work due to societal norms that regard housework as women's work. Similarly, women may have less agency to refuse domestic work because they face and internalise gender norms that places value on their performance of household tasks. The sociological study of personal choice and agency implies that individuals have the ability to make decisions about all major aspects of their lives. However, they have to manage social, economic and family circumstances (Evans and Strauss, 2010). In the context of my study, analysis of the daily lives of rural female stayers therefore needs to focus not only on their own accounts of their lives and how they make choices, but also on their social and cultural position with society. Given that individuals enact agency in the context of their social environment and culture, understanding the Chinese social context is integral to the present study. Accordingly, in the following section, I will elaborate on existing research on gender in the Chinese context.

## 2.3 Research about gender in China

### 2.3.1 Societal background—characteristics of patriarchy

When we look at gender, the background to the origins of the differences between men's and women's lives is something we must try to understand. In this case, a key aspect of the cultural context is Confucianism. Confucianism is the core of traditional Chinese culture and has dominated the entire system of Chinese society throughout its historical evolution. It was first developed in the pre-Qin peroid, established during the Han dynasty, and then further rationalised during the Song and Ming dynasties (Li and Zhang, 2008). Confucianism has had a profound influence on the socialisation of gender equality (Li and Zhang, 2008). Confucian culture has been a historical and enduring presence. Its influence changes flexibly with the times, remaining

Chapter 2 Literature review

important today. As Jackson, Ho and Na (2013) pointed out, even when cultural precepts and practices have a very long documented history, they may be reinvented and their current form maybe the product of successive revivals and revisions, as is the case with Confucianism in East Asia (Jackson, Ho and Na, 2013, p669).

As such, as well as influencing changes in gender relations and women's roles in contemporary China, this influence is also changing in tandem with the ongoing evolution of society (Li and Zhang, 2008). All the negative elements for women of the family ethic advocated by Confucianism are summed up in the concept of feudal patriarchy. Confucianism, for example, 'takes focusing on internal family matters, like housework'[1] as a role for women and considers 'assist[ing] the husband and educate[ing] the children'[2] to be the vocation of women. This is further explained by the Confucian doctrine that the functions and roles of women as wives and mothers, are measured and reflected by the social status and value of men—their husbands and sons (Li and Zhang, 2008).

Patriarchal cultures are typically characterised by male-centrism. Patriarchy creates a male-centred worldview by devaluing the experience and status of women (Ye, 2009). It treats men as models and places women on the margins of social regulation (Gao and Ye, 2009). As the concept of patriarchy enters Chinese scholarship, how it is translated into Chinese actually reflects the scholarly understanding of the concept. There are several main understandings of patriarchy (Zhou, 1998; Shen, 2019). I agree with Zhou's (1998) expression of patriarchy, which is further interpreted to mean that the power of the father

---

1  In Chinese, *Zhu nei*.
2  In Chinese, *Xiang fu jiao zi*, from the Analects of Confucius.

and the husband make up the concept of patriarchy, although they are both similar and different in real life. Although patriarchy places more emphasis on the relationship between the sexes, in the Chinese context it also has a specificity which manifests itself in terms of age or generation (Shen, 2019). This is further explained by the fact that the subordination of married women to their husbands is accompanied by the need to defer to the older men in the family, and this is actually accompanied by their need to defer to the older women. The elders, including the in-laws, are seen as one, the elder women are seen as subordinate to their husbands but also have some of their husbands' rights. As Jaschok and Miers (1994) characterise it in relation to Chinese patriarchy, the woman often becomes the subject of oppression of the other woman. In patriarchal societies, where the core of society is formed by men, women are merely the nurturers of children. An order of gender relations that protects the universal primacy of men is formed under this ideology (Tong, 2011).

One of the most obvious effects of patriarchy is gender preference. Gender preferences are influenced by family practices, i.e. patriarchal authority, and the existence of these practices determines the structure of a patriarchal family system composed of certain social, political, economic and cultural factors (Li, 2000, as cited in Ye, 2002). The family system is an intermediate variable that directly determines the gender preferences of reproductive subjects, emphasising the gender utility of sons over daughters in a patriarchal political model. It ultimately constructs gender orientations that are skewed towards men (Ye, 2002). Although some women have achieved success in Chinese society and gained prestige and recognition, they still need to transition into a more traditional role when they return to their families (Jin, 2000). As Kan and He (2018) found in their study, women still perform most of the household chores, However, the division of labour in the household depends on factors such as the gender ideology of the area. One of the institutional arrangements of family patriarchy is that sons inherit property, family names and prestige, which are passed on from father to son and from son to grandson, whereas daughters cannot inherit these. At the same time, the male inheritance system transcends class and hierarchy. In other words, women must follow the institutional arrangement of male inheritance regardless of their status (Li, 2012). This gender preference has evolved somewhat over time and as society has changed. Indeed, as Chen's study (2017) shows, in urban areas, more and more families are beginning to prefer daughters. However, in rural areas the male gender preference has not changed significantly. According to Yin et al. (2018), rural households still prefer to have at least one son. The mother will gain a higher level of decision-making power if she had a son.

'The patriarchal family is undoubtedly rooted in tradition. As Max Weber said, the legitimacy of patriarchal authority comes from tradition' (Jin, 2011, p27). At the same time, the patriarchal family could be perpetuated and reconstructed because, on the one hand, it did not impose the cost of reproducing the population on society and on the other hand, it raised the free labour needed for industrial society (Jin, 2011). The impact was accompanied by the continuation and reconstruction of the patriarchal family in terms of relational patterns and ideologies (Jin, 2011).

It is useful to use the concept of patriarchy to analyse the status of women and how male heads of household control resources and construct hierarchies in rural Chinese society (Jin, 2000, as cited by Du, 2001). Within the framework of patriarchy, the marriage of a man and a woman has a completely different meaning. Men do not have to leave their homes, family members or the villages where they grew up, and they only need to take care of their parents, whereas women have to enter the man's home and village when they are married and take care of their husband's parents (Li, 2012). Further explaining Li's point, the reason a family needs to have at least one son is that the son will be responsible for the care of the parents in their old age. Because the predominant marital residence pattern in rural areas today is that daughters live in the same village as their husbands' families after marriage, and many even live with their husbands' parents. Inevitably, daughters will focus their attention on their husband's family, and this leads to the origin family's son becoming the main carer of his parents. Here, I find I disagree with Li (2012) that 'raising a son for old age' is a realistic choice in the absence of a change in the pattern of marriage between men and women. The fact that married daughters are beginning to care for their own parents is the best rebuttal to this view (Weng and Li, 2019).

There are many studies (Jin, 2011; Liu, 2017; Jin, 2010) on the disintegration of patriarchy. Some scholars (Yang, 2016; Liu, 2017) argue that the modernization process will inevitably weaken or even break up the patriarchal family in China, and Jin (2011) states that the tendency for rural families to gradually follow the urban family model will eventually lead to the destruction of the patriarchal system. I do agree with these views, and it is important to recognise that patriarchy is not set in stone. At the same time, a focus on patriarchy will help to explore the interaction between rural female stayers and families. This will form an important part of the focus of my thesis on the relationship between married rural women and their parents in their families of origin. And this thesis will explore the interaction between married daughters and their families of origin through an analysis.

## 2.3.2 The gender situation in China

In the context of Chinese society, as a matter of fact, changes in the social context and policies from 1949 onwards have had a great impact on women. In Mao's era, the status of Chinese women greatly improved (Su, 2004). Women's full participation in the workforce helped to reduce discrimination against women. It was guided by the Marxist idea that women's emancipation depends on their participation in society (Croll, 1983). During the 1950s, the essentialist fusion of sexuality and gender remained quite influential, with the assumption that female gender identity was inextricably linked to female reproductive function (Evans, 1995), and the female subject was defined through the issue of reproduction (Evans, 2008). Although the law supports equality between men and women, the reality is that 'scientific' differences between men and women result in women being seen as vulnerable and subordinate in marriage (Evans, 2008). In addition, the emancipation of women is expressed in their equal access to the public sphere of production and labour (Evans, 2008). Women were guided by government policy to move out of the home and into various jobs, although gender differences were still prevalent, and women earned less than men (Su, 2004). According to international standards, the gender wage gap in China before the economic reforms was very small, which was caused by the government's equal pay policy for equal work. Socialist standards for dual-income families, full employment, and equal wages have led to very small income gender differences between urban households (Ding, Xiao, and Li, 2009; Ma, Liu and Song, 2019).

Since the 1980s, government policies such as macroeconomic adjustment, reforms and public sector downsizing have not appeared to have affected gender equality (Su, 2004). However, market reform measures have inadvertently had a negative impact on a equitable gender division of labour in a socialist system. Providing childcare support made it more expensive for employers to hire female workers. In that case, female workers were disadvantaged in a market economy. State-owned enterprises abiding by market discipline, abolished the state's protection of women workers. The reformatian of the property rights system and labour market increased the number of laid-off workers and reduced women's wages to transfer some of the childbearing expenses incurred by the state and workplaces to women, and childcare became a woman's duty (Ding, Xiao, and Li, 2009). The reform strategies pursued by Chinese cities in the late 1990s have similarities with the structural adjustment policies of the 1980s, and neither recognized the role of women in social reproduction.[1] Before the economic reforms, under the policy of 'equal pay for equal work' (*tong gong tong chou*), women and men enjoyed the same remuneration. After the reforms, under the market economy, the government could not force companies to implement the previous policies, so women were gradually placed at a disadvantage (Wu, 2019a). So, it is not surprising that women are more likely to be laid off than men and it is more difficult for them to find reemployment in the private sector (Ding, Xiao, and Li, 2009). In the late 1990s, the government implemented several reforms aimed at increasing women's social labour participation, for example, the promulgation of the 'Programme for the Development of Chinese Women (2021–2030)' and implementation of the 'Law of the People's Republic of China on the Protection of Rights and Interests of Women'. The current employment rate for women is slightly above 70%, but this is still one of the highest in the world (Ye and Zhao, 2018).

China's transition to a market economy has led to changes in family norms

---

1 Social reproduction includes two aspects, material data reproduction and population reproduction (Wu, Yang and Wang, 1980).

and gender relations. The country's efforts to create gender equality in the workplace have shrunk, and restored traditional normative gender roles and the division of labour within the family. The restoration of normative gender roles has, in some ways, been linked to elaborated interests in gender difference and gender identities in the transition to post-socialism (Rofel, 1999). A lot of research on the division of labour in Chinese society shows that women take more responsibility for care (Yu and Chau, 1997; Chen, 2018a; Tong, Shu and Piotrowski, 2019). From this we can expect that in China, like other countries, women's labour market activities will be more affected by family roles (Zhong and Pan, 2012). Research on gender in China has gradually increased in recent years, and the research on gender has gradually deepened, such as the division of labour, equality and other issues (Sun, 2020). The research on gender in China in sociology, mainly from the perspective of women, analyses the conflicts between the modern social gender division of labour and the attitudes to female gender roles at the social level and stress (Ji et al., 2017; Wang, Ma and Guo, 2020). Furthermore, under the influence of Confucian culture, femininity is closely related to people's stereotype of weak, submissive and inferior women (Ghate, 2018, as cited by Shi and Zheng, 2020). Living in an expanded family is a reflection of the patriarchal family system which controls women. The role of the Chinese woman is defined by her absolute obedience to and respect of her husband's family authority in the marriage, as well as her affirmation and maintenance of family authority (Leung, 2003). Therefore, the traditional Confucian gender concepts of 'good wife and loving mother' and 'promoting men and degrading women' are the basic principles for evaluating a woman's behaviour and desires, and her status relative to men. Confucianism defines women as social subjects in terms of their relationship with men (mothers, sisters, wives), so women are expected to play secondary roles in the family and community

(Leung, 2003) and women's subordination also limits their self-determination rights (Li, 2005). Although women's rights are protected, demographic data suggests that strong cultural values still privilege men (Rosenberg, 2009, as cited by Navaaro, 2012). Moreover, as women have become more educated and as society has developed and people's mindsets changed, the need for women's own initiative is becoming more important, particularly in the urban context. Urban women are beginning to have more of a choice in how and what they do. They are breaking away from patriarchal 'control' to a certain extent, and the new image of women as independent and active is being established and widely accepted (Gu, 2020). They rely on notions of individualism that contradict Confucian norms and ideals about women. Women living in cities have a higher level of education than rural women (Wu, 2021) and as discussed in Chen's study (2015), the level of education influences Chinese people's identification with individualism to a certain extent. To sum up, as urban women have more employment opportunities, it is easier for them to establish a new image of themselves. It should be noted, however, that although educated urban women do have a degree of freedom compared to rural women, they are not completely free from patriarchal norms, for example, the leftover women[1] (Fincher, 2016).

We have considered the changes to patriarchy but this has primarily been done with reference to urban women, however when the subject of study becomes rural women, the situation is different. The majority of urban Chinese women combine family with work, a result of the mingling of a patriarchal culture and the idea of gender equality guided by various reform policies. As explained above, patriarchy has evolved with the times and there is no longer

---

1  Leftover women in Chinese is called "sheng nv", which means a woman who is past what society considers to be marriageable age but is still unmarried.

a disincentive for women to work outside the home in China. However, when the subject becomes rural women, the situation of women working outside the home is different because of the social conditions in the countryside. Rural areas are more conservative in habits and therefore expectations of women there are more concentrated within the family. As a result, rural women tend to operate as family-centred women, whose energy is mainly concentrated within the family.

Much existing research regarding Chinese women's lives has been conducted in terms of one or several gendered roles, such as mother or wife. Most research has focused on the division of labour between men and women due to gender and on differences in family and social roles. Due to gender, women in 'wai and nei' are in completely different situations, but of course these two situations are also mutually influential. The term 'nei' refers to women's lives within the family, while the corresponding term 'wai' represents the situation of women in society outside the home. For greater clarity, I will discuss the two situations—women in society and women in the family—separately. After that, I would like to consider the research about rural women and gender.

### 2.3.2.1 'Wai'—Outside the home: Women and working

Although the life of the 'wai' is not normally associated with rural women, research on this does at least provide us with a complete picture of women's lives in the urban area. The life of the 'wai' is more associated with urban women, but the study of these social contexts provides a rich source of information about the lives of migrant women in the city. At the same time, the decisions and perceptions of rural women in their daily lives are also influenced to some extent by the lives of urban women, so it is valuable to understand the lives of the 'wai'.

Work and family are two important areas that shape a woman's gender, and in China, women's roles are greatly influenced by patriarchy in both the job market and the family (Fang and Walker, 2015). This family-employment relationship emphasises women's socioeconomic security and social identity (Fang and Walker, 2015). Kmec (2005) argues that women's career paths are determined by organisational practices rather than women's own preferences (Luo and Chui, 2019).

Many studies have focused on the different circumstances faced by men and women at work due to gender differences and the reasons that lead to women being at a disadvantage. A study of gender differences in the contemporary China labour market shows that households have different effects on different genders in terms of changing jobs. For example, when women change their jobs, they are more driven by family reasons, while men's changes are more caused by career pursuits (Cao and Hu, 2007). Only women are negatively affected by marriage and family in terms of income and employment status (Zhang, Hannum and Wang, 2008). The existence of young children only negatively affects women's income, but does not affect men's income, because women spend more time on childcare, and this is likely to hinder their promotion (Shu, Zhu, and Zhang, 2007; Chen, 2018b). Among laid-off workers, marriage reduces women's possibility of re-employment, but men do not face this issue (Du and Dong, 2009, as cited by Zhang and Pan, 2012). And furthermore, the role of women as wives, mothers and caregivers in the family can lead to work-family conflicts and limit their job choices. Many women choose work that is suitable for the family in order to maintain work and family balance. It is usually a typical job of devaluation and low wages, and has limitations in wages and career development (Budig and England, 2001). Furthermore, marketisation has led to the privatisation of the economy. Due to the lack of effective labour market discrimination and regulation policies, women are subject to various forms of discrimination in the labour market, from job hunting, salary increasing to promotion. This discrimination is underpinned by employer stereotypes that women's time and energy costs in pregnancy, childbirth and childcare are high, and that this can distract them from work and make them less efficient (Xio, Zhang and Li, 2017). In addition, women face discrimination from employers because they are expected to put more emphasis on their family responsibilities and this leads to stereotyping that women work less productively than men (Zhang and Pan, 2012).

These previous studies have demonstrated that women are in fact treated unequally in the life of the 'wai' because of society's inherent expectations of women. They are often restricted to a position where they need to be reactive to family needs when making decisions. However, I would like to point out that more and more research is actually starting to focus on urban women who do not exactly meet the social requirements or customary definitions of society (Li and Zhang; Sun and Li, 2017). For example, some of the more distinctive images of contemporary women are also hotly discussed by researchers, such as the so-called 'strong woman' or the female doctor. In Chinese society, 'strong' women[1] are respected for their ability and success in the workplace, but these women are not acceptable to all. People sometimes think that work success in work is in conflict with achieving gendered social norms and women's values (Navaaro, 2012). The emergence of these 'new' women, who are successful in the world of work, has gone some way to

---

1 'Strong' women are able to stand alone in work and life. They usually have advanced academic qualifications, high income, and have achieved a certain amount of success in their careers.

breaking the stereotype that all women face difficulties in their 'wai' lives, despite the fact that society views them in a more negative light. They try to break the stereotypes that society assigns to women by expanding ways of 'doing' gender.

There is also a tendency for some studies to explore women's perceived oppression that arises from having different working conditions than men because of their gender. Researchers who study gender perception in China have found that women understand and articulate the nature of gender discrimination in society and the workplace. According to research from Gaskell et al. (2004), women attribute the causes of differences to social structures: family responsibilities and social ideologies. Other studies, however, suggest that some women try to rationalise these experiences and believe that it is due to what they see as the inherent weaknesses of their own gender, which means they ascribe this difference to biology (Jin, 2000; Navaaro, 2012).

To sum up, it is easy to find studies that have focused on urban women. It is important to note that rural women are often overlooked when talking about the external life of women and there is limited research on rural women in the 'wai' studies. This is due to multiple factors; on the one hand, the social environment in rural areas lacks the opportunity to work outside the home because of the custom gender division (Ye, 2018). On the other hand, for the rural migrant women who work in the cities, the focus of their lives is still seen as internal to the family and working is only recognized as a transient option (Tong, Shu, and Piotrowski, 2019). For this reason, I have separated out women with urban experiences for discussion, but I have not placed too much emphasis on their lives in the 'wai'. Rural women's lives are mainly focused on the 'nei' part of their lives and, as I mentioned earlier, the lack of job opportunities makes it difficult for rural women to associate their lives with the 'wai'.

### 2.3.2.2 'Nei'—Inside the home: Women and family

Women's lives in the family have been the focus of academic attention from a gender perspective. Previous studies have usually discussed urban women in terms of their roles in the family.

First, women play a role as a wife in the family. The Maoist reform did not end the traditional division of labour and the public's impression of the roles and responsibilities of men and women in the family. In Chinese families, the role of husband as a breadwinner and wife as a housewife remained stable (Wang, 2006), even though women already had equal access to work. Bruin and Liu (2020) used the 24-hour time module data from the China Family Panel Studies, and they point out that this pattern in the division of labour between men and women seems to have changed over time, as working wives have also been able to bring in financial income to the household and their husbands have gradually taken on more of the household chores. However, as expressed in Zhang's research (2020), despite the fact that women earn money to contribute to the household income, they are still primarily responsible for the work within the household. Additionally, Ye and Zhao's (2018) study showed that wives are still guided by their husbands, their labour market behaviour is influenced by their husband's gender role, and all generations have this feature. For the wife, in Chinese culture, it is their job to help the husband take care of the family, educate and discipline the children (Ye and Zhao, 2018). In the historical Chinese gender order that 'man is responsible for the outside, woman is responsible for the inside' (*nan zhu wai, nv zhu nei*), both urban and rural women are required to be good wives and good mothers. In the context of Confucian culture, women must 'obey their father, husband and son'. In conventional marriages, men contribute their income in exchange for women's domestic work (Becker, 1981, as cited by Zhang and Tsang, 2012). This is a social custom, based on the longstanding division of labour between men and women. As men are more likely to have a better position in the labour market, they can make their maximum contribution to the family through their economic income; whereas women's contribution is reflected through their housework and childcare, which in turn is a reflection of the gender specialisation model (Zhang and Tsang, 2012). The research of Zhang and Tsang (2012) also highlights that both spouses in this model have a high rating of marital happiness. Both men and women are satisfied with what society requires of them, and both acquiesce to what society requires as 'reasonable'. The status of a woman is decided by the gender order (Fang and Walker, 2015).

These previous studies on the division of labour between men and women in the family have concentrated on women being more often asked to take on the domestic tasks of the family, and less on women's perspectives on this division of labour within the family. At the same time, with the improvement of living standards and the rise of individualism, more and more people regard a better family life as a right. Zuo and Bian's (2001) research showed a new gender division emerging in families whereby men and women share the housework, and couples no longer pursue an inherent order in household responsibilities, but choose according to the actual situation. Therefore, we need to recognize that the days of men's complete indifference to housework are over, although as Fang and Walker's (2015) research shows, women are still the main bearers of housework, as many families are still affected by the traditional gender order. According to Wang and Zhang's (2007) research, men do some of the housework, but they are mostly involved in less time-consuming and occasional tasks, such as buying groceries and other temporary tasks. And society's demands for women to take more care of their families remain unchanged (Wang and Zhang, 2007).

A second strand of research focuses on women as mothers in the family. Chen's (2018b) research found that although women's work identities are increasingly stable, expectations about women's role as mothers are relatively unchanged. In addition to this, the emergence of the concept of the "all-round mother" has placed new demands on working women, who are being asked to combine childcare with work (Yang, 2018). Conversely, Zhang's (2007) study showed that the one child policy reduces the requirement to be a good mother. Under the one-child policy, mothers become the greatest influence on the one-child family's only child (Chang, 2013). The family planning policy directly changes the size of the family and also changes the women's role inside and outside of the family. Meanwhile, a study by Xie, Zhang and Li (2017) demonstrates that there are new options for mothers, because they no longer have to spend so much time being pregnant and raising children, and can therefore devote more time and energy to personal interests and development. The above studies suggest that although motherhood remains an important identity for women, this does not mean that they cannot make their own personal choices. It is worth noting that most of these studies focus on the perspective of urban mothers, with rural mothers not often being the focus of attention.

A third strand of research focuses on women as daughters in their birth family when exploring gender roles in the family. Since traditional agricultural production is dominated by men, male status and patriarchal culture requires women to enter their husband's family, although this occurs more often in rural areas. Xie et al. (2017) claim that sons are favoured for their value in agriculture, old-age care, and family inheritance. Male offspring means blessings and happiness (Xie, Zhang and Li, 2017). However, an unexpected result of the family planning policy may be to empower the daughter. For example, they have a higher likelihood of receiving more support from their families (Fong, 2002; Tsui and Rich, 2002). In addition, the parents of only daughters have no choice but to rely on the daughter to bear family responsibilities, such as the responsibility of caring for the elderly (Xie, Zhang and Li, 2017). As a result, the urban family's attitude towards their daughters has also changed in response to changing social circumstances and policies, so that we can no longer suggest that a daughter is automatically treated negatively in her family because of her status as a woman.

In conclusion, we need to recognize that under the influence of patriarchy, women's gender is often formed by social demands, and the spaces inside and outside of the home available to women are very limited. Gender is something that women are experiencing, and because women's gender is given by social standards, this creates a different division of labour and standards than men. Moreover, with the changing social environment, women have indeed gained more space to play their roles. For example, the emergence of female managers and businesspeople who break social stereotypes, even in the face of disapproval, is evidence of this. Urban women have been given more space to expand ways of doing gender than rural women.

### 2.3.3 Research about gender in rural China

Rural women face gender-based inequalities, and these inequalities are much more acute than they are for urban women, because rural society is more conventional (Tian, Yu and Klasen, 2018). Village family culture has had a great influence on rural family life. After the founding of the country in 1949, the state led four political waves, the first three of which severely weakened village family culture (Wang, 2010). Since the 20th century, China's rural areas have gradually undergone an overall transformation from traditional to modern, with accelerated commercialization and population mobility. Consequently the inherent patterns[1] of people interaction in rural areas are beginning to change, and the lifestyles of stay-behind women and migrant women are becoming different (Chou et. al, 2020). With the development of production and under the guidance of the government, family relations and attitudes have gradually changed and the role of women in the family has been affirmed, yet traditional thinking still plays an implicit role (Wang, 2010). For example, women are the main domestic workers and the tradition of 'female subordination' has not changed (Luo and Chui, 2018).

The concept of 'domestication' was developed by Mies (1997) and the gendered division of labour arose from the demand for labour in the capitalist economy, Ochiai further identifies 'housewifization' as an important factor in the modernization process (2008b). According to Ochiai et al.'s research about East and Southeast Asian societies, 'modernization led to the gender division of labor between the "breadwinning" husband who labored in the public sphere and the housewife who specialized in housekeeping and childrearing in the domestic sphere' (Ochiai et. al., 2008, p4). However, since the market economy was not well developed in the countryside and there was a lack of job opportunities, rural women were seen as housewives even more, especially after they got married. As Ma and Guo's research shows, the organisation of rural families means men take care of everything outside the home and women decide on the affairs of the home. For women, they are

---

1   Means the a relationship-oriented society.

merely responsible for the domestic labour, and the men still have the power to decide on things (2020). This is the way of life that rural female stayers are accustomed to and this is also their traditional division of labour and way of life they inherited from their parents (Ma and Guo,2020), even if some researchers, represented by Zhang, have expressed the view that women are disadvantaged by the inequalities they face as a result of this division of labour (2011). As Wang and Ye argued in their study, the effect of this division of labour being inherited is that the husband leaves home to work in the city and the wife has to stay at home to take on the domestic work and the increased farm work due to the absence of the husband (2020). Using data from a research report on the protection of the rights and interests of rural women left-behind in Shanxi Province, Ma's study (2018) further goes on to point out that in this situation, left-behind women are under enormous pressure and heavy workload. However, the emergence of research on left-behind women has been accompanied by some opposing voices. For example, Wu and Ye's study argues that due to the division of labour and complementary role functions between couples, couple separation can enhance couple bonding and lead to more stable and harmonious marriages for left-behind women (2009). My research aims to understand family divisions of labour in the daily life of rural female stayers, as well as exploring women's perspectives on this.

The specific culture of families and marriage systems often determine the status of women in the family and society (Li, 2005). Young women in rural areas are very vulnerable. On the one hand, it is because of the lack of opportunities and choice in rural areas (for both men and women); on the other hand, young women are at the age of marriage and they will face pressure from their husbands and mothers-in-law after they are married, especially when their children are daughters (Pearson, 1995; Yin et al.,

2018). In rural China, women's status changes from independence to dependence on their husbands as they marry, and their rights also change due to their attachment to their husbands (Wang, 2006; Wang and Ye, 2020). Meanwhile, Tong, Shu, and Piotrowski's study (2019) draws on data from the Chinese Family Panel Studies, where they show that for married rural women, their migration experience is seen as a short-term absence from rural home, and married rural women migrating alone for long period happens in only very few cases. This is a relatively common phenomenon. Wang's research (2006) also argued that as rural women get married, many lose the villager status of the original village and the rights they receive under this qualification and their rights as women in general depend on the condition of their husbands. The qualifications lost here refer to some original village welfare, such as eligibility for land sharing. Although women face unfair treatment, especially in rural areas, they still possess rights in their family. For example, the research from Chan (2013) contrasts with Wang's (2006), and she acknowledges the rights of women in their families of origin, although she also points out that these rights come with many problems. Chan points out that rural women have the right to receive cash dividends for family property and/or ancestral property, although the principle of male inheritance is a deep-rooted custom of descent. It is worth noting that although female inheritance is allowed, it applies only to cash, not to housing because village housing is still an essential part of maintaining a clan community and its associated identity (Chan, 2013). In addition, Sun's study (2019) indicates that inheritance is customarily predominantly male in rural areas and that women's rights to inherit land are more vulnerable. Moreover, Xiong, Yun and Hu's study (2020) analyses inheritance preferences using data specific to older people from the Chinese Women's Social Status Survey, and shows that while there is a clear tendency for older people to inherit equally between men and women in terms of property distribution, there is still a preference for customary male inheritance in rural areas.

At the same time, in the rural areas, the idea of valuing the male child only (*zhong nan qing nv*) still exists. Giving birth to a boy means adding another important member of the workforce that can create economic value for the family in the future (Pearson, 1995). It is worth noting that this situation has improved with the gradual emergence of the opposite view of '*yang er fang lao*', which is a Chinese proverb meaning 'bringing up sons can give you security in your old age' (from the book *Shi Lin Guang Ji* of the Song Dynasty). Originally it meant to raise children in case of old age, but gradually it was interpreted to mean raising sons. It is clear that rural women are not valued within the family in the same way as men, but arguably the advent of the family planning policy did go some way to improving this situation (Xie, Zhang and Li, 2017). According to the family planning policy, most rural families can only have a maximum of two children. This means that rural daughters can get more family resources because they have fewer 'competitors' compared with before. As families have more resources (for economic development) and fewer children, rural daughters are given more opportunities to develop themselves. This means that the status of daughters in rural families has also improved (Xie, Zhang and Li, 2017).

To sum up, when researchers have discussed the issue of gender, as the previous section shows, when it comes to the situation of women in 'wai', their research has focused on urban women and relatively little has been conducted with rural women as subjects. Researches on urban women's gender perceptions is difficult to apply to rural women because of the differences in lifestyles between urban and rural areas. At the same time, the few studies on rural women's gender perceptions are mostly focused on rural women in general and there is still relatively little research into a more refined classification of rural women according to their life experiences. Since the situation faced by rural female stayers is not exactly the same as that faced by rural women in general. They may face more complex circumstances, like their husbands' prolonged absence from home. It is necessary to conduct research on the subject of rural female stayers as well. It is also important to note that, as urbanisation accelerates, rural women who have experienced urban life are a new group of interest, influenced by both rural and urban environments. Unlike rural women of the past, they are likely to be influenced by both 'nei' and 'wai'. It should be noted in particular that the 'wai' component is becoming more influential for these rural women because of their experience of urban life, such as the experience of urban work and the influence of other women around them while living in the city, making it a valuable new direction for research to focus on how they understand their own life experience. Having explained why research on gender and rural stayers is important, in the following sections I will explore what is already known through research about this group of women, and explain how my research contributes to this field.

## 2.4 Research about the rural female stayers

The increased scholarly attention to rural women, especially left-behind women[1], would have initially started from research related to urbanisation. 'Urbanisation refers to the population shift from rural to urban residency, the gradual increase in the proportion of people living in urban areas, and how

---

[1] Although I have used stay-behind women instead of left-behind women in my study, I will follow the convention of using left-behind women in the literature review, given that this is the term that most studies in the past have used.

each society adapts to this change and it is a vast field, incorporating changes in the processes of politics, economy, culture, regulation, and so on (Yang, 2012). According to the UN Commission on Human Settlement's World Cities report in 2008, the urban population is more than half of the world, and by 2030 an estimated every seven in ten people will be urban dwellers (Wu, et al., 2013). According to Zhang and He's research, based on the data from the National Bureau of Statistics of China, the first time urban residents exceed rural residents was in 2011, and the urbanisation rate was 52.57% in 2012. Although the level of urbanisation in China is continuously growing, compared with the 81% urbanisation rate of the U.S.A and 90% rate of the U.K, it is a long road for China (Zhang and He, 2015). According to a report by the National Development and Reform Commission in 2021, the urbanisation rate of China's resident population has reached 64.72% and the urbanisation rate of the household registration population has increased to 46.7% (National Development and Reform Commission, 2022). With increasing levels of urbanisation, the gap between urban and rural areas and the positive and negative impacts of urbanisation are becoming focuses of academic research. Rural women, as an important part of the rural population, especially the long-term population, have also been one of the main focuses of researchers.

In fact, with the development of economy and society, urbanisation has become a necessary condition for the emergence of left-behind women and return women. The imbalance between urban and rural development motivates more rural people to go to cities to seek better opportunities (Chen and Xu, 2016). Since 1978, China's economy has been transforming, and the reduction in the government's control over the flow of people has led to an increase in rural-to-urban migration (Chang, Dong and Macphail, 2011). Most migrants are young and middle-aged men and young, single women. Although male migrants are of different ages, most female immigrants are of premarital age (Liu and Zhang, 2005). They leave their family and then go back to the rural area months or years later (Jacka, 2014). The sixth census in 2010 showed that there were more than 150 million left-behind people which includes left-behind women, left-behind children and left-behind elder and about 47 million were left behind women (Wang, 2015). The formation of left-behind women in China is due to the current economic situation, cultural heritage and strict household registration system (Liang, Tang and Huo, 2014). Since the 1990s, many rural women have come to the city to find jobs, but because after marriage they become mothers very quickly and are expected to take care of their families, marriage usually causes them to end their urban sojourn and return to rural life, which in turn makes them lose the opportunity to engage in non-agricultural work (Fan, 2004). Most research data show that most migrant women are single, and these researchers believe that marriage has a negative impact on rural women's migration decisions-making (Song, Zheng, and Qian, 2009) and married women usually stay in the rural areas to look after their families (Shan, Liu and Li, 2015). There are also studies that show some rural people are trying to overcome the inequalities between urban and rural areas. As Xu's research (2020) which used in-depth interviews demonstrates, some rural women have overcome the disadvantages of their rural origins to pursue higher education and eventually become academics. From the perspective of rural migration history, Chinese rural female stayers are mainly divided into three age groups. The first category is women around the age of 45, who have little experience of migration; the second category is about 35 years old, who usually move to the city before marriage and then return to the rural area to take care of their children; the third category is people in their 20s or early 30s who have worked in urban areas for many years and are eager to move, but they have to return to the rural areas because they are the only people who can support their family (Ye et al., 2016).

Since the 1990s in China, the theme of urban and rural migration has gradually attracted the attention of the academic community. In these academic studies, the causes, influences, and social integration of migrants have become mainstream. Since 2005, the issue of left-behind women has also begun to become a subject of research (Ye, Wu et al., 2016). The study of this issue has focused on the impact of labour migration on left-behind women (Ye et al., 2016). However, more papers now focus on their emotional or mental health. For example, Wu and Ye's study (2010) used a combination of questionnaires and interviews to analyse the psychological impact on left-behind women of husbands going out to work. My research is conducted from a sociological perspective, so this research will focus on the everyday experiences of rural female stayers. This study will show how rural female stayers interact with other family members in the home and with those around them outside the home, and it will also show how they understand life. Although there is a large body of literature on Chinese urban women in terms of family life and related topics, I will review the literature using mainly empirical research on rural female stayers in rural areas, given the different living environments of urban and rural women.

### 2.4.1 The reason and result of migration

The employment of migrant workers in China continues to increase and reached around 281 million in 2016, with 169 million migrant peasant workers and 112 million in situ peasant workers (National Bureau of Statistics, 2017). According to estimates by the National Population and Family Planning Commission, out of a population of 1.5 billion, one third live in urban areas, one third in rural areas and the remaining third will move between urban and rural areas (Lv, 2009, cited by Ye et al., 2016). The 2021 Migrant Worker Monitor put the total number of migrant workers in 2021 at 292.51 million, an increase of 6.91 million over the previous year (National Bureau of Statistics, 2022). Migration to the urban area has become a common way of life for young people in rural areas, and family separation has become the norm in rural areas of China. Therefore, rural residents tend to pay more attention to the beneficial effects of migration, while seeing the adverse impacts as something that has to be tolerated for the sake of the benefits (Ye et al., 2016).

The urban-rural dualism system of China's means a system of allocating resources differently using the *hukou* division between urban and rural areas, and it has made great contributions to its industrialisation and modernisation (Chan and Wei, 2019). However, the benefits that farmers receive from this process are relatively limited. Provision of social security and public services for rural migrants and their families, including basic health care and compulsory education, lag behind those for residents who have the urban *hukou*. In contrast to rural areas, urban areas have better welfare, education and services, which are largely related to the individual's living conditions (Zhang, 2013). On the one hand, land cannot guarantee the basic livelihood of rural residents, so rural labourers migrate to urban areas to make a living; on the other hand, migrant workers cannot get corresponding social security and welfare in urban areas because of the *hukou* system (Ye et al., 2016). It is understood that women, children and the elderly who are most in need of welfare and other social services cannot obtain benefits and other social services in urban areas without being registered as urban citizens (i.e. without urban *hukou*).

'Gender is a key factor, in terms of earning opportunities and family responsibilities' (Razavi 2012, as cited by Ye et al., 2016). As described previously, it is constructed as 'traditional' for women to be responsible for the family while men work outside the home and this gender concept is particularly ingrained in rural areas (Shan, Liu and Li, 2015). For many families, the couple fulfil their different responsibilities in different places, and thus the paradigm of traditional rural Chinese couples living together has ended. Economic development and labour migration have reconfigured marriage and family in rural society (Ye et al., 2016). In normal circumstances, women would stay in rural areas while men would migrate to urban areas (Fan and Chen, 2020). This is a decision made after careful calculation of the family's livelihood needs. In fact, given many factors such as education and marital status, most rural families have no other choice (Song, Zheng and Qian, 2009; Wu and Ye, 2014). Obviously, the left-behind wives need to bear the heavy work burden and the family's economic pressure, and they may be under extreme emotional pressure too (Ye et al., 2016).

In summary, this section focuses on showing the context of rural life under urbanisation. The section presents research related to the creation and outcomes of urban migration, and I attempt to show the reasons why returning rural people deserve our attention, as well as the reasons for the emergence of left-behind women. In the meantime, it is important to note that it was the migrants that led to the emergence of the group focused in my research—rural female stayers.

### 2.4.2 Research about rural female stayers in recent years

In this section, I provide an overview of relevant past research based on the two categories of women included in my definition of rural female stayers.

In recent years, there has been much researches concentrated on rural areas and rural women in China. Many of these studies concentrate on how to solve the left-behind issue and the difficulties which rural women face. Less research has considered rural women's life experience. In the case of return women, more attention is focused on working in the city against the background of increasing urbanisation than on life back in the rural home. I will illustrate these aspects of existing research in the following sections, and explain how my research develops these.

### 2.4.2.1 The research about left-behind women

Many researchers argue that left-behind women are easily vulnerable in many ways: increased workload, difficulties of fulfilling family responsibilities and basic survival, and emotional loss and stress (Gulati 1987, Rodenburg 2000, as cited by Ye et al., 2016). Family division of labour in rural China is a dual system[1] of men and women, with women mainly devoting their time to household work. However, with men migrating to urban areas, women inevitably have to do more agricultural work (Chang, Dong and Macphail, 2011) to avoid a drastic decrease in their household incomes (He and Ye, 2014). The agricultural work of left-behind women has increased significantly, and the relatively low income of it leaves left-behind women at a disadvantage in the family (Gao, 1994, as cited by Ye et al., 2016). Therefore, many studies have concluded that with husbands working outside the home, the heavy work needs to be done is the biggest challenge for women, especially for those who have very young children and very old parents, both of which require care from them (Ye, et al., 2016; Zhao, Hu, and Yang 2009, as cited by Ye, et al., 2016). Within much of the literature then, left-behind women are seen as a vulnerable group who are always in a position of needing support.

---

1  Dual system here means women working inside (in family) while men working outside (in Chinese, *nan zhu wai, nv zhu nei*).

Jiang and Zhou have argued that left-behind women bear the dual burden of agriculture and housework, and rely on men psychologically as well as economically. These relationships place women in rural areas in subordinate positions relative to men (Jiang and Zhou, 2007, as cited by Ye et al., 2016). Men who have migrated to cities still keep in touch with their wives by phone to determine family decisions, especially decisions related to production investment (Zhou, 2006, as cited by Ye et al., 2016). Research data obtained through interviews using a qualitative analysis approach suggests that left-behind women are still in a secondary position in the family, with men doing the managing and women the producing (Ye et al., 2016). The pressure on these rural wives stems not only from the heavy workload, but is also financial (Ye et al., 2016). The impact of migration on time spent on agriculture and household work is more positive for men, but for women, it means they need to spend more time on household duties (Chang, Dong and Macphail, 2011). Most of the work done by women is not paid, and men become the economic backbone of the family. Money is an important factor in maintaining a relationship between husband and wife (Ye et al., 2016). However, Wu's research using interview questionnaires found that left-behind women do not think they need to worry about earning money, because their husbands are working in the urban area and will bring money home (Wu, 2011). Luo (2017) argues that most left-behind women consider their family's economic position as good, and they don't feel much pressure. The above studies show contradictory representations of the lives of left-behind women after their husbands have moved to urban areas to work, to some extent, the impact of economic conditions on these rural women as well. This contradiction is therefore an aspect that my research will inevitably focus on.

In the long process of feudal society, the Chinese formed a family-centred culture.

The interests of the family replaced the interests of each member in the family (Liang, Tang and Huo, 2014). Left-behind women may pay more attention to the family finances than meeting their own needs. Although their husbands are not around, they need to plan for family expenses to ensure that these can be met (Liang, Tang and Huo, 2014). In terms of marriage and husband-wife relations, studies have shown that there are many risks involved in the husband and wife living apart, including increased risk of divorce, mental stress and sexual stress (Xiang, 2006 and Wang, 2007, as cited by Ye et al., 2016). Besides, under the virilocal marriage system that controls rural China, women's land use rights are attributed to the husband's family after marriage. After divorce, in most rural areas of China, women lose their rights involve land issues in the village of their husbands, and they do not regain land rights in the villages where they were born (Jacka, 2014). In addition, in terms of the psychological aspects, the mental health of left-behind women is worse than that of other women (Ye et al., 2016). For example, it is not easy to take care of children, which may lead to physical and mental strain for left-behind women (Wu and Ye, 2016). In some areas, poor mental health has led some left-behind women to seek religious consolation (Wu and Ye, 2010; and Xu 2010, as cited by Ye et al., 2016).

While I agree with the majority of scholars about the negative physical and psychological effects that left-behind women face when their husbands migrate to the urban area to work, I am equally aware that some scholars paint a different picture (Ye et al., 2016; Luo, 2017). It is thus difficult to conclude that all left-behind women have been negatively or positively affected by the urbanisation process (Ye et al., 2016). The research by Guo, Yang et al. found higher levels of marital well-being among left-behind women with high levels

51

of emotional interaction with their husbands in the long term. This led to improved quality of family life or improved ability to educate children (2016). Besides, the study of Ye et al. (2016) uses questionnaires, case studies and other methods to show that the separation of husband and wife is not the key factor affecting the lives of left-behind women, and that migration can have a positive impact. For example, left-behind women may gain more power to decide on family matters (Ye et al., 2016). This is an interesting point because it highlights the possibilities opened up for left-behind women to exercise their agency, and again this is something that I intend to explore further in my study. From this alternative perspective, the lives of left-behind women are more positive, and this is a view I would like to further elaborate. The impact of their husband's migration varies among left-behind women, depending on factors such as family, region, and culture. These new perspectives remind me that I need to be aware of more factors in my research that may influence the representation of left-behind women. In other words, my respondents may have completely different representations due to factors such as family status, regional differences, etc. This will be something I need to pay attention to.

### 2.4.2.2 The research about return women

In previous researches, scholars have focused on the changing identity of return women, the stages of migration and the impact of urban life on their return home.

According to the concept of social exclusion status proposed by Akerlof and Kranton (2000), until citizens are fully integrated into the community, the negative effects of social exclusion will continue (Afridi, Li and Ren, 2014). The identity and experience of rural migrant workers in Chinese urban areas is formed by their gender, class, local/external, urban/rural and regional locations within the social hierarchy. However, among all these factors, the two key divisions are between locals and outsiders and between urban and rural residents, and it is these two divisions that largely determine what being a rural migrant woman means in the urban area (Jacka, 2015).

Rural migrant women are not a homogeneous group with the same attributes. The various aspects of women's identity negotiation, construction and performance determine the changes and efforts of rural women (Zhang, 2014). Indeed, rural women are more likely than rural men to change their family role because they have several roles: being the daughter of the family and the role of the 'outside stranger' wife when they enter the husband's village after marriage. Their multiple roles do not mean that they have more options to chose their roles. As Zhang (2014) argued that it is still too early to say whether settled migrant female workers have actually given up their farming status. When they migrate to the urban area, their urban role is also likely to be a temporary presence. Relatively speaking, the experience of urban life and working makes them more aware of their identity as rural people. For others, especially young unmarried migrant girls, moving to the urban area not only poses a serious threat to individual self-understanding, but also creates exciting opportunities for new job positions (Jacka, 2015).

In fact, many studies situate return women in the family, focusing more on women's staged choices and how the family factors influences their choices. With the development of society, more and more young women chose to take urban employment, and rural women in most parts of China have similar life trajectories: graduate or drop out of school; work in cities; marry and have children; and return to the rural area to take care of children and the elderly after marriage (Chuang, 2016; Chen and Fan, 2018). As Ye et al. explained in 2016, the early migration experience of the rural women gives them independence, and they struggle to find a balance between migration and caring for children and the elderly (Ye et al., 2016). Tang and Yang's research in 2008 argued that as migrants, rural women have crossed rigid ideological and administrative borders of the urban and rural, but they are not only discriminated against because of their lower status as workers, but also because of patriarchal gender ideology and structural gender inequality. In particular, restrictive policies and regulations related to the household registration system and urban and rural class division are the barriers to eliminating discrimination (Tang and Yang, 2008). The social status and temporary nature of rural migrant women disconnects them from urban residents due to the welfare gap created by the *hukou* system (pensions, educational resources, health care coverage, and so forth) (Zhang, 2014). Although in recent years the government has proposed a number of policies[1] to try to address the negative impact of the *hukou* system on migrant workers moving to the city, Chen and Hu's research (2021) uses quantitative data from the China Migrants Dynamic Survey (CMDS) to show that the negative effects of *hukou* on migrant populations continue to exist. The patriarchal marriage and family system and the gender-biased labour market also limit their livelihood choices, their placement possibilities, their marriage prospects, and their future (Gaetano, 2015). According to Zhang's study, return women found themselves marginalised in the city through their interactions with those around them (urbanites), despite their seeming integration into urban life (2014). Zhang also mentions that when their interpersonal relationships in urban areas are restricted, rural female migrants will concentrate even more on family members and relatives, which in turn reinforces their blood ties with their rural family network (Zhang, 2014). Shen (2016) has the

---

1  For example, migrant's children can attend school without *hukou* under some circumstances.

same opinion: rural migrant women are deeply immersed in the overall rural kinship network, which makes it necessary for them to balance the pursuit of modern and non-rural desires with the traditional morality of rural people and women.

At the same time, a number of studies have looked at the impact of the urban experience on return women. Migration is more than just a change of living place. Whether rural women choose to migrate, return or stay in the rural area, it affects all stages of their lives (Mills, 1997 and Murphy, 2002, as cited by Zhang, 2014). Under the influences of industrialisation and urbanisation, a large number of rural residents, including rural women, have changed their occupations and places of residence. Once rural women are employed in the urban area, they face less pressure to perform traditional gender roles and become more independent (Xie, Zhang and Li, 2017). Statistics show that in 1990, only 23.9% of women were engaged in non-agricultural work. In 2015, this proportion increased to 58.2%. Urban or/and non-agricultural employment provides women with personal income, and with economic independence, their voice within the family also become more important. Studies have shown that female migrant workers, even after marriage, still show strong filial piety to their birth family (Shen, 2016). This is despite the fact that urban work can, to some extent, help them resist the patriarchal control that dominates their lives (Zhang, 2014). For women who eventually return to rural areas, returning home is seen as a temporary suspension of the migration programme rather than a long-term end result. By distinguishing themselves from their 'fellow peasants', they reaffirm their memories of urban life and plans for future migration, and successfully reconstruct the imagined role of the 'urban migrant' (Zhang, 2014). This is why many later studies have wanted to focus on the life choices or stages of choice of return women. For example, some researchers have studied the lives of return women after they return to the rural area, where return women's entrepreneurship is gradually becoming a new theme (Gao, 2020). These studies focus on the dilemmas that return women encounter when starting a business and how they can take subjective initiative to solve the problems. Using a case study approach, researchers have attempted to present the plight of return women in terms of the impact of the gender division of labour (Gao, 2020). However, these studies have focused more on the entrepreneurial component and less on the return women themselves.

For some researchers, represented by Ye, taking care of children is also a key factor that cannot be avoided when discussing return women. They use a combination of case studies, questionnaires and interviewing to try to illustrate how taking care of children play an important role in rural women's migrant lives (Ye et al., 2016). In Chinese family culture, children are the centre of family interests, so taking care of children is the first task for rural families (Wu and Ye, 2016). Giving birth to children is not only an important stage of rural women's lives, but also a turning point for their lives as migrant workers (Ye et al., 2016). A study by Connelly et al. reached similar conclusions by means of a quantitative study. Compared with older mothers, rural women with young children are more likely to migrate to the urban area to work, and are more likely to live with their children in the city (Connelly, Roberts, and Zheng 2012). In other words, the time of return is closely related to the age of the children. When they decide to return to the rural area to live, they will sometimes become part of the left-behind group, as some of their husbands will still work in the urban area.

### 2.4.2.3 Summary

Overall, through previous research, it is easy to see that most studies to date have focused on the emotional experiences of left-behind women, or the reasons for and effects of their husbands' migration to the city as a result of the economic burden on their families (Li, 2018; Fu, 2019). Relatively few studies have focused on rural female stayers themselves in terms of their experiences of everyday life. In terms of return women, there is more research on the reasons for their return to their hometowns. In existing studies, researchers are more concerned with the external influences on returning migrant workers, such as the study of Li and Long (2009), and even when some studies have focused on returning rural people, they have mostly concentrated on the male perspective, such as the research of Zhu et al., which use interviews to analyse the situation of migrant workers returning to their hometown (2007). Yuan and Shi's research discusses the theme of migrant workers' decision to return home by using the data of the national rural fixed observation sites (2019), while a few studies have used qualitative data to focus on the reasons why women return to rural areas (Gao, 2020; Zhang, 2014). As noted in the above review, existing research highlights the importance of attending to the potentially positive impacts of marital separation for left-behind women, and I aim to consider this further in my thesis in relation to women's accounts of their life experience. In addition, I include return women who are less studied in the existing literature, and I will analyse this group's understanding of their own life experiences, providing explicit comparison with the experiences of stay-behind women. And in contrast to most existing research, my research uses interviews instead of questionnaires, in order to generate a more in-depth analysis of women's experiences. I detail my data collection methods subsequently in Chapter 3.

Under the government's 'poverty eradication' strategy for rural areas in recent years, the environment and policies in rural areas are different from those previously in place, and this has led to a very different situation for rural women. With the guidance of policies, some work opportunities have emerged in the countryside, while rural families have also been given favourable policies such as collective contract farming and farmers receiving dividends through their land. All these aspects have potentially changed the living conditions of rural women to a certain extent. As a result of these new factors, new research on rural female stayers continues to be valuable.

## 2.5 Conclusion

In summary, in the existing literature discussed in this chapter, given the influence of patriarchy on gender identity in China, I introduced the culture of patriarchy as a background. I present existing studies on gender identity in China, where gender factors influence the division of labour between men and women and their situation within the family. Secondly, I critiqued previous research related to rural female stayers in China, by contrasting the different situations in which left-behind women and return women find themselves. The existing literature provides a wealth of detailed analysis for understanding gender, particularly in relation to urban women, with a large number of studies focusing on them in the domestic and work spheres. However, there is still a lack of relevant research on rural women. Although there has been much research on left-behind women, most of this research focuses on the difficulties they encounter rather than on their understanding of life. In addition, few studies have explored the everyday lives of return women who have lived in urban areas. Therefore, my research starts with rural female stayers and focuses on their daily lives. The next chapter will discuss the methodology used, including the interplay of theory, methodology and data analysis, and I will present my research design and the status of field investigation in this chapter.

# Chapter 3  Methodology

I viewed methodology as a plan and a guide, but in fact, as the Chinese say, 'plans can't keep up with change'. In practice, I found methodology to be a process with the actual fieldwork and it needed to be constantly re-planned, redesigned, Even though it seemed to be well prepared and perfect, I still encountered unexpected situations. However, I think this imperfection in adapting to change is what allowed me to treat uncertainty positively Although the uncertainties are not what I had hoped for, I gladly accept their existence. Unpredictability is a rollercoaster ride, always thrilling and exciting, and I would not wish to minimise uncertainty, but rather to reflect on the 'unpredictable' in order to improve it.

I conducted my fieldwork in two villages in central Inner Mongolia[1], in northern China, with rural women aged between 30 and 45. As I mentioned in the previous chapter, I refer to them as rural female stayers, who can be divided into two sections, return women and rural female stayers, based on their life experiences. Some had lived in the city and then returned to rural areas ('return women'). As for the others, their husbands were working in the city and they were left in the countryside to take care of their families (so-called 'stay-behind women'). The biggest difference between these two groups of women is whether or not they have had experience of urban life.In that case, I

---

1  Given the vast size of the area (1,183,000 square kilometres in the Inner Mongolia Autonomous Region) and the large number of villages, even pointing out that the area where I did fieldwork is in central Inner Mongolia would not reveal specific information about these two villages.

designed two different outlines for the interviews based on this characteristic (See Appendix 5: English version and Appendix 6: Chinese version for more details).

I have divided this chapter into four parts. The first part is the study design. I will explain how my research priorities were determined and how I prepared my fieldwork based on these priorities. The second part describes the data collection process. I will briefly introduce my interviewees and provide details of my data collection procedures. The third part is about the challenges of fieldwork and my reflections on this. I will discuss the difficulties I encountered in fieldwork, and will further explain how I dealt with these challenges. The final part is about data analysis, and I will explain the chapter division of the thesis. In sum, this chapter does not simply describe the methodology of how I envisaged the project and the ways I collected the data. It also considers the barriers and dilemmas that I encountered throughout the fieldwork. The design and practice of fieldwork helped me gather data to explore how rural female stayers describe their daily life and the possibilities of agency in their lives.

## 3.1 Research design and preparation

### 3.1.1 Choosing a research method

Qualitative research methods can help us better understand phenomena that are not yet clear (Strauss and Corbin, 1990, as cited by Hoepfl, 1997), while at the same time reveal a wealth of detail and insight (Stake, 1978). In order to better present the details of the interviewees' accounts and better understand their explanations of their behaviour, I wanted my study to be focused on the interviewees themselves. I decided to use qualitative research methods.

Chapter 3 Methodology

As this is a qualitative research, the interview is both a data collection strategy and a research method (McIntosh and Morse, 2015). Interviews are one of the most commonly used methods of data collection in qualitative research. Interviews help researchers gather 'facts' that interest them or get opinions, attitudes, experiences, processes, behaviours, etc. (Rowley, 2012). Besides, 'Interviewing is one of the most common and powerful ways in which we try to understand our fellow human beings' (Fontana and Frey, 2000, as cited by Clough and Nutbrown, 2012, p141). And one of the reasons I chose qualitative interviews is to understand people's lives (Schultze and Avital, 2011). Interviewing is often understood as the researcher and participants talking together, which can create an opportunity for participants to respond 'naturally' (Griffee, 2005). Besides, in-depth interviews are designed to better understand the experience, perspectives, and characteristics of a phenomenon (Curasi, 2001). Interviews show richer detail. It's more meaningful than quantitative surveys. They can more easily seek and develop narrative responses (Hollway, and Jefferson, 1997). Bryman (2012, p466) maintains that 'in qualitative interviewing, there is greater interest in the interviewee's point of view'. In other words, the qualitative interview is one of the most effective methods to study an interviewee's subjective experiences. Also, qualitative interviews are the most effective and direct way for knowing how these rural female stayers express their life experience, make their choices and give their personal accounts. Hence, the qualitative interview method became the research method for my research project. Within the framework of qualitative interviews, my research focused on the life experience of these stay-behind women and provided the basis for me to analyse them from a sociological perspective.

Both unstructured and structured interviews are common forms of data collection in fieldwork. The unstructured interview, also known as the free-form interview, has only one topic or scope of the interview and the interviewer and interviewee talk more freely around this topic or scope and the questioning style is always informal (Bryman, 2012). However, unstructured interviews are more demanding for the interviewer and the resulting data is more difficult and time-consuming to process analytically due to a possible lack of uniformity (Feng, 2013). Structured interviews require as much uniformity and standardisation as possible in terms of process, content and formality (Feng, 2013). The goal of the structured interview is to have the same questions for all interviewees and the interviewer asks the questions in the same order according to the interview schedule (Bryman, 2012). However, the structured interview lacks the flexibility and elasticity to obtain more specific and detailed information and to discuss the interview questions in greater depth (Feng, 2013). Overall, based on the advantages and disadvantages of these two types of interviews, I choose the semi-structured interview to design my interview outline. The semi-structured interview is the most common type in qualitative research (Doody and Noonan, 2013). A semi-structured interview means 'the research has a list of questions or fairly specific topics to be covered, often referred to as an interview guide, but the interviewee has a great deal of leeway in how to reply' (Bryman, 2012, p321). The main advantage of the semi-structured interview is its flexibility in both use of questions and question-order (Bryman, 2012), and thus there is more freedom in how the communication between the interviewer and the interviewee unfolds (Reinharz and Chase, 2011). Further, the use of open questions enables researchers to solicit in-depth answers. Thus, the data collected are more abundant (Dearnley, 2005; and Hand, 2003). Besides, the interviewer can pay attention to any new path during the process of the interview that may not have been considered at the beginning of the interview outline design

(Doody and Noonan, 2013). I decided to choose semi-structured interviewing rather than the structured or unstructured interview because it not only ensures that the interview revolves around a given topic, but also in the light of the different situations of different interviewees. The questions can also be cut or adjusted according to the actual situation of the interview (Rowley, 2012). In a semi-structured interview, the interviewer follows an interview script to some extent (Bryman, 2012), so it does not require advanced interviewing skills or the rich experience of the interviewer, unlike the unstructured interview, which demands prior experience and expertise. Besides, the semi-structured interview is more accurate when the interviewer has a clear focus, as it tends to make the interview more specific and targeted (Bryman, 2012). I wanted to give my interviewees the freedom to express their views but in a relatively structured format. I did not want them to be influenced by my perceptions and I tried to get their subjective ideas through more flexible questions. At the same time, as I grew up in the city, the lives of rural women were very different from what I had experienced, and most of my knowledge about them came from mass media or television programmers, as well as from brief encounters with some rural women. Therefore I wanted my questions to be not completely limited and fixed, so that I could go deeper into certain topics during the interviews, depending on the situation. To explain further, I wanted there to be scope for women themselves to be able to shape the agenda and so it did not become determined by my 'outsider' perspective. I will discuss the interview guide in

## 3.1.2 Ethical approval

My research involves human participants, so according to the relevant regulations, before conducting the fieldwork, I needed to ensure that my research was compliant with the relevant codes of practice and ethical guidelines. Accordingly, ethical approval for my research was granted by the University of York's Economics, Law, Management, Politics and Sociology Ethics Committee in July 2019, prior to the commencement of fieldwork (ELMPS 2018 version). The University ensures compliance with the Code of Conduct on Research Integrity and the University's Data Management Policy, as well as the British Sociological Association's Statement of Ethical Practice. Given the sensitive nature of the study, I needed to ensure the security and confidentiality of the data in order to protect the privacy of the participants. Therefore, all recorded interviews and text transcriptions were stored in an encrypted format in my encrypted laptop with password, with pseudonyms used in place of real names.

It is worth noting that since my fieldwork was carried out in China, I also needed to comply with relevant Chinese laws, regulations and ethical standards. The participants are Chinese citizens, and they are protected by the law of China[1]. As a Chinese citizen who is familiar with the local cultural tradition and ethics code, I respected all participants and used my knowledge to protect their rights. In order to make the interviewees feel comfortable, I used the local dialect for interviews. Also, I used different titles for the interviewees according to Chinese cultural habits. For example, if they were older than me, they were called 'sister' (in Chinese, '*Da jie*'). On the other hand, investigation and research in the rural area has its own particularity. Interviewers have many advantages such as social status and information (Chang, 2017), so I also attempted to decrease the inequality of status between the rural women and myself by using dialects to reduce the distance, avoiding

---

1 The right to privacy of natural persons is guaranteed by a number of laws in China, and the personal information of natural persons is also protected by law. For example, articles 101, 1032 and 1034 of the 'Civil Code of the People's Republic of China'.

academic language, etc. Secondly, rural residents are relatively conservative and sensitive (Chang, 2017; Huang and Pan, 2009), so I took note of their emotional changes and maintained a good communication environment by ensuring that the interview space was private (just me and the interviewee). By observing the changes in their moods, the interview could be paused when necessary. In addition, to make the research conform to ethical guidelines, I followed suggestions from the *Social science research ethics in developing countries and contexts* (2004) and *Thoughts on moral standards in social investigation* (Wang, 2012). For example, I insisted that participants had to participate voluntarily, as well as stressing to participants before the interview that their privacy would be protected and that my interview was legal, etc.

In addition to focusing on the well-being of the participants, it was important to consider my own safety and wellbeing as a researcher. Firstly, there was the issue of safety. It is important to emphasise that I do not think I was in any kind of danger when conducting these interviews. However, some of my interviewees felt more comfortable being interviewed at their homes. As this was a private location, rather than a public place, I did provide the phone numbers of the village leaders and the local police officer telephone number (I didn't give the name of village, they only knew the general area) to my parents or my friends before the interviews and then sent a confirmation text message to my parents or friends after the interviews were finished. And if they didn't receive my text message, they would contact the leader of the village to ask him to go to the place. My parents and friends live in the city which is not far from the area where I did my fieldwork, so using this 'buddy system' is an appropriate means of ensuring that I could be located. Additionally, I stored all the emergency contact numbers (for example, the police number is 110) in my phone before the interviews, and I also ensured that my phone was always charged. If in the highly unlikely event that I was in danger, I would be able to call the police immediately.

The second aspect of researcher safety to consider was my psychology and reaction when faced with a 'sensitive' story. I am not an experienced qualitative researcher. However, my previous experience in school clubs has helped me a lot. During my time in the club I had the opportunity to meet different people. For example, we would visit nursing homes. These people had different circumstances and situations, and one of the main things we did was to talk to them and listen to their stories. The experience I gained from the activities of the society has been a valuable asset to me as a researcher. On the one hand, I was able to react appropriately when I heard sensitive stories, and on the other hand, I developed the ability to be a good listener. At the same time, while focusing on the interviewees' stories, I was also able to manage my emotions well, which is an easily overlooked but important part of the process. In addition, my supervisors have been a strong support to me. Before the fieldwork began, we set up a plan to keep in touch on a regular basis. During the course of the fieldwork, we kept in touch via email as I was doing fieldwork in China. I reported my progress and any unexpected situations I was facing via email and they made suggestions via email. We also had online meetings to make it easier and quicker to discuss how to deal with unexpected situations in the interviews.

### 3.1.3 Interview questions

Typically, the interview lasted about 40 minutes, but some interviews took about one hour. Interview questions are listed in the appendix. The interview outline was divided into four sections.

The first section was about my participants' daily lives and families. Paying attention to these rural women's daily routines (schedules for the day) gave me a sense of the focus of their lives and their usual activities. By acquiring knowledge of their daily lives, I can gauge the difficulties they face and their everyday experiences. This helped me to understand how they made their decisions and their real living situation. Family and village space is the basic context of rural women's daily practical activities and family life is an important aspect of rural women's lives. By asking them questions about their families, on the one hand, I could get a quick overview of their information, such as family members. On the other hand, I could also see their position in the family (where they place themselves) and how their role in the family influences their choices. Collectivity is the essence of Chinese culture, which is characterised by family relationships and support (Xu et al., 2007). Families are usually closely connected units and it is an important part of life for Chinese people. Chinese culture emphasises social stability and family harmony, so the needs of the family and society are placed higher than those of the individual (Xu et al., 2007). As I set out in the literature review chapter, collectivism is not essential and it is subject to change. Thus, it is important to note that family ties are strong in rural areas, yet its influence is declining in rural areas as urbanisation and social change occur. For example, young people who have moved to the city to work demonstrate an emphasis on the individualised notion of self (Jin, 2010). Some people who have had an urban experience are beginning to place increasing emphasis on self-determination, believing that urban life represents the right to 'free' choice. At the same time they cannot be completely separated from their rural families, which creates ambivalence when it comes to making decisions between themselves and their families (Shen, 2016). The tension between self and family becomes a contextual factor that cannot be ignored in the analysis of women's daily lives.

For part two, I designed questions to explore my participants' satisfaction with their current lives and the impact that their living conditions have on them. Since the interviewees are divided into two situations (staying behind and returning), in the second part, I designed different questions according to their different situations. The second section for stay-behind women is about their stay-behind life. The questions, such as enquiring about what their stay-behind life involves and how their long-term separation affects their lives, helped me understand how these women view their current living conditions and their thoughts on rural female stayers' life. These questions allowed me to find out if these stay-behind women were happy with their lives and then to take a look at how they described their lives and how they coped with the choices they made in their lives. In the second section, for return women, the topic was about going back to the rural area. I asked questions about their reasons for returning to the rural area, and whether they had a preference for living in the city or the countryside. These questions helped me understand their lives before returning to the rural area and their satisfaction with life now, as well as how they feel about their return life and how they relate these feelings to their status in society.

As Peter et al. argue, people are often more willing to share other people's stories than their own (Peters, Kashima, and Clark, 2009). Knowing others is easier than knowing yourself, and when talking about other people, expressing your opinions is more direct and easier than when talking about oneself. So, I designed the third section to ask questions about people who live around these women: their acquaintances. Acquaintances may be their friends, neighbours or relatives, and so on. Most of the questions in this section are about the situation of the women around the interviewees (migrants, returning home or staying behind), and how the people around them think of these women. From an interviewee's description of her surrounding acquaintances, I could obtain

Chapter 3 Methodology

her views on women in different living conditions, so as to draw her views on her own living conditions. By asking these questions, I could not only understand their views but also the prejudices they may have suffered because of their status. To some extent, I could get a sense from them about how they treat these prejudices.

The fourth section is about external sources of information, like social media, newspapers and so on. Questions about the 'outside' world, such as whether they have heard news or media reports about women who are in the same situation as them, helped me understand whether and how these particular rural female buyers attend to information regarding similarly placed women. As with section two, the answers to these questions not only facilitated an understanding of how they see women in the same situation as themselves, but also how they frame their own lives and whether they are satisfied with the present situation, or simply forced to accept reality. I wanted to know if they can get support (from the outside),if these outside sources have a positive or negative effect on their descriptions of their life experience.

In addition, I did not directly ask questions about participants' personal information like their income. This was for two reasons. First, directly asking these questions about themselves or their families was likely to be viewed as insensitive because many people are not willing to answer such private questions from a stranger. For example, income is a more private matter and they might have been reluctant to reveal the exact amount of their household income, which is a measure of their family's situation and may have caused them to lose *mianzi* (face). Second, during the interview process, it was possible to get relevant information (such as family members and income sources) through asking other questions. For example, I would ask them about their sources of income for the year. By using their household's sources of

69

income, I could roughly derive the household's income level. It is easy to find information on government subsidies and crops to get specific figures, and I also can get some idea of what kind of work their husbands do in the urban area. At the same time, most of them also mentioned their husband's approximate income from working outside the home, 'a little over 5,000' or 'less than 3,000', which is a good reference point.

To prevent the omission of personal information, I also designed a personal information checklist (see Appendix 4 for details) to check if I had obtained the necessary details. If I did not get relevant information during the interview, I would be able to add indirect questions about that information before the interview ended.

### 3.1.4 Interviewee recruitment

By contacting rural women I knew and then using a snowball sampling approach to recruit other potential interviewees, I recruited over 30 potential participants, out of which 25 actually participated in face-to-face interviews. They included so-called stay-behind women and rural women who had returned to a rural area following migration to an urban area. According to the existing research, the age of stay-behind women is mainly between 36 and 45 years old, and among these the proportion aged 26 to 35 years old is 29% (Ye and Wu, 2008). 18 to 40 years old is the concentration period of marriage and pregnancy for women (Huang, 2006). And the main reasons for rural women returning to rural areas are caring for the elderly, taking care of their children and breastfeeding (Ye, Pan and He, 2014). So, I set age limits for my participants, and all of the participants needed to be between 30 to 45 years old. This is because rural women in this age group are at a life stage that has multiple choices about migration or returning. Previous research shows that rural women's choices about migration and returning are framed by their life stage (Fan, 2004). Rural women who are too old or too young don't have all the choices to some extent (to stay in the rural area, migrate to the urban area or return to the rural area). To further explain, when rural women are old, they have difficulty finding work in the cities and therefore they face having to stay in the rural area; when they are too young, they may not be married or have children and also some of them have to follow their parents' opinion. Their families need care, which is the main reason for them to return to rural area. To sum up, I wish that each participant could be in a period where they have multiple choices.

I have chosen two villages in the middle area of Inner Mongolia. Inner Mongolia, which is a region located in northern China, contains a majority population of the Han and the Mongolian ethnic group living together with various other ethnic minorities. With an average altitude of around 1,000 metres above sea level and a large east-west span, Inner Mongolia has marked differences in climate and geographical factors. In 2019, the resident population in rural areas was 9.31 million and has declined in the last five years in the Inner Mongolia. In 2020, the GDP per capita was 72,062 yuan, while the national GDP per capita was 72,447 yuan in the same year, making Inner Mongolia's GDP per capita lower than the national average. In addition, the per capita disposable income in 2020 was 41,353 yuan for urban residents in Inner Mongolia and 16,567 yuan for rural residents, which is about 2.4 times higher in urban areas than in rural areas (National Bureau of Statistics, 2021b). Although Mongolians are the main minority ethnic group in Inner Mongolia, the main population in the two villages considered here is Han. Since ancient times, the Mongolian and Han ethnic groups and other ethnic groups have lived together here, so their living habits are integrated with each other. In particular, the two villages in which I interviewed were farming areas with a large number of Han people, and their living habits were no different from other regions. I did not think it was necessary to stress the particularity of minority areas here.

As Hohhot is the nearest major city to these two villages, it is often the preferred area for local people to work, due to its ease of access and the lower cost of living compared to other cities (especially some traditional labour-demanding cities in southern China), as well as the similarity of living habits and language (meaning the dialect used in everyday conversations). In my interviews, apart from Hohhot, there were also individual migrant families who chose cities such as Beijing and Baotou, which are also relatively close. Hohhot is a third-tier[1] city in China and different from other big cities, as there are relatively limited jobs and women who live nearby face a different situation, compared with those next to big cities. Hohhot lacks medium- and large-scale labour intensive industries, so most of the jobs available to migrants are ones with low technical requirements such as construction site work and community security, although these roles do at least tend to come with accommodation. However, most of these jobs are not suitable for women due to the heavy manual work involved. Therefore, the problem of finding a job may also affect the decision of women to work in cities here. Some of them may decide to remain in the rural area. Many women who migrate to the urban area have to remain in their temporary urban homes taking care of their children[2] and husbands as housewives because they cannot find paid

---

1  The third tier of cities refer to large and medium-sized cities with strategic significance, a relatively developed economy and relatively large economic aggregate, which are comprehensively evaluated according to the city scale, population, economic development level and GDP.

2  Most of the time, if children are under school age, they will live with their parents in the urban area but they will go back to the rural area when they start school.

jobs outside of the home. For these families, this also leads to big financial burdens on the husband. As noted above, my research enriches the data on the lived experiences of migrant families in northern China, particularly in areas lacking large labour intensive industries, given that most research and data on migrant families is concentrated in the south and central regions, where there are more large enterprises that need labors.

I had existing contacts with some rural women who live in the county near Hohhot and they indicated that they would like to take part in my interviews and help me contact other people for my interviews. The reason why I chose the two villages is that they are small enough. Most people there would know others living in the same villages. In order to better protect the privacy of participants, I decided to choose two villages for the interviews. The two villages I chose are close to Hohhot and both located in the central region of Inner Mongolia. This region is predominantly hilly and mountainous in distribution, inland and with distinct seasons. The villages I have chosen are administrative communities formed by the merging of several natural villages, which are close together and where the inhabitants know each other very well. The main crop in this area is potato, due to the severe lack of water, low temperatures and plenty of sunshine all year round. The villages I interviewed were close to the main road and the county town could be reached by tarmac roads in good condition. The villages' convenient location also makes it easy for the villagers to travel to Hohhot city. Due to the government's hardening project[1], most of the houses in these two villages are newly built brick cottages. Most households in the villages rely on the income from potato farming, but some are also able to receive financial subsidies from the

---

1   The hardening project is a government funded initiative to build and renovate rural areas with concrete roads, houses and dilapidated buildings.

government as part of their household income. There is a nursing home in these two villages employing a number of female staff, which is one of the jobs that some rural women would like to have. There are no larger factories around these two villages and the nearest factory is in the neighbouring county, while the few new establishments that have opened around the villages in recent years provide only a limited number of jobs for residents.

I started fieldwork in Inner Mongolia in mid-September 2019. For the most part, the interviewees were recruited during the fieldwork. I did not find enough interviewees beforehand because I personally knew very few rural women who met the interview requirements. So, except for the first few women who participated, I recruited the rest while interviewing via snowball sampling. I contacted the rural women I already knew, and expressed my hope that they could introduce me to other potential participants. They were happy to help me and successfully recruited new participants. Later, with the help of new participants, I found other participants through these new people. By the end of my fieldwork, I had successfully invited 25 interviewees to participate in the research.

Snowball sampling is the most widely used sampling method in the qualitative social sciences (Noy, 2008), and it is also widely used in Chinese social research (Yan et al., 2014; Geng, 2010; Mi et al., 2016). It is an appropriate way to do research in an acquaintance-based society, where prior relationships are essential to establishing trust and are the basis upon which people take part in research within this cultural context (Zhang and Wildemuth, 2017). Snowball sampling is a method used to recruit participants when it is difficult to find members of the target population. It involves some interviewees being initially selected for the interview, then asked to recommend other participants who meet the requirements of the research objectives (Geng, 2010). The sample is like a snowball growing bigger as it rolls down the hill. Snowball sampling can help researchers enrich sample groups and visit new participants and social groups when other access channels are exhausted (Noy, 2008). Participants with a large number of social relationships are more likely to provide the researcher with other participants who have similar characteristics to the original participants (Etikan, Alkassim, and Abubakar, 2015). Since I did not know enough interviewees prior to starting, snowball sampling provided me with an opportunity to reach the target population that I was interested in, and because it was through the introduction of acquaintances, these 'new' people were more likely to agree to participate in the interview. In addition, the participants I was looking for have a certain similarity, so it was easier to find the interviewees who met my research conditions by snowballing.

## 3.2. Data preparation

### 3.2.1 Interviewees

As shown in Table 2 below, I interviewed 25 eligible rural women. To ensure their privacy, I named them according to the order of the Chinese surname book. The table contains information on their characteristics, family demographics, education level and source of income. Generally speaking, these women have completed primary or junior high school education. In fact, of the women I interviewed, only two had completed higher education. Seven of the 25 had not completed formal education at any stage. Although compulsory education was established in China in 1986, implementation of this policy has been uneven in rural areas, especially for girls (Li and Tsang, 2003). The majority of interviewees (16/25) were return women and the remaining nine were stay-behinds.

The number outside the parentheses in the family member column is the number of all members of the household, and the number in parentheses is the number of children of the woman. The final column of the table relates to household income sources. In the section on sources of income, odd jobs refer to unstable work, usually short term (perhaps six months or less), such as construction site workers; also, land includes farming as well as income from livestock such as cows and sheep.

**Table 2. List of interviewees**

| Name | Education | Stay-behind /Return woman | Family[1] (children) | Source of Income |
|---|---|---|---|---|
| Zhao | Primary school | Stay-behind | 4 (2) | Land and husband's odd jobs |
| Qian | Primary school | Return woman | 3 (1) | Land |
| Sun | Primary school | Return woman | 3 (2) | Husband's restaurant (urban) |
| Li | Primary school | Stay-behind | 1 (3[2]) | Land |
| Zhou | High school | Return woman | 2 (1) | Her odd jobs in rural areas |
| Wu | Primary school | Stay-behind | 2 (2) | Husband's odd jobs |
| Zheng | Junior middle school | Return woman | 7 (2) | Husband's odd jobs |
| Wang | No[1] | Stay-behind | 2 (2) | Husband's odd jobs |
| Feng | Primary school | Stay-behind | 3 (2) | Husband's odd jobs |

1 This refers to family members living together. The number of children is in the parentheses.

2 Although under the one-child policy, a family can only have one child (excluding ethnic minorities' family), families in rural areas can have two children because agricultural work requires more labour. At the same time, some families exceed the policy and therefore have three children.

continued Table

| Name | Education | Stay-behind /Return woman | Family (children) | Source of Income |
|---|---|---|---|---|
| Chen | Junior middle school | Return woman | 5 (2) | Husband's odd jobs |
| Chu | Junior middle school | Return woman | 3 (1) | Odd jobs |
| Wei | No | Stay behind | 1 (1) | Husband's odd jobs |
| Jiang | No | Return woman | 5 (2) | Husband's odd jobs |
| Shen | Junior middle school | Return woman | 2 (2) | Odd jobs |
| Han | College | Return woman | 1 (1) | Odd jobs |
| Yang | College | Stay-behind | 4 (1) | Husband's odd jobs |
| Zhu | Junior middle school | Return woman | 3 (1) | Husband's odd jobs |
| Qin | Primary school | Return woman | 3 (2) | Her odd jobs |
| You | Primary school | Return woman | 3 (1) | Husband's odd jobs |
| Xu | Primary school | Return woman | 2 (3) | Husband's odd jobs |
| He | Junior middle school | Return woman | 5 (1) | Husband's odd jobs |
| Lv | No | Stay-behind | 3 (1) | Husband's odd jobs |
| Shi | No | Return woman | 2 (2) | Sons' odd jobs |
| Zhang | No | Return woman | 5 (2) | Husband's odd jobs |
| Kong | No | Stay-behind | 2 (2) | Husband's odd jobs |

## 3.2.2 The process of gaining informed consent

Obtaining informed consent was not as difficult as I expected before I started the fieldwork. I was introduced through acquaintances of earlier consenting participants, so it was easier to gain trust than it might have been if I had been a complete stranger. In order to enable the interviewees (participants) to understand what was involved if they consented to participate in the

---

1  It does not mean that the participant has not received an education; here, 'no' means that she has not completed (primary) school.

research, I prepared project information and informed consent forms for them. Because the women I interviewed did not speak English and members of the ethics committee and my supervisory team did not speak Chinese, I have provided versions of the project information and informed consent form in both Chinese and English. All participants were given an opportunity to ask questions before they consented. If they did ask questions, I provided specific and detailed responses to help clarify things before they agreed to take part in. In addition, the information sheet provides contact information for organisations such as the Women's Union so that the interviewee can receive support if needed. I always checked that the participant was still willing to start the interview before it began and I was also attentive to their emotions during the interview. I also informed them that they could refuse to answer questions that they did not wish to answer, as well as terminate the interview at any time and withdraw from the study. All my participants came across as positive and upbeat women who were strong even when talking about difficult situations.

In addition, when introducing my project and explaining informed consent to them, I also emphasised that their participation would be anonymised. I would keep their information confidential and they would have the right to withdraw from the project even after consenting, without giving a reason. Given that my interview would revolve around the daily lives of the interviewees, in preparing for it, I also anticipated that stories with strong emotions or conflicts might emerge. I wanted to make my participants feel safe and supported. So before the interview began, I addressed any concerns about the possible risks of being interviewed, such as emotional distress or anonymity.

To a certain extent, the women who participated in the interviews focused more on my description of the project than on the content of the project information sheet. They generally skimmed through the project information sheet quickly, but still asked me questions that were already on the sheet. This may be due to the fact that some of them were not very literate and may not have fully understood the content of the information sheet. Also, when I explained that they were required to sign the informed consent form, most of them were happy to cooperate and did not worry about any adverse effects of signing or participating in the interview. They showed a great deal of trust in me. At the same time, there were a few people who were quite cautious about signing. Therefore, they repeatedly asked questions about their concerns to ensure that their signature or interview would not cause problems for their future lives. In some cases, women gave just their verbal consent, which was a provision I had made knowing that not all participants were necessarily literate. So although five women decided not to be interviewed after listening to my introduction to the project, most women were still happy to join my project and together we successfully completed the interview. The five women who eventually refused to participate expressed their concerns about the interview. For example, some were afraid that they would not understand the questions, while others were worried that their answers would become known to family members or friends.

Lastly, I informed my interviewees that I would be recording the interviews using a recording device. I also stressed that the recordings would be encrypted. I uploaded the recordings to an encrypted computer after each interview, and the folder where the files were recorded was also encrypted.

### 3.2.3 Face-to-face interviews

I had used the face-to-face research methods (Duncan and Fiske, 2015; Sappleton and Lourenço, 2015) to collect my data. Gooch and Vavreck (2016) have found that when people are asked the same question, but through different channels, for example, by online survey or face-to-face discussions, they give different answers. With this in mind, when I was preparing for the interview, I had practised mock interviews with my friend (using some interview scripts found on the internet for the interview, with a different topic to my research). Through the mock interviews, I tried both face-to-face and telephone interviews. During the telephone interviews I found that I had to repeat the questions and confirm the answers several times, that my voice and the interviewee's voice tended to overlap, and that there were short periods of silence when I was not sure if the connection was poor or if the mood of the person on the other end had changed, so I decided to go for the face-to-face interview.

In order to encourage the interviewees to express their ideas more candidly, it can be very effective for interviewers to also express their opinions openly in some cases. However, when the interviewees' opinions are different from those of the interviewer's, keeping quiet maybe the best way to gain trust from interviewees (Reinharz and Chase, 2011). When my interviewees asked questions, some of them were curious about me. For example, when I asked return women about whether they prefer to live in the countryside or the city, several interviewees wanted to know how I would respond to this question. To prevent my answers affecting their point of view, I usually gave relatively neutral answers. In other words, I aimed to make my answer more objective rather than too subjective. From my personal point of view, I prefer city life. However, when we talked about this topic, I would talk about the advantages

Chapter 3 Methodology

and disadvantages of city and rural living. In this way, I hoped to gain their trust while preventing my answers from guiding them.

All my interviewees were rural women. Harmonious relationships with interviewees are an important part of interviewing women (Reinharz and Chase, 2011). Although many women may easily establish a harmonious relationship with others, the establishment of such a relationship depends more on listening skills (Reinharz and Chase, 2011). In order not to be treated as a 'stranger' by the women I interviewed, I did not start the interview immediately. I wanted them to feel relaxed in front of me, so I usually chatted about something relaxing or interesting to them before beginning the formal interview. For example, if they were watching TV when I went in, I would naturally talk about TV shows and other related topics. I also went to the square in the centre of the village to chat with other villagers. This was not part of the fieldwork, but it gave me a quick insight into their way of life and the talking points of the villagers. In fact, some of the interviewees already knew me and even chatted with me before I went to interview them. In both ways, I felt that the interviewees were able to start the interview formally without being nervous. In that case, I was not treated as a complete stranger. This worked. During the interviews, some of the villagers would happily tell me that they had seen me before in the village square, which on the one hand made us relaxed with each other and on the other made me feel welcome. At the same time, some women were more introverted and not used to being asked to talk about themselves. When facing these women, giving them enough time to think and organise their responses, and listening to their sometimes simpler and shorter answers were important ways to keep the interview going smoothly. In fact, although some questions were occasionally difficult for these rural women to answer (in some cases they had difficulty understanding them), they would always tell me that 'we are not sure how to help you to complete your research, but we will try our best to answer your questions'. At the same time, I realised at this point that the interviewees' confusion about my questions was probably due to my status as an 'outsider', as I had a preconceived notion that they would understand my questions. For example, I would ask them about their day, such as what they had done today and what else they planned to do today. In fact, my question is to try to know how they spend a typical day. However, their first reaction when they hear the question is often that they haven't done anything all day. By explaining my questions and learning about their understanding of the questions, I found out that what they think of as 'things' are something special, such as going to weddings and other so-called 'big' things. They do not think that the experiences of daily life can be called 'things'. We have a different idea of what 'things' are. This difference in understanding not only causes them to fail to understand my questions accurately at times, but also causes them to lose sight of their own contribution and value to the family. I will discuss these issues in more detail as part of my analysis.

During the second half of my fieldwork, the area where I was doing fieldwork went into winter and it started to snow. The snow disrupted my interview plans as I had to drive to the fieldwork sites. Due to the bad weather, several scheduled interviews were cancelled and I had to reschedule. In fact, I could have actually chosen a telephone interview instead of a face-to-face interview in such cases, but I did not do this, even though telephone interviews can improve efficiency, and save time and money (Mahfoud et al., 2014). An important part of face-to-face interviewing is the observations made during interviews. People's emotions are not only conveyed through words but also expressed through actions and expressions. Therefore, the observation of interviewees during the questioning also becomes a part of the interview. What's more, face-to-face interviews increase the affinity of interviewers and respect for participants (Yan, 2002). If they are facing with living people rather than cold screens or sounds, participants' attitudes would also be more positive when they answered the questions (Yan, 2002). In addition, face-to-face interviews can yield more detailed information. It can have better response rate, compared with telephone interviews (Mahfoud, Ghandour, et al., 2014). Observing the participant's attitude in answering questions, hesitation between pauses in words, and even unnatural small movements, the details expressed by these body languages helped me answer the questions like whether they were confident in their answers or hesitant, etc. Besides, with the questions prepared in the outline, based on their expressions and body language, I could be more flexible with follow-up questions, such as questions closely based on their response. However, face-to-face interviews also provided an opportunity for the interviewees to observe me. My body language would betray my heart, and my expressions would show on my face when I heard their answers. Although I tried to hide it, I couldn't completely erase the emotions I felt.

In addition, I used a notebook to make field notes during the interview process, to record and organise the interview. In reality, it was difficult for me to take detailed notes on the interviewees' characteristics, expressions and other details during the interview, as I needed to listen carefully to their answers and then continue with in-depth questions. So, immediately after an interview, I would usually start to record details that were not captured in the audio-only recording of the interview, such as the interviewee's appearance, her living conditions and even the way she was dressed. I wanted to create a complete and three-dimensional picture of the interviewee as much as possible. In addition, I also recorded my thoughts and feelings after the interviews, and I marked the topics that the interviewees mentioned several times when I took notes. The process of taking notes also served as a review of the interviews. On the one hand, this review allowed me to collate and record the interview while it was still fresh in my memory, and on the other, it also allowed me to identify issues with the interview in time to avoid problems in subsequent interviews. The interview notes became my second dataset (Flick, 2009), which made up for the parts that I was not able to record in real time, and also made my data more three-dimensional and fuller. The interview notes played a big part in the organisation of my data later on.

## 3.3 Fieldwork's challenges and reflections

### 3.3.1 How to be professional—the relationship between me and interviewees

In order to ensure that the interviewees' opinions were accurately expressed, I needed to pay attention to "emphasizing the importance of not starting out with too many preconceptions" (Bryman, 2012, p470) during the interview. Apart from this, I also had to 'be professional', because the project required me to adopt a dual status. During the interview, I listened to women's stories and shared their feelings, and became a participant. After the interview, as a professional researcher, I recorded their lives, and at this point, I became a spectator. During the interview, I asked questions about interviewees' lives, about their children, marriages and so on. It may have caused some emotional distress for both them and me. In some cases, this emotional impact on us was likely to last until the end of the interview.

How to clearly distinguish my dual relationship with the interviewees was the key ethical issue I needed to address during the fieldwork. How I saw myself and how these rural women saw me was crucial. Theoretically, I was a research student going to a rural area to investigate and explore rural women's daily lives. My goal was 'simply' to collect data and information useful for my research project and it was highly possible that I would end up imposing my academic ideas on them during our interactions. I was faced with how to deal with my relationship with the interviewees during the fieldwork. Therefore, how to deal with the relationship with the participants was the first ethical issue which I needed to address during my fieldwork. During the interview, I was a bystander to these rural women's lives. Because the questions are closely related to their daily lives, and even touch some sensitive places, the emotions of the respondents when answering the questions also affected my emotions. This occasionally made it difficult for me to maintain the expected professional stance. But if I behaved too academically at these times, and tried to ignore the feelings of the interviewees, it may have been easy to have come across as aloof or even offensive, which is not conducive to the smooth conduct of the interview. 'Respondents may be more willing to share their experiences with a researcher whom they perceive as sympathetic to their situation' (Berger, 2015, p220). In other words, when interviewers show their empathy, interviewees will believe the interviewers more, and they will be more willing to share their stories. Thus, I regarded myself as both a participant and an observer in the fieldwork. And the interviewee was more like a sharer, sharing their life with me. During the interview, I observed and talked to people, to understand and explore what they were thinking. But after the interview, I reinstated myself as a researcher, thinking about what I observed during the interview rationally. In other words, I tried to find a way to think about and acknowledge the role I played in the interview process.

Moreover, how the local people regarded me was another important point throughout this project. I had two identities, a university student doing fieldwork in the village and a person who comes from Hohhot, one of the provincial capital cities in China. Most of the villagers knew my background when I talked to them. I had few concerns about how to build relations with them, because I was introduced to them by their acquaintances. Meanwhile, they were very curious about me. Some of them thought urban life was far away from them. They could only imagine what it was like in big cities. As a result, they usually asked me personal questions, like 'What are your parents' jobs?' 'How is the income of your family annually?' 'How long will it take you to finish your studies?' 'Is the UK very far away from China?' 'What is a Ph.D.?' 'Why do you want to do a Ph.D.?' 'Do you have a boyfriend?' In these villages, most women are married, and have children in their early 20s. Now, I am in my late 20s, and I am still single. This is a strangeness to them and made me a particular example in the village. They tended to conclude that women in big cities have high standards for boyfriends and husbands. For me, in these daily conversations, their answers also provided me with another way of thinking about what they care about and what they are curious about. What they are more interested in is why I chose their villages, a 'stay-behind' place in China, to develop my research.

I focused my research on rural female stayers' life experience and agency, a topic that is not well accepted and even unpopular in their lives. How to explain this obscure principle to the villagers was another barrier that I met with. Therefore, I could not ask them what they think about their life experience directly. I had to ask other things that are related to their daily lives. According to Yu (2014), rural populations are more interested in topics which are closer to their lives, such as agricultural production and income problems. I tried to get the information I wanted from the topics that they cared about, to understand how they conceive of a daily life.

## 3.3.2 Improving interview skills and dealing with unexpected problems

As a non-professional interviewer with no experience in interviewing, I worried most about how to start the interview and whether the interview could be conducted smoothly before the fieldwork. So, before I started the interviews, I went to my friends and conducted pilot interviews with them. In these pilot practices, I also used my mobile phone for recording. After the interviews, I was able to identify my weaknesses by listening to the recording and hoping to improve my interview skills. In fact, practising with friends helped me become more confident during interviews, especially when asking questions. Through these practices, I was able to ask expanded questions based on the respondents' answers while listening to their responses. Listening is an important part of the interview. Only when you understand the answer can you ask better questions and make a better analysis. Through practice, my interviewing skills improved and I was more able to observe interviewees.

Despite extensive interview practice, some unexpected things happened in fieldwork. Coping with these unexpected situations in fieldwork was another challenge for me. For example, during the interview with Ms. Zheng, because the questions about her daily life and family involved some sensitive and stressful things for her, she cried without warning. For me, whether the interview was continued or not had become a matter that needed to be decided very quickly. I was invariably flustered by the emotions that the interviewees suddenly fell into as a result of their stories, especially when they were in some of the more emotionally charged situations. However, this also speaks to the authenticity of the story, as authenticity is always expressed in emotion (Ezzy, 2010). At the same time, to a certain extent, I was also highly trusted by the interviewees. Telling stories of grief and loss can be useful for interviewees who have not had the opportunity to share their stories in other contexts or to other people (Shaw, 2011, as cited by Cain, 2012). When Ms. Zheng cried, I didn't comfort her or ask other questions, and what I did was give her time to let go of her sadness. I quietly waited for her to recover. After her emotional recovery, the interview continued after she indicated to me that she could continue the interview. I then indicated to her that the interview could end if she wanted, but she declined and said she could continue. This situation only happened once in my fieldwork. Because it was very sudden, it raised my vigilance and provided an effective practical experience for how to deal with similar situations later. In the middle and later stages of fieldwork, it was quite common to encounter the situation that individual interviewees were facing difficulties. I did the fieldwork at the end of autumn and the beginning of winter. Due to the cold climate and other factors, this was a relatively sparse period in the north. As a result, many women's husbands or other families working outside began to return home one after another. Due to the large population and small rooms in the countryside, it was difficult for me to conduct one-on-one interviews with women alone. In order to solve this problem and avoid the interviewees being unable to fully express their opinions due to the other people nearby, I initially tried to interview outside in the yard. Due to the cold weather outside and occasional interruption, the interviewees wanted to finish the interview as soon as possible, so it was difficult for them to fully explain their stories or express their opinions. After that, I solved the problem by inviting the interviewees to my car for a separate interview. At the same time, I tried to arrange interviews with them when their husbands were not at home (e.g. when their husbands were out shopping for

New Year's Eve, visiting their relatives, etc.) after communicating with them in advance.

### 3.3.3 The difficulties of transcription and translation

Since my interviews were conducted in Chinese, I sorted the data in two stages before the analysis. The first step was to organise the interview into text (Chinese) according to the content of the recording, and the second was to translate the interview data from Chinese into English. When sorting the data, the difficulty I faced was the dialect. The place I interviewed was in a rural area in northern China and the interviewees all used local dialects. When transcribing the recordings, I found that it was difficult to transcribe the dialects into written words. This also led to certain restrictions when translating them into English. In addition to the meaning expressed by the speaker, dialects also have an emotional extension (Li and Wang, 2008), leading to the problem of how to accurately convey emotions and express them in written language (*Putonghua*). This is particularly challenging for some dialects it is difficult to find the corresponding Chinese characters to use instead. Finally, in response to this problem, in order to reduce the loss of content and emotion during transcription and translation, my solution was to use *pinyin* instead of text to retain the tone of the interviewee when speaking. And when translating to the English version, for which I did not translate the dialects, I added notes in places to specifically explain the meaning of the word and the emotions it conveys in this context. Of course, I also know that the process of transcription is a process of selection, which is not a mechanical activity (Tessier, 2012). And translation is even more complex and takes considerable thought to arrive at a translation that not only carries literal meaning but also the right resonance. However, I hope that I have managed to convey as much as possible during the process of transcription and translation.

To sum up, in order to ensure the accuracy of the data and to reduce the loss of nuance in translation, I analysed the data in the original language, which is Chinese. Afterwards, I translated this data during the writing of the thesis.

### 3.3.4 The limitations of sample

First of all, when I selected the participants, I concentrated on the two villages adjacent to Hohhot city. From a geographical point of view, the environment they live in is consistent, and the difficulties they face are similar. However, this also led to the situation that my sampling frame can only represent the northern area around Hohhot. It has a certain reference for rural women living in areas with a similar geographical environment, but for completely different areas, whether these conclusions can represent the women in these areas needs further investigation.

Secondly, there are the limitations of the interview object. At the beginning of the fieldwork, because the interviewees involved two groups—return women and stay-behind women—I hoped that the participant numbers of the two groups would be similar. However, during the process of field investigation, due to age and other restrictions on the participants, in the end, more return women were interviewed than stay-behind women. This was caused by two factors. The first factor was the age limit. In the areas where I conducted interviews, the age of stay-behind women mostly exceeded the conditions I set. The second factor was that the area where I did my fieldwork was relatively close to the city, and the locals thought it was relatively conservative. Convenient geographical conditions make it easier for these rural people to go to urban areas to work than people living far away from urban areas, while conventional thinking makes it difficult for these rural women to stay at home alone. Therefore, many people choose to go out to work together or stay in their hometown together, so the number of stay-behind women is also relatively small.

## 3.4. Data analysis and themes

### 3.4.1 Data analysis

When I started to analyse the data, I wanted to be able to use professional sociological language. I also hoped that my data would convey the feelings of the interviewees vividly and accurately. As Back (2007) says, a good sociologist is a good listener. In other words, when analysing data, it was important for me to balance the relationship between academic language and data. Literature is only for better interpretation of data, making data easier to understand. Literature is not the protagonist. Data is the key to the research direction (Back, 2007). So I decided to use thematic analysis to analyse my data.

> 'Thematic analysis is not simply to summarize the data content, but to identify, and interpret, key, but not necessarily all, features of the data, guided by the research question (but note that in TA, the research question is not fixed and can evolve throughout coding and theme development) '(Clarke and Braun, 2017, p297).

In order to show the details and avoid omission, recording field notes during the fieldwork are useful for analysing the data. This is because field notes play an important role in connecting researchers and their subjects (Wolfinger, 2002). According to Emerson et al., if researchers are 'to preserve and agree that closure, they must describe situations and events of interest in detail' (1995, p243) and field notes are a shorthand reconstruction of events, observations and dialogue that take place on the spot (Wolfinger, 2002).

In other words, the details recorded in field notes make the data vivid and more close to the original expression and meaning. As I have explained above, the field notes I made mainly consisted of several parts: what the audio-recorder could not capture, like the expressions and body movements of the interviewees when answering questions, the living environment of the interviewees, and my thoughts on the interviewees' current answers. For example, when I entered a participant's home I could usually get a brief insight into the daily life of the household, by observing the level of decoration in the home or the newness of the appliances, etc. It was hoped that these annotations would be useful in data analysis.

After sorting out and translating all the interview materials, I tried exploring the data through NVivo 12. However, I found that it was more efficient for me to transcribe the interview into a printed text version and combine it with the field notes. Then I can code it in pen. As I eventually decided to process the data manually, I found that I could concentrate more on the text itself. To process the data manually, I needed to read it several times. In this iterative reading I could focus on the data itself, discovering more about it. A narrative and sequence that in itself was worth investing more attention in. Then, I divided the answers into themes according to their responses, such as children, parents, husbands, neighbours, working experiences, city life, domestic work. These themes gave me a picture of the interviewees' daily lives. After that I read each interview again, looking for common themes that recurred among them. Another benefit of hand-coding the analysis data like this is that it retains more sentiment for the dialect parts, while placing them in the correct topic. Although I conducted the interview in Mandarin, there were many dialects in the participants' responses. Some of these dialect words have similar meanings to Mandarin, but are more emotional in expression. For example, *benku* means the same thing as manual labour, but the word 'benku' also emphasises the person's lack of ability. Therefore, in the process of hand coding, I grouped these parts with similar meanings under the same theme, and then marked certain dialects differently to preserve their sentiment.

### 3.4.2 Three themes in the project

I collected a wealth of data through interviews as well as field notes during my fieldwork. After collating this data, I coded it, and my analysis was based on qualitative thematic coding of the interview texts. The themes I developed were derived from the data. That is, after I had coded the data collected, the codes were then constructed into generalised themes. These themes embodied the main issues relevant to addressing my research questions and I have organised my analysis chapters according to these three key themes.

The first theme is about family relationships. This section shows the everyday experience of rural female stayers and how this life affects them. To explain further, it examines the relationship between rural female stayers and their families. In other words, rural female stayers and their family responsibilities. These roles include their roles as mothers for their children, their roles as wives, and their roles as daughters or daughters-in-law with their parents or parents-in-law. I will discuss this topic in Chapter 4.

The second theme is *mianzi*. Regarding the second theme, I found that there was a focus on the rural female stayers' relationship with the people around them. Among the many community relationships, I would like to focus on how acquaintances such as friends or neighbours perceive them and how they maintain *mianzi* in their interactions with others. In the process of collecting data, rural female stayers often compare their living conditions with their neighbours or friends. They care about what people around them think of them, but don't agree with (or refute) the misunderstandings of people around them. When it came to this topic, I therefore wanted to focus on the issues behind the stigmatisation of women by those around them and how they are able to maintain *mianzi*. I will discuss this topic in Chapter 5.

The third theme is happiness. In my interviews, I felt that these rural female stayers rarely talked about their desires and pursuits. Besides, they gave little thought to happiness and described their lives as flat, but were nonetheless satisfied with them. Although not explicitly mentioned, their words and expressions often carried expectations about the future. Based on what these rural women had to say about their life experiences, how they see their lives and their childhood dreams, I will discuss how they define their lives as happy in Chapter 6.

## 3.5 Conclusion

In sum, this chapter not only introduces my thoughts on fieldwork preparation and the process of data collection, but also explains how I dealt with the challenges faced during the interviews. Doing fieldwork provides researchers an opportunity to redescribe what they have experienced in the field (Hancock and Algozzine, 2016). However, there are still some barriers that I could not overcome from time to time. For example, I needed to keep my questions simple and easy to understand, avoiding words that tend to confuse rural female stayers. When I was preparing questions, I didn't think they were far away from life and difficult to understand. However, in the field interview, I found that some of the questions I originally designed for were not relevant to my interviewees. I think this is because, as a relative outsider, I needed to communicate with a community whose experiences are very different from mine. Therefore, during the process of the interview, I was also constantly revising my interview outline, hoping that the questions would be closer to their lives. Despite this, I have to admit that although I tried my best to modify the interview outline, in many interviews, I had to spend a lot of time explaining my questions so that the interviewees could understand what I was asking. For example, when I asked questions about their value or contribution to their family, the most common reaction was a confused expression and hesitation, with some women answering that they do not think they have value to their family. I think this was caused by two factors. On the one hand, they might have never considered this aspect of their lives before; on the other, they might think 'contribution' is too important and complex a concept, too far away from the reality of their everyday life. Generally speaking, I always explained to them what I meant by contribution or value, after which they could understand what the question was asking. As an 'outsider' researcher, I also gained more by explaining the questions. It actually proved analytically fruitful, as the gaps in conversation, the hesitations and the parts where I had to offer explanations helped to bring me a closer understanding of what rural female stayers' lives were like. I am going to bring out these aspects of the analysis as I continue with the analytic chapters. In the next chapter, I will move on to the first themes, which is the daily life of rural female stayers.

# Chapter 4   Chinese rural female stayers in the family

In this chapter, I examine the picture of everyday life that emerges through rural female stayers' detailed descriptions of their daily lives. I suggest that a key aspect of this picture is the way that gender shapes the division of responsibilities in the family. Studying gender is clearly related to agency and helps to understand why some people (especially women) may choose to take on more housework, even though it may not be in their own best financial intentions (Grunow, 2019). Given the influence of Confucian culture on Chinese society, this gender division of labour is based on a patriarchal social context (Sung, 2003). Drawing on an understanding of gender as a product of social relations between men and women (Jackson and Scott, 2002), and West and Zimmerman's (1987) concept of doing gender, I argue that rural female stayers have a limited set of cultural resources for enacting appropriate femininity, and they are not free to construct gender however they like. Nonetheless, rural female stayers try to show how they can be good mothers, wives and daughters (daughters-in-law) through their agency, despite insufficient space and resources. Their exercising of agency is expressed within the limited possibilities of doing gender. It is important to note that, as I have elaborated in the literature review, the space for rural female stayers to exert their agency is limited as agency is made within the constraints imposed by the structures of their personal, social and cultural environment.

First of all, in the context of the Chinese practice of a 'child-centred' family, I will discuss how rural women as mothers take care of their children, and how they face conflicts between their children's interests and their own or even family interests. Secondly, I argue that although family life is still affected by the idea of 'husband singing and wife following', as women's importance in daily life is manifested, the relationship between women and husbands and their roles in the family have gradually changed. My focus will be on how rural women as wives participate in family decision-making and 'assisting' husbands in family life. In the third part, I will explore the role of rural women as daughters or daughters-in-law in their native family and husband's family, and how they manage the relationship with their parents (in-law) as daughters.

## 4.1 Rural female stayers as mothers

In Chinese culture, children are considered to be the flesh and blood of their parents. In other words, their connection is viewed as natural and unchangeable.

In Chinese culture, children are usually taught to have strong family values and believe that family and kinship are indispensable to a happy life (Ho, 1986, cited by Chang, Stewart, et al., 2003). In Chinese society, filial piety and parents' reciprocal commitment to children's happiness not only idealise the parent-child relationship with young children, but also the parent-child relationship between teenagers and adults (Chang, Stewart et al., 2003). In terms of Chinese family relations, the relationship between mother and child is often closer (The China National Children's Center, 2013). In other words, the mother's influence and 'control' on the child are more comprehensive and it is not unreasonable for a mother to put the focus of her life on her children. On the contrary, when a woman who has became a mother is busy with career or other things, this will be considered abnormal by the people around her in all contexts. In fact, when describing women who are successful in their careers, they often use the term 'strong women'[1] (Liu, Yang and Jiang, 2015). Although 'strong women' is a positive compliment, in everyday use it can also be a derogatory term. 'Strong women' is a term used to emphasise women's ability to be successful at work, an assessment that in practice ignores the contribution these women make to their families. So when evaluating whether women are good mothers, strong women are often described as women who only pursue career success at the expense of their families and children, and thus becoming a derogatory term. At the same time, when describing men as successful, the gender factor is ignored in the use of words and they are referred to as successful people rather than 'strong men'. Hence, the term strong women is somewhat biased, because the Chinese would never call a successful man a 'strong man'.[2] Therefore, when women are willing to sacrifice their own interests to become a 'perfect' mother, society often gives them more praise. The perfect mother means that she concentrates more on the inside of the home and the children rather than concerning herself with factors outside of the home, such as work. Unlike rural mothers, urban mothers face the dual pressure of having a career and being a good wife and mother. The rural mothers I interviewed recognized this and, as I will illustrate through my findings, were also proud of their roles as mothers because society's evaluation of women is based on

---

[1] 'Strong women', called '*nv qiang ren*' in Chinese, is usually used to describe successful women to show that they are very capable.

[2] 'Strong man' in Chinese is literally '*qiang ren*'. In reality, there is no such saying in Chinese.

their contribution to the family, and here, children are the most important part of the family. Although some of these rural female stayers have lived in the city and returned to the countryside, and some have not lived in the city, they often seem to share the same goal as mothers.

### 4.1.1 The 'child-centred' model in everyday life

Ms. Wang is a stay-behind woman and her living situation is representative of most stay-behind women in my study. She has two sons, one of whom is an adult and lives in the city. Her second son is of school age and Ms. Wang's typical day revolves around caring for him. Due to poverty, her poor health and long-term medication, she always feels great pressure.

> 'What things can I like in daily life? Every day is to take care of my little son. Nothing else can be done. Now, if I'm not feeling good in one day, my bad health condition makes most work hard for me to do. Now every day, what I can do is to take my son to school and pick him up from school, and then cook for him. I used to farm when I was not ill, but I can't do it now. It is too heavy for me... My husband has no contribution either. Look at the bungalow. I lived in this bungalow with him when I got married. If the bungalow is unoccupied, it would have collapsed long ago. He can't make much money and the money he earns is just enough to maintain a basic life. We just enough suffer from *BenKu*[1], because he has no skill, and I have no skill. The focus of my life now is my youngest son, and I need to send him to school and

---

[1] *BenKu*, in the northern dialect, refers to unskilled and low-paid labour with few qualifications required to work these kinds of jobs. *Ben*, means stupid. It emphasises that there is no selectivity or requirements involved; while *Ku* means that the work is laborious and really hard to do, and that the people doing this job are coolies.

pick him up every day (she repeats again). He is the priority; the child comes first in everything. Last year, my husband and I borrowed money to buy an apartment for my eldest son in the city, so now our finances are very tight. In this case, I can't go to the city. Living in an urban area costs a lot of money. My financial situation is worse because of the cost of buying a house for my older son. I have to spend less on me in order to provide enough money for my younger son. I don't want the child to suffer. I have this younger son and I can't work even if I go to the city… When the second child grows up, I may go to live in the city, because the child needs to attend the cram study session. But I don't really want to go. Living in the village saves money because the house is my own, I can plant vegetables myself, and I also raise sheep. Things like these do not cost money… I know, urban life is great. Without the second son, I might also like to work in an urban area. After all, I can earn more in the city. Due to the situation now, I don't want to go.' [Ms. Wang, stay-behind woman]

In interview with Ms. Wang, the conversation always turned to her children. Her life seemed to be closely tied to her children in every way. When talking about her daily life, her descriptions unfolded entirely with the children at the centre, and although she shared with me aspects of her attitude towards her husband, her evaluation of herself and so on, the criteria for generating the evaluation were actually based on whether they benefited the children.

Just as Ms. Wang centred the conversation on her young son, most of the other women I interviewed also talked a lot about their children in the interview. In rural areas, mothers play the more traditional role of housewives, and they stay at home most of the time. To a certain extent, the interaction between the child and the mother is more frequent (Li, et al., 2015). Although Ms. Wang constantly denies her and her husband's usefulness when talking about their contributions, her answer still shows that she is completely dedicated to her children. Just as Ms. Wang compromised step-by-step on her choices for the sake of her children, her children became the basis for her decisions and ultimately for their implementation. She puts the interests of her children first and chooses to ignore her own interests and desires in order to maximise the benefits for her children. In fact, even though she has never experienced city life, Ms. Wang did not completely rule out going to the city in the future. All her assumptions and plans are made around the children's schooling. Although it can be expected that the higher consumption levels in urban area will bring more economic pressure, this did not matter to Ms. Wang. According to my participants' accounts, parents should help their children regardless of the personal consequences. Despite some regrets because of their sacrifices, they want to put the focus on their children. They try to show their focus on their role as mothers. As Ms. Wang stresses, while her interests can be sacrificed, she cannot let her children suffer. This corroborates the study by Bi and Oyserman (2015), in which mothers reported the only thing that gave them hope was helping their children to succeed.

### 4.1.2 Being a good mother

Ms. Zheng, who lives in a typical three-generation family together with her parents-in-law and children, describes how she defines a good mother and enacts this role through an account of her everyday life. There are seven people living in Ms. Zheng's household. After dropping out of junior high school, she started to work in the city.

And after getting married, she worked in the city with her husband. Then, she returned to the countryside with her husband and now takes care of the family at their rural home. Ms. Zheng said:

> 'At that time, the child (elder son) went to high school. The local textbooks were different from Inner Mongolia, and (as we do not have urban *hukou*[1]) my son had to take the exam at my home (in the rural area where they have *hukou*). In addition, my father-in-law needs to be taken care of and he wanted us to move back to the rural area. So (me and) my husband decided to come back to the rural area. I want to go to the city to work, but the second child (my little daughter) is now in primary school and needs to be picked up every day. Because the price of food in the city is high and my family is large, we cannot all go to the city together. So, I don't think I can migrate to the urban areas in the near future. Housework at home (including farming) depends mainly on me, and earning money outside depends on my husband. The economy is quite tense now, and in fact, the family was not as well-off as when my husband and I were working in the city.'
> [Ms. Zheng, return woman]

Higher wages were their reason for migrating to the city to work in the first place. However, when the children and others for whom they care were on the opposite side of their wish to go to the city, these mothers seem no choice. Their decisions are always child-centred. Many of the women I interviewed expressed to me that earning more money is nothing more than saving some

---

1 *Hukou*, China's household registration management system divides the household registration into urban and rural households based on blood inheritance and geographic location. It stipulates that citizens enjoy education, medical care, public services and other resources in the place of household registration, and the state also grants subsidies based on household registration.

money for their children's future. In fact, for these rural women, whether they move to the city, stay in the countryside or return, the decision is made with their children at the centre.

For these mothers, returning home is a sacrifice they make for their children. As mentioned in the literature review, in recent years, the government has gradually introduced various policies to help migrant workers' children study in urban schools. Consequently, more schools for the children of migrant workers have been established in the cities and more public schools for the children of migrant workers have begun to accept the children of migrant workers. However, these children still need to return to their hometowns (in rural areas) where they have *hukou* (household registration) because they cannot take the entrance examination of high school and university in an urban area if they do not have urban *hukou* (Wu, Tsang and Ming, 2014). So, many people, such as Ms. Zheng, choose to take their children back home. As Ms. Zheng mentioned, when she returned to the countryside, her income dropped and her family's life was 'more stressful than before'. Although caring for her father-in-law was also a factor in Ms. Zheng's return to the countryside, it came second to the children in terms of priority.

In contrast, Ms. Xu demonstrates another way to be a competent mother—going to the city. There are five people in Ms. Xu's family: her, her husband and their three daughters. Now, she and her husband live in the countryside. Her daughters all work in the city. After the youngest child went to university, she and her husband returned to the countryside and now the family's income mainly depends on them doing odd jobs in the village. The reason why Ms.

Xu went to the city was primarily to accompany her daughter.[1] After her daughter finished her studies, she and her husband returned to the countryside. Ms. Xu:

> 'I don't have any major sources of stress in my life now. My children all have their own jobs and I did my best to support their education. I feel that life is much easier after I have returned to living in the rural areas. I don't hate city life, but I have no reason to stay in the city now. In fact, living in the city has a lot of expenses, such as renting an apartment. My husband was not earning a stable income from his part-time jobs in the urban area, and we were living in the city just for our children.... When I was living in the city, I made breakfast for my daughter, and she went to school after eating it; then I could do some housework, and then it was time for me to buy foods and cook for my daughter again. At noon I had to help my child keep track of the time to avoid her being late for school, and then I had cook again in the afternoon... That was the case for the past few years.' [Ms. Xu, return woman]

Cities undoubtedly have better educational resources and teaching conditions. For example, in terms of progression rates, a much higher percentage of students from urban areas go on to major universities (Yang, Yang and Huang, 2018). There were also some rural families in my study who had decided to send their children to school in the city. Just as qualified urban parents hope to choose better schools for their children, these rural families with lower

---

1   Accompanying reading refers to the behaviour of parents participating in the whole process of the child's life and learning. Since many schools do not have dormitories, parents often choose to rent an apartment near the school to facilitate their children's education. The accompanying reading parents are mostly women. They usually put their body and soul into the care of their children and they do not work outside.

incomes and insufficient education are also very aware of the importance of education. Some mothers like Ms. Xu decided to become accompanying parents. After their children enter university (usually after the college entrance examination), these accompanying mothers would go back to the countryside, and their short-lived city life revolved around their children. These accompanying mothers hardly had any friends in the city. In fact, they didn't have the opportunity or time to get to know the people around them:

> 'The children go to school and the husband works outside all day. I occasionally feel lonely. However, most of the time I am very busy and there are many places where my children need to take care of. In fact, wherever I live, I spend my life just the same.' [Ms. Xu, return woman]

When I asked Ms. Xu about her own life, she answered me this way. Her brief sojourn in the city was a difficult decision that a mother has to make for her child. According to her description, life in the city was not easy, but she wanted her children to have a better education. So she and her husband had to live in the city for several years and then quickly returned to the countryside after her daughter graduated from high school. Ms. Xu's urban experience is not unique. For example, Ms. He also used to take care of her children in the city, which resulted in her family income being entirely covered by her husband, and the expenses of city life also put a lot of financial pressure on the family. Before accompanying her children, Ms. He also used to work in the city, but when her children needed care, she decided to become a fulltime mother. She said that:

> 'I considered working and taking care of the child at the same time, but it would have been difficult. My main task was to take care of my daughter, who was busy with school work, and my schedule was

completely built around her study schedule. So I didn't have time to go out to work and my family had to rely on my husband's income.' [Ms. He, return woman]

Many rural mothers who choose to go to the city to accompany their children have to give up their lives completely. They cannot work in the city because they are worried that they will not be able to take care of their children, and their work and rest time is completely arranged according to the child's time. The experience of accompanying mothers may be different from the image we have of return women, given that we know more about migrant women who work in the city. Despite their entry into urban life, accompanying mothers still perform housework within the family and may even lose the little social space they have due to a lack of friends or acquaintances in the urban area.

Ms. Xu is proud of her daughter, who has made it to university, and she feels that her hard work and dedication have been rewarded. The success of her daughter has also boosted her reputation in the village and overall, raising a child is what Ms. Xu considers to be her greatest contribution to the family:

> 'I have worked very hard to bring up the child and she is now able to earn her own money. It's the biggest contribution I've made to the family. I've almost always taken care of the child from a young age. I (and my husband) didn't care about anything else.' [Ms. Xu, return woman]

While praising herself for being a good mother, she expresses that the husband's involvement in the process is minimal. To a certain extent, the success of the child is more of her success as a mother. As a result, children have become the label by which the good mother's competence is measured, rather than the measure of a good father. And 'successful mother' has become the criterion by which these rural women define their own contribution to the family. This is because their lives are, to some extent, organised around their children. In the meantime, they recognize this criterion for evaluating 'good mothers'.

Ms. Han's husband usually works outside the home, and she is a stay-behind woman, and she only has a child. When it comes to being a good mother, Ms. Han said that a key issue is to ensure that you do not have too many children:

> 'The family is not well-off. If I raise two children at the same time, it will be a great burden for my family. Especially in terms of finances. On the other hand, if I raise two children together, I don't have the confidence to do well (the role of mother)...I hope he can get the best (that I can give). Of course, the older generation (referring to her parents) want me to have another child, but I only want him (the child). It is enough.' [Ms. Han, stay-behind woman]

As times change, the old idea of having more than one child is disappearing. In fact, the one-child policy in rural areas has always been distinct from that in urban areas (Murphy, Tao and Lu, 2011). Before the liberalisation of the one-child policy, in a rural area, if the first child was a girl, then the family could have a second child. This was because of the need for agricultural labour. Under the influence of factors such as the influx of rural labour into the cities and the mechanisation of agriculture many, rural families are no longer looking for more labour. Therefore young stay-behind mothers are more likely to stick to their idea of raising only one child. Rural female stayers are beginning to emphasise securing more and better resources for their children, something which is at odds with having more than one child. According to my study, in recent years younger rural female stayers have become less willing to have a second child because they want to be good mothers. Their limited experience and lack of resources does not allow them to have a second child. This desire to have only one child has nothing to do with the gender of their first child. Most of Ms. Han's generation have siblings, and from their own experience, they feel that mothers who lack the resources are in fact less able to set their children up for socially defined success. As a result, when they became mothers, they tried to discover new ways to maximise their limited resources to raise their children and thus achieve their goal of being good mothers. As the number of children increases, the resources provided to specific children will decrease (Li, Liu and et al., 2015). In the one-child family, the mother devotes all her time and energy to the child, which undoubtedly increases the chance of contact between mother and child and deepens the relationship between them (Hao and Feng, 2002). In addition, since the parents only have one child to invest in, they will have higher expectations for their offspring and a greater desire for control and protection (Jiao, Ji, and Jing, 1992). At the same time, government policy emphasises the need for quality not quantity. In 2021 the 'better natal and prenatal care and better upbringing' initiative was introduced, so that every family will have healthy children and every child born will have a good education (Hao, 2021). Against this background, as my data shows, in order to give their children what they have, many rural female stayers are choosing to be good mothers of one child rather than (less adequate) mothers with many children, though what they can give is limited.

### 4.1.3 The sacrifice of being a good mother

Stay-behind woman Ms. Shen was one of the participants who very directly illustrates how her choices as a mother were made for the sake of her children. For most of the year, Ms. Shen lives with her young son. Her husband works outside the home, so she is responsible for all the household and farm work. Ms. Shen said:

> 'Whenever it is definitely for the children, it doesn't matter how much hard work is needed for my child... My husband is not here, I can take care of my family and the children by myself, although it is not easy. When my husband is not living at home, I sometimes feel very tired because there is no one to share the housework and the bad emotion... however, I encourage him to go out to work...save more money for the future of the child.' [Ms. Shen, stay-behind woman]

For these stay-behind women, the fact that their husbands have gone to the city to work also puts more pressure on them, but it is the only way to improve the family's financial situation (Li, 2018). In Ms. Shen's case, the heavy work of agricultural production and the household chores of caring for the elderly and children are all carried out by a woman alone, and in the absence of a husband, there is nobody to share the ups and downs of life with. These rural women prefer to define themselves as mothers willing to give their best for their children. In the meantime, as Ms. Shen and others describe their daily life, the rural female stayers at home in the countryside lack other resources and their children become the focus of their attention. These stay-behind women are separated from their husbands and living alone in the countryside with their children. Although they may not be able to prioritise their role as wives, they have fulfilled what they describe as their most important mission—to be a good mother. As Ms. Wu says, 'It is clear to everyone that whether they are in the rural area, going to the city or returning to the rural area, mothers will be there when the children need care.' In addition, these mothers show they have higher expectations for the development of their children and they think that this is their responsibility (Ma, 2018). These elevated expectations for the children are mainly due to the mothers putting the family at the centre of their lives. Rural female stayers follow the custom whereby Chinese women will sacrifice themselves when confronted with a conflict of interest between self and family. They gave up the opportunity to live with their husbands in the city or to earn money in the city. As a mother, there are limited resources that can be provided for children by rural female stayers. This is because they themselves lack resources and most do not have the power to decide on family matters and resources. However, as mothers, rural female stayers seek more for their children by sacrificing their own interests. They are dedicated mothers who always put their children first.

At the same time, Ms. Shi notes that rural female stayers blame themselves for their children's failures. When Ms. Shi, who used to work in the city, talked about her regrets, she expressed sadness that she could not take care of her son by herself:

> 'I never took care of him when he was young, because I was working in the city... He could not study well and went to work. How I wanted him to have good (school) grades and then go to university so that he can have a good life in the future. I think if I had taken care of him at home then, maybe he could've gone to high school or even college. However, my family was too poor and I had to go to the city to work to feed and clothe him .' [Ms. Shi, return woman]

Ms. Shi blames herself for her son's academic failure, as she feels that her own inadequacies as a mother have led to her son's lack of academic success, which in turn has led to the fact that his life is not as smooth and easy as it should be. At the same time, she emphasises the reasons why she had to go to work and tries to find a justification for her 'failure' to be a good mother through these reasons. As Ms. Shi mentioned that a mother's greatest responsibility is to enable her child to have a 'successful' life, of which learning becomes a measurable criterion. My data shows that the child's academic failure is seen as evidence that she is not a good mother, even though her reason for working is to provide better material conditions for her child. Although poverty is not her fault, she sees this as part of what she has failed to do. And it affects the children as a result, which becomes a failing that a mother needs to take on. As for the child's father, who also works in the city, he is not the target to such criticism. With the development of urbanisation, the interaction between urban and rural areas has become more frequent. It has also become easier for farmers to go to cities to work. As parents leaving the countryside, many rural children are 'left-behind'. Rural families have little choice in this. However, with regard to the issue of left-behind children, mothers have been criticised by society more than fathers (Xiao and Tang, 2021). People seem to acquiesce that the mother of a left-behind child is by no means a competent mother. It is not easy to be a good mother. The criteria for good motherhood are clear, but the difficulties of being a good mother vary depending on material circumstances. My data show that it is not easy for rural female stayers to affirm themselves as a qualified mother, even though they have made a lot of sacrifices for their children. The old custom requires rural women to confine their attention to the family, and place the children at the centre of the family. They are not allowed to be left in the hands of others. Migrant mothers are therefore at a disadvantage when it comes to being a good mother. They face the dual pressures of the economy and their status as mothers. They need to meet the material needs of their children, and at the same time, they have to abide by the social standards of fulfilling the obligations of mothers (To, Lam and So, 2020). Due to the objective reality of rural people living in cities without *hukou*, many return women had to leave their children behind in the countryside while they worked in the cities, which resulted in them being unable to take care of their own children. These mothers feel that they have not done their job as mothers by their own or society's standards. Rural female return women ignore the fact that they have had to leave their homes because they are trying to provide a better material situation for their children. In Ms. Shi's story, women are asked to take primary responsibility for the care of the children because their gender dictates it. However, when they fail to do what is expected of them, they feel guilty and think that they have 'failed'. At the same time, however, they try to rationalise their 'failures' because it is important for them to be 'good' mothers.

In order to take care of her children, Ms. Zhang gave up her job in the city and returned to the countryside. As Ms. Zhang says, for some rural women, going back is actually a kind of relief:

> 'I finally have the opportunity to be a real mother. Even though I cannot earn money for my children, I am safe by his side and I feel at ease now. I try to do what a mother should do, for example, taking care of her children by herself.' [Ms. Zhang, return woman]

In my study, when motherhood conflicts with other options, being a good mother is the first choice for rural female stayers, if they have a chance to choose. Although by giving birth to a child, women become mothers, rural female stayers try to emphasise that their goal is successful or good motherhood. Despite the limited options available to rural female stayers in order to be good mothers, the interests of their children are given the highest priority. The media and schools have discovered that left-behind children have more learning difficulties and psychological problems, and have spoken out about this, hoping to attract attention (Bi and Oyserman, 2015), and my data suggests that rural women are aware of such discourse. With the attention of society and schools, the problems of left-behind children are also a concern for their families. Many mothers are returning to the countryside to take care of their children themselves, describing this as important and conducive to the healthy development of their children. Although society's expectations for women to become mothers have not changed, unlike urban mothers who want to balance themselves and their families (Hu, 2015), these rural mothers often have no requirements for themselves, and the family is their only focus. This is due to the different living conditions of urban and rural mothers. At the same time, as my data shows, there are fewer job opportunities in rural areas, which leaves many rural mothers with less personal space or resources than their urban counterparts. For example, in one of the villages where I did my fieldwork, the main source of employment for women was in the village's nursing home, which needed some staff to look after the elderly. In my interviews, I found that more and more rural women are choosing to return when their children reach school age or stay in the rural area because their children need to go to school in the countryside, while some women are moving to the cities because their children need their company to school. If working in the cities provides a better material foundation for the family, especially the children, then when more and more families realise the importance of parenting to the growth of their children, then mothers will decide to return to their families and sacrifice their own interests. This confirms that the child is the centre of the family. Rural female stayers as mothers are trying to make the best choice for their children. At the same time, it is a choice that rural female stayers make in order to become good mothers.

## 4.2 Rural female stayers as wives

In China, marriage is the foundation of the family, and the relationship between husband and wife is one of the most important relationships in the family (Ye and Wu, 2009). The family, as the basic unit of society, is a very important institutional arrangement and functional institution (Liu, 2016). In traditional times, the marriage of a man and a woman was a cultural arrangement to form a family community, and marriage and family relations were highly compatible together (Yi, 2019). In the countryside, the establishment of marriage not only means the establishment of a new family, but also marks the beginning of independent adulthood for both sexes. For rural female stayers, some of them live separately from their husbands, who work in the city. At the same time, many of them live with their in-laws or even their husbands' unmarried siblings. The sense of responsibility and pressure that marriage and family bring to men encourages them to go out to work, while their wives take care of the elderly and children at home. When face-to-face communication is not possible, the telephone becomes the main communication tool between husband and wife (Ye and Wu, 2009) while new communication technologies like WeChat have become another way for couples to connect (Qiu, 2022). In the process of contact, husbands are dominant and they often take the initiative to contact their wives. In the process of this connection, the husband and wife create a situation in which the husband feels at home. On the one hand, it reflects the husband's concern for the family; on the other hand, it also gives the wife the chance to talk about her emotions and her daily housework (Ye and Wu, 2009). Domestic chores have traditionally been women's responsibility, even when they work outside the home, and balancing work and household chores is a necessity (Benston, 1997). Men can give their views in the domestic sphere as well as

Chapter 4 Chinese rural female stayers in the family

outside the home, but for women, the home is often the only place where they can express themselves (Sun, and Cheng, 2013), and this is even more so in rural areas.

The relationship between husband and wife in rural families can be analysed from two perspectives. The first is the household division of work between husband and wife. The second is the discourse rights of the family.

### 4.2.1 The household division of work between husband and wife

As a return woman, Ms. Zhang's answers show her thoughts on returning to her home village and are very representative of the return women in my data. Ms. Zhang said:

> 'I spend most of my days at home looking after my children and my parents in-law, cooking or doing other household work after coming back to the rural area. My husband is responsible for working outside the home to earn money. My husband's contribution to the family is the greatest, and the family's income depends entirely on him. I've thought about getting a job, but it's difficult in the village. And my husband always says that you should just work at home, don't be like other women (referring to the women who are working in the urban area)... The only thing I ask of you is that you take care of the family and that's enough. He doesn't want me to leave home too much and go out to work. In his opinion, it is the woman who stays at home and does the housework, which is their *benfen*[1]. I'm already busy enough with the housework at home, so it's just imagining for me to go to the city to work.' [Ms. Zhang, return woman]

---

1 Here it means their own duties and obligations.

Ms. Zhang's statement demonstrates the division of labour between her and her husband in the family. Her husband has the right to decide on family matters, where the right to decide means, on the one hand, that her husband is deciding on family matters and, on the other hand, that his views also influence her decisions. In the family, her husband is the one who is responsible for earning money to support the household, while she is responsible for other tasks within the home. Influenced by conventional thinking, the constructed gender difference between men and women is reflected in the different division of labour between husband and wife. In fact, many husbands would assume that it is the wife's job to take care of the family and his main role is making money outside of the home. The historical mindset of 'men outside, women inside', which means women take care of the family and men become the source of income, still greatly affects the Chinese family where traditions persist (Hu and Scoot, 2016). In the rural areas, many rural husbands are more conservative in their mind and in my study they were not very supportive of their wives' choice to work outside the home, as Ms. Zhang also mentions. One of the criteria for assessing whether a woman is a good wife is whether she is '*benfen*', and the 'honest' to stay at home, following the old division of labour is the most acceptable state of the family for a husband. Their wives, on the other hand, accept this situation. 'My husband is the main earner in my family, and I don't contribute much, except for doing these chores around the house and taking care of the children and the elderly.' quoted from Ms. Zhang The observations of Ms. Zhang demonstrate that the ideology of gender roles justifies the gender division of labour bias in the couple's relationship. The husband is seen as the one who needs to provide for the family, while the wife is not. In family life, the general requirements of rural female stayers for their husbands are mainly that they have sufficient income to support the family normally and they do not expect their husbands to take responsibility for the household chores or child and elderly care. Rural women are very happy when their husbands take the initiative to share some of the household chores, seeing it as an unexpected bonus (Hu, 2015). In my data, while rural female stayers did not require their husbands to be involved in household chores, a few rural female stayers made it clear that they felt happy and more relaxed when their husbands came forward to help. However, the majority of rural female stayers that I interviewed expressed that their expectations of their husbands were only about their husbands' income, and that housework was not part of their evaluation criteria for a good husband. Even to the extent that Ms. Shen, who is a stay-behind woman, said of her husband's housework, 'He doesn't have the skills to do housework, and if he does do some housework, it will lead to more work for me. It's better and faster for me to do it myself.'

In fact, economic pressure has been affecting most rural families. In many families in my study, the husband's going out to work does not bring a stable income to the household, but the wife still affirms the husband's great contribution to the family. From the perspective of the wife, the actual economic contribution is far greater than the 'invisible' contribution of taking care of the family by doing housework at home. As Ms. Zhang put it, her husband makes the greatest contribution to her family. The reality is that the wife recognizes the husband's value and contribution to the family. Housework does not bring visible economic value, and these tasks are categorised as women's obligations, which makes rural female stayers' contribution to the family easily overlooked (Sun and Cheng, 2013). As Sun argues, in rural areas, both rural female stayers and their husbands evaluate a woman's value and contribution from the standpoint of men, which makes it difficult for people, including rural female stayers themselves, to recognise women's contribution to the family (2013).

Indeed, it is not only the idea that women should take care of their families that prevents rural female stayers from working, but also the lack of job opportunities in rural areas. Although there may not seem to be a conflict between women caring for the children and elderly at home and working outside the home, it does pose a problem in rural areas where there are fewer job opportunities. As Ms. Zhang said, finding a job in the rural areas is difficult. In order to find work, most rural women have to leave the countryside for the cities, which makes it difficult for them to care for the elderly at home. At the same time, in the interview with Ms. Kong, she also mentioned a reason. 'I feel that even if I went into town, I wouldn't be able to find a job ... I'm not very educated, I know very little and I'm afraid of being cheated.' Ms. Kong lives in the rural area with her son and her husband works in the urban area as a junk collector. Some rural female stayers still have a sense of fear or apprehension about finding work outside the home, which has a negative impact on changing the existing division of labour between men and women. Although some women hope to get some income from going out to work, the subordinate status of rural women in the job market makes it difficult to find a job. The interviewees suggested that the extremely limited range of options and resources given to rural female stayers, coupled with their definition of themselves as good women who should be taking care of family, prevent them from becoming the main breadwinners of the family like their husbands. In Ms. Zhang's case, we can see the influence of the wife's role ideology in the division of labour in the household. The wife's work is not seen as valuable to the family, while the husband's financial income is seen as extremely important or as the only contribution to the family. This makes it difficult for rural female stayers to avoid the division of labour that comes with family responsibilities in family life. At the same time, rural female stayers agree with their husbands' demands for them to maintain *'benfen'*. They expect themselves to comply with their husbands' demands and to do their household chores without question.

## 4.2.2 The right of decision in rural female stayers' families

Ms. Chu returned to the countryside with her husband, having previously worked as a cashier in a small supermarket in the city. Despite the tiring and fast-paced city life and the monotony of her cashier's job, she had wanted to stay in the city but followed her husband back to the rural area. Ms. Chu said:

> 'They (meaning husbands) make decisions, and in the village it is mostly men who make decisions. A woman married to a husband has to listen to him, and women always lack knowledge. There are things that the husband can do if he is happy. If he is not happy, although I want to do it, it is useless. I don't care if this matter is good for me. If a husband wants to do it, I will just follow his decision... A good wife should obey her husband. I do not want to go back to the rural area, especially when my family (natal family) are living in the city. It was easy to go to see them, but I had to listen to him (my husband)... After all, my husband is the backbone of the family and earning enough money is just one aspect. I definitely listen to what he has to say.' [Ms. Chu, return woman]

After marriage, most women will abide by their husband's decisions, honouring the Chinese saying, 'Follow the man you marry, be he a cock or dog'[1], which was always quoted by the rural female stayers in my study. Ms. Chu's statement suggests that listening to her husband is seen as a quality

---

1  It is believed that when a woman is married, she must live in harmony with her husband and follow the rules that he asks her to follow, regardless of the circumstances or whether he is a good or bad man.

of a 'good wife'. If rural female stayers want to establish themselves as good wives, then they lose the right to make decisions and are seen, to some extent, as followers. This relationship takes away from the equality of the couple. Rural female stayers in my study did not believe that they are being treated unfairly in the daily routine of their husbands making decisions for the family. They took this situation for granted, as they tended to recognise that their husbands' decisions were worth more. The rural female stayers in my study thought that since financial income could make a real difference to the family's living conditions. The ability to earn money in rural households became an important criterion for evaluating whether a person is capable. However, the dominance of women in domestic work keeps them away from 'economic activities' (Singh and Pattanaik, 2020). To a certain extent, the criterion is mostly directed at men. The rural female stayers believed that the 'visible' contribution of the husband to the family gives them the absolute right to make decisions. Furthermore, rural female stayers have become accustomed to this state of unrecognised value. Ms. Lv, a stay-behind woman, repeatedly expressed the importance of her husband when talking about the respective contributions to the family. 'Our family's income comes mainly from my husband, and all I can do is cook and take care of the children and things like that, which cannot be considered (as a contribution) at all. ' When stay-behind women do not recognise their own value, they indirectly put themselves in a lower position than their husband, which also affects their decision-making power in family matters. Although unpaid domestic work, as an important aspect of productive activity, contributes to family and economic well-being (Singh and Pattanaik, 2020) as Ye and Wu (2009) argue, for stay-behind women, the husband is the pillar of the family. What Ms. Chu said was similar to the findings of Ye and Wu's study, and she went a step further in her description, even though rural female stayers are not necessarily satisfied with their husbands' income, they do follow their husbands' advice. Besides, as rural female stayers believe that people (husbands) who contribute the most should make the decisions, and the husband's greater contribution is recognised by his wife, the husband automatically gets the power to decide on family matters.

The situation of return women is not exactly the same as that of stay-behind women; however, this positioning of the husband as the decision-maker was not without nuance in my data. Ms. He is a return woman who now cares for her husband's parents mainly in the rural areas. Ms. He said:

> 'Generally speaking, I can decide on small things, but I have to ask my husband about big things. The experience of living in the city has allowed me to speak my mind in the family. When I was in the city, I found that city women would argue with their husbands over disagreements and these (city) women were not ashamed of it ... City women like to make their own decisions and go along with their own ideas… I feel that I can now make some decisions. For example, I sent my child to go to a school in the city which has a good reputation. I also have more confidence to speak up when I earn money and my husband is more willing to refer to my advice because of the income I can bring into the family. Of course, my family continues to live mainly on my husband's income.' [Ms. He, return woman]

According to what Ms. He described to me, most of the things she decided were everyday things, such as what to eat and so on. For things that cost a lot of money or do not happen very often in daily life, it's really up to her husband to decide, for example, whether or not to pay more money for the children to attend the school in the city, even though her husband lives far away from her for the most of the year. At the same time, husbands make most of the decisions in the household, but they do not tend to do the actual household work themselves. The experience of living in the city, to some extent, has changed the situation where wives are completely at the mercy of their husbands' decisions. Return women with migrant work experience have greater discursive power in some respects (Sun, 2012). This is because their income has improved the living standards of their families. At the same time, the broadening of their horizons after leaving their communities also makes them aware of their status in the family and they start to yearn for some power. As my data shows, a visible income is more likely to help women improve their status in the family, which increases their voice and sense of confidence in the home. Return women also recognise their importance to the family and have the courage to express their indispensability (although most people express it indirectly). Their experience of working in cities allows them to see themselves and their husbands on more equal terms, and they break the habitual thinking of rural areas where they are their husband's accessory. The old standards of a 'good' wife have changed and return women are finding that women's independence, reflected by their deciding family matters and disagreeing with their husbands, is not a reason to deny their value and contribution. As Ms. He expressed when she talked about her own value to the family, 'the family does everything by discussing, and not talking about how much they pay and the size of the value.' While she praised her husband's contribution and sacrifice to the family, she also affirmed her efforts. Return women put themselves on a more independent platform. This is because their income has improved the living standards of their families. At the same time, their broader vision after migrating also makes them begin to emphasise their status in the family and yearn for some rights. Although they cannot always make choices according to their wishes, they are happier now that they have been given the right to express themselves. Moreover hand, even though Sun's research showed that return wives are still dependent on their husbands (2012), my study reveals a different result that it is better to say that return women still find it difficult to make decisions entirely on their own. By comparison, rural female stayers follow the decisions of their husbands, and even if they express their opinions occasionally, they do not care whether these opinions are adopted. As a return woman, Ms. Sun says, 'My husband makes the decisions in our family, but I say what I have in mind and it's up to him whether he cares to listen or not.' For them, expressing opinions is more about participating in family affairs, rather than wishing to decide something for the family. I would argue that the return women who I interviewed are trying to create a new image of themselves as more independent by having a voice in family matters and showing that they can get enough respect and support from their husbands. Although a woman's income contributes to her voice in the family, men still have more decision-making rights due to the dominance of customary thinking.

To sum up, there are two main answers to the question of who has the right to make decisions in the family: one is a situation whereby it is the husband who makes all the decisions, and the other is one in which the wife becomes more involved in the process. On the one hand, as more and more women experience working in the city, and are exposed to new ideas, many are gradually taking on more responsibility in the family—they are sharing or have shared the financial burden, and thus they have a greater right in the family than before. On the other hand, although working away from home makes it difficult for husbands to be involved in family decisions in a timely manner, they still have absolute decision-making rights in the family. Indeed, the family is a space where men have ultimate authority, while at the same time there are limited demands on them when it comes to family responsibilities and child rearing (Mallett, 2004). As a wife, the rural female stayer is gradually gaining the right to make her own decisions or at least express an opinion about the family in some situations.

## 4.3 Rural women as daughters in the natal family and daughters-in-law in the husband's family

Married women actually straddle two living spaces—their mother's home and their mother-in-law's home—and are able to deploy resources from and implement strategic activities between both spaces (Chen and Wang, 2012). In fact, given the change in rural women's living situation from living in the father's home to living in the husband's family, married women are often seen as outsiders to the parents-in-laws and guests in the natal family (Weng and Li, 2019). In the process of gradually integrating into the husband's family, although rural female stayers also play the role as 'daughters', they define their role differently in their natal family and in the husband's family.

### 4.3.1 Daughter-in-law—living with the husband's family

Under patriarchy, women's living mode is mainly composed of the paternal residence and the husband's residence (Weng and Li, 2019). When a woman marries in China, it means that, to some extent, she leaves the natal family and enters the husband's family. There, she will have another new role—daughter-in-law. On the one hand, the newly wed daughter-in-law will take on the responsibility of raising children, and on the other hand, she will take on the duties of the husband's household and share in her husband's family obligation to take care of her parents-in-law and even other family members.

Ms. Li, who is a stay-behind woman, lived with her husband's family after she got married. She said,

> 'I used to think it was good to go to work in the city. I was fined for having a second child, because of the one-child policy. At that time, my husband had a plan to migrate to the urban area with me. However, my husband's parents wouldn't allow me to go to the city to work, as they thought that it's hard to make a living in the urban area. The best choice in their mind is to cultivate land in the village, which is a kind of stable life. After losing that chance, I decided to follow my parents-in-law's advice, and take care of our children in the village. Now I don't think about migrating to the urban area anymore. Now I think it's right not to go out. In fact, I can't really help at home with either farming or housework; it's mainly my father-in-law and mother-in-law who do it. My parents-in-law make most of the decisions in the house and I can't interfere with anything and I also don't need to worry about other things. My parents-in-law would solve the problems. What is certain is that in the future, my husband and I will be the head of my family like my parents-in-law.' [Ms. Li, stay-behind woman]

Generally, sons and daughters-in-law who live with their parents need to follow the parents' advice on many matters. Ms. Li's story is highly representative of my participants and is not an isolated case. When rural female stayers are married to their husbands, if they live with their husband's parents, the head of the family is by default the husband's father. At the same time, mothers-in-law indirectly have more decision-making rights, as they represent their husbands' rights to a certain extent. They are usually the ones to convey the decision of the father-in-law. In other words, the right to make decisions about family matters belongs to the husband's parents, not only in terms of household chores and the use of income, but they also have a say in the education of their grandchildren and the work of their children. At the same time, in many rural families, the young daughter-in-law does not take on the burden of household chores, and it is still the mother-in-law who bears the burden of housework. The parents-in-law have the power to make decisions and also have to bear the burden of household chores, finances, and other pressures. Despite the fact that women are to some extent separated from their natal family after they get married, men are more closely connected to their natal family after marriage (Weng and Li, 2019). The wife who enters the husband's family does not have the right to make decisions in the parents-in-law's home, and most family decisions are made by the father-in-law or mother-in-law. The Chinese notion of filial piety is a longstanding and important cultural mechanism that involves listening to and respecting elders. The Chinese tradition praise the act of following their elders' advice (Zhan and Montgomery, 2003). Indeed, marriage in China means women entering their husband's family. Therefore, making the parents-in-law happy is an important thing for daughters-in-law. A daughter-in-law's integration into her husband's family requires the approval of the in-laws. According to my interviews, during this integration process, conflicts of interest become unavoidable and rural women are more likely to choose to sacrifice their own interests in order to keep their parents-in-law happy. During my interviews, many of the rural female stayers would stress that reputable daughters-in-law are usually respectful and dutiful to the elderly, and one of the key emphasises here is to be submissive to the elders. Under the influence of patriarchy, men are seen as more 'wise', so listening to the father-in-law is not oppressive to rural female stayers, although their ideas may differ from those of their in-laws. In addition, rural daughters-in-law are well aware that they will take second place in the event of any conflicts of interest with their parents. However, they do not see this as unreasonable. For many rural female stayers,

Chapter 4 Chinese rural female stayers in the family

it is a perfectly normal choice and they are not forced to do so. This is what filial piety demands. But submissive daughters-in-law don't last forever. As Ms. Li says, in the future she will also become a mother-in-law in her own right. If the father-in-law passes away, the husband of the rural female stayers will be given the right to decide on family matters. Therefore, for rural female stayers, accepting the decisions made for them by their in-laws may be the only option available to them at present.

Ms. Chen is a return woman. Her family consists of five people: her children go to school in the city (and live at the school), her husband has a part-time job in the urban area, and her life in the countryside is mostly spent taking care of her husband's mother, who is paralyzed and bedridden. For Ms. Chen, although she would like to live with her children in the city, her paralyzed mother-in-law makes it impossible for her to leave the countryside. Ms. Chen said,

> 'I went back to the countryside because my children were studying in the rural area at that time, but now my parents-in-law are older and need care, so I can't go out to work. ... Since last year, my child has been studying in the city. I would like to go there to look after him, but the situation does not allow me to do so. During these years, I worked in the urban areas. I relied on my parents-in-law to take care of things at home. It's my responsibility to take care of my parents-in-law and I don't want to shirk it.' [Ms. Chen, return woman]

The rural female stayers insist that they should take care of their elders, even if this is not what they would rather do. According to my data, when a stay-behind woman marries into her husband's family as a daughter-in-law, she has to accept that she is part of the husband's family, that on the one hand they are cared for by their husband's parents, and that on the other they have or will have to take on the responsibility of caring for the family in the 'new' home. Although the children are the centre of the family, for these rural female stayers, caring for their parents is a responsibility that cannot be abandoned. When the child no longer needs the care of the mother or the care of the child and the elderly can be carried out at the same time, the focus of the daughter-in law's life will be put on the parents-in-law. At the same time, according to my data, the role of daughter-in-law is more important than the role of wife. In fact, as mothers, they put the interests of their children first. Migration is not seen simply as a desire to move to the city, but rather as a desire to do more for their children, fearing everything that might prevent their children from being 'successful'. The demands of being good daughters-in-law, however, can make it difficult for them to get what they want. Thus, when it comes to being a good mother and a good daughter-in-law, the fact is that rural female stayers have to make certain compromises to balance both sides. While acknowledging that it is rural female stayers' responsibility to care for their parents-in-law. Indeed, many women who returned home after working in the city expressed in the interviews the importance of their in-laws in the family life. 'When we were working away from home, we relied on them (parents-in-law) to take care of our children; now that they are old and in need of care, we naturally have to come back,' Ms. Chen said. Rural female stayers emphasised the contribution that in-laws make to the family in everyday life, but also their undisputed role in caring for their parents-in-law. In fact, this conveys a thought. In classical Confucian filial piety, children are expected to be filial to their parents and to take responsibility for their care. Just as the elderly take care of their children or grandchildren, the children take care of the elderly—it's a cycle of care. Parents-in-law tacitly acknowledge that they will be cared for by their sons and daughters-in-law in the future, and their sons and daughters-in-law naturally acknowledge this fact. This is a kind of care circulation (Liu, 2016). In the old custom, the women are expected to be good wives and good mothers and to be filial to their parents. In China, the family is the institution traditionally responsible for the care of the elderly (Liu, 2016) and these daughters-in-law will take on the responsibility of caring for the parents-in-law, but do not have the same responsibilities in their natal family (Lee and Xiao, 1998; Liu and Cook, 2017).

## 4.3.2 Daughter in their own family—the married daughter

Ms. Sun is a return woman. She originally worked with her husband in the city, but decided to return to the countryside to take care of her parents:

> 'My father is over 80 and he can't take care of himself. And now my mother's health is not so good, so I came back to take care of them. My brother and sister-in-law are working outside and do not live in the village, and they only come back during the festive season, like the Chinese new year, so my parents mainly rely on me... My family was poor when I was young. It was difficult for my parents to pay for all their children to go to school, so some of my sisters would leave school early and go to the city to work or stay at home to take care of other brothers who went to school. I was the one who had to stop my education earlier. My parents have actually done their bit for me, and when I was younger, I was jealous that my brother had more love and care. However, I no longer have that thought.... (My parents') family is still largely dependent on my brother... All I can do is do some housework for my parents, and it is not worth mentioning.' [Ms. Sun, return woman]

According to Ms. Sun, as a daughter she did not get the same resources as her brothers in her family of origin, but was still happy to take on the responsibility of caring for her parents and felt that this situation was not a case of her being treated unequally. Rural female stayers tacitly acknowledge that after marriage she and her family of origin have become two families, but emotionally they still have a strong connection to their family of origin. Rural female stayers have less access to resources than sons in their families of origin, and they are often the part of the family that is sacrificed. However, this does not affect their sense of belonging to their original family, and this attachment to their family of origin is likely to become stronger after marriage, as my interviews suggest, and more and more daughters are realising that their close connection to their natal family does not stop when they marry. Culturally, when daughters get married, their ties to their biological family become shallow (Lu and Chen, 2021). This changing of ties refers not so much to the emotional but to other parts of the relationship with the natal family, such as the financial relationship. Daughters who marry will live with their husbands' families, hence the old Chinese proverb, 'A daughter who marries out is water that is poured out'. In other words, a married daughter will be supported by her husband's family and is therefore of 'no use' to her own family (Shi, 2009).

The stability of the paternal line means that the son remains part of an economic community with his parents, but the daughter who marries becomes a member of someone else's family and is economically isolated (Weng and Li, 2019). The impact of this thinking is even more profound in rural areas. As a result, rural families tend to favour their sons when dealing with both daughters and sons at the same time (Yi, et al., 2016). It is easy to give examples to show that these daughters face unfair treatment in their original family. As Ms. Sun says, she had to leave school earlier than her brothers to take on household duties. Daughters, because of the discontinuity of their identity and the ambiguity of their subordination, will not be supported by the their family of origin, and they will not be bound to support their parents (Weng and Li, 2019). Family ties are not completely severed when a woman marries but in rural areas. Aalthough the contact between the natal family and their daughters is not interrupted after marriage, the natal family's thought towards their married daughters changes to a certain extent, with the natal family changing the position of the daughter from that of a child to that of a relative (Weng and Li, 2019). This change in status also makes their family of origin long able to demand more from them.

However, unlike the patrilineal kinship system, the kinship system for women is to some extent influenced by emotional factors (Judd, 1989). In other words, a daughter's dependence on her natal family and the strong bond with her natal family when she is not married will encourage a married woman's long-term ties with her natal family. Although married daughters do not think they can give much to their families of origin, as times change, it has become rare for a daughter to marry and be completely disconnected from her birth family (Lu and Chen, 2021). This 'change' has in fact been hidden in the parent-child relationship and is not contradictory to the change in the relationship from daughter to relative in the natal family. Because the relationship with the natal family is mostly reflected in the economic, discursive and other parts of the relationship, the daughter who marries has a relationship with the family of origin like a relative in these respects (Weng and Li, 2019). To explain further, the married daughter enters her husband's family, thus separating herself from the natal family in terms of finances, family discourse, etc. At the same time, emotionally, the daughter's dependence on her natal family has also become more evident in recent years. As a result, their interaction with their natal families becomes more frequent (Bi, 2019). Just as Ms. Sun looks after her parents, married rural female stayers do not identify themselves as having become outsiders to their natal families. Most of them remain close to their natal families even after marriage. In Ms. Sun's case, it is easy to see that the daughter is willing to take care of her parents, while the parents do not refuse the care from their daughter. Daughters are often seen as more caring than sons. In terms of care given, parents are more satisfied with their daughters than their sons (Yi, George et al., 2016). Despite the cultural requirement for sons to take care of their parents, for many rural female stayers, they are the ones who actually fulfil the responsibility of looking after their parents. This is also due to the gender division of labour in which women are asked to take care of the home. Despite the fact that married daughters are seen as outsiders, the practicalities of caring for their parents and the expectations placed on them to care for their parents each contribute to the strong relationships they typically have with their families of origin.

Ms. Feng still lives in the same area as her parents, and her mother is living with her brother's family, who live in the two-room house left by Ms. Feng's father. 'When my mother passes away in the future, the house will be my brother's. It's nothing to discuss.'

> 'I visit my mother many times a week, but I just visit, and I can't say anything. I sometimes see my brother and sister-in-law doing badly and I just have to pretend that I don't see it… Although I am usually the one who looks after my mother, cooking and cleaning for her, when a major decision needs to be made, it is definitely my brother who decides. After all, it is their (meaning her brother's) business and I don't have the right to make the decision.' [Ms. Feng, stay-behind woman]

When rural female stayers get married and leave their birth family, they actually indirectly lose their voice and inheritance rights in the family (of their natal parents). When there are important matters to be discussed and decided in their family of origin, even though they retain the right to give advice, it is mainly up to their parents or brothers to decide whether the advice will be followed (which is especially true when one or both of the parents is deceased). When their parents die, it is usually their brother who inherits the parents' property, even if it is also customary for the brother and sister-in-law to look after their parents while they are alive (Liu, 2011). In fact, the loss of the right to have a say in parental matters indirectly supports the fact that rural female stayers become outsiders to their families of origin when they get married. To a certain extent, rural female stayers also see themselves as 'outsiders', taking care of their parents more out of daughterly love and the demands of their role as good daughters.

Ms. You had worked in the urban area but went back to the rural area because she was pregnant. Ms. You said:

> 'I usually ask my mother if I need help. Although I can also see if my mother-in-law can help me, I find it more comfortable and easier to get my mum to help me.' [Ms. You, return woman]

Although she has entered her husband's family, When Ms. You need help, she turns to her own parents as her first choice for assistance. When the natal parents need care, they also turn to their daughters for help. This two-way interaction allows them to maintain a close relationship with their original families. Therefore, the network of relatives has the colour of 'women's preference' and the main manifestation of this is an emphasis on the birth natal family and a distancing from the mother-in-law's family (Bi, 2019). The colour of women's preference refers to the fact that in family interactions, female preferences largely influence the choice of people to associate with and the frequency of interaction. In other words, women influence the composition of kinship relationships. Most women in my study maintained more of an emotional closeness to their birth families, especially in the form of dependence and closeness to their mothers. In contrast, they have a certain detachment from their mother-in-law. Married rural female stayers' strong ties to their families of origin focus on their close relationship with their mothers. This bond is reciprocal, as on the one hand the family of origin gradually becomes dependent on the married daughter's care, and on the other hand the married daughter is more inclined to look to the family of origin, especially the mother, for help. Although the married daughter maintains a relatively close relationship with her maternal family, this relationship is determined by the emotional basis of the past. As mentioned in Ms. Qin's interview, 'When my mother died, my relationship with my family of origin became less strong than before, although I still keep in touch with my brothers.' The main link between a stay-behind woman and her family of origin will be her parents. When the parents pass away, the link between them and their birth family will gradually become lighter. As with Zhou's research, as the time goes by, their sense of belonging to their natal family fades and they gradually move on to the in-laws and their own small family (Zhou, 2016).

In conclusion, the resources and power given to rural female stayers as daughters-in-law entering their husband's family are quite limited. Rural female stayers are expected to be filial, so they choose to sacrifice their own interests to be good daughters-in-law. At the same time, when the role of daughter-in-law conflicts with that of mother, they will abandon their own intentions and become filial daughters-in-law. This is because the tradition of respect for the elderly comes before the care of children.[1] There is some controversy on this issue, however, as some mothers will in fact challenge their mother-in-law's authority and want to be able to make decisions for their children themselves, and when conflict arises, the decision will largely depend on the decision of their husband or father-in-law. Rural female stayers receive fewer resources than their brothers in their families of origin, but they accept that this is due to their status as women. At the same time, their status as daughters gives them a degree of responsibility for the care of their parents that is not required of them, and it is difficult for them to completely disconnect emotionally from their family of origin. Their status as daughters allows them to accept the role of caring for the family that the female gender imposes.

## 4.4 Conclusion

In this chapter, I have discussed my participants' accounts of their roles in the family. These accounts reveal the daily lives of rural female stayers and how their gender shapes the possibilities of everyday life. The discussion in this chapter argues that the domestic responsibilities that rural female stayers take on are due to the division of labour they are given because of their gender. In addition, women have limited support to exercise their agency. However, in spite of this, women still actively use their limited resources to clearly demonstrate how they exercise initiative in their daily lives, in order to actively position themselves as 'good' mothers, wives, daughters-in-law and daughters. It is important to note that agency is limited and it is culturally and socially framed (Man, 2016).

As mentioned in the literature review, Confucianism has had a profound

---

1 *Zun lao ai you*, from the Confucian classic *Mencius* and passed down as an idiom.

influence on Chinese society, and its advocacy of women focusing on things within the family is attributed to patriarchy. Under the influence of the patriarchal culture, a male-centred social model was established in which women became subordinate to men (Ye, 2009). Confucian culture therefore influenced the division of labour within the family. The rural female stayers accept their multiple roles in the family, and assume the responsibilities that the family places on them. Most unpaid domestic work is not optional for women; instead, social and patriarchal norms require women to take responsibility for the work of the household. Unpaid domestic work prevents women from entering the labour market and limits women's earnings and earning potential (Kabeer, 2012, as cited by Singh and Pattanaik, 2020). To rural female stayers, their responsibility for the family comes from taking care of the elderly, husband and children, but also from sacrificing their own interests as a mother, as a wife and as a daughter or daughter-in-law. Firstly, as mothers, they place their children at the centre; secondly, as wives, they have accustomed themselves to following their husbands and being subordinate to them; and finally, as daughters or daughters-in-law, they not only take on the responsibility of looking after their in-laws and their husbands' families, but they also assume their obligations as daughters in their own natal families. At the same time, through these accounts of self-sacrifice, rural female stayers showcase the full extent of their efforts as women in the home. They try to exercise their agency to meet the expectations of society for women and this choice is made within the constraints of their environment. As Hitlin and Elder (2007) argued, agency derives from the individual environment and the external environment that directs the individual's attention. At the same time, given that agency is limited, not infinitely free (Man, 2016). It needs to be stressed that within these constraints, rural female stayers mobilise the resources available to them to position themselves as successful. In summary,

Chapter 4 Chinese rural female stayers in the family

rural female stayers are trying to live up to society's expectations of them by exercising agency in a limited space within the constraints of their social and cultural context.

It is worth noting that migration itself generates tensions and changes in women's expected roles. Rural female stayers may face a choice or balance. For example, they need to decide whether their main obligation is to provide for children materially or be with them physically. Caring is important throughout the lives of rural female stayers in all families. And rural female stayers play a key role in caring and supporting their families (Liu, 2014). And as Liang and Wu argued, rural women are constrained by established structures of markets, power, and so on, but they are able to adapt their actions and strategies to their situation (Liang and Wu, 2017). When facing conflicts between their own interests and the interests of other family members, rural female stayers tend to give priority to caring for family members. They do not care whether their own interests are harmed, and they are even willing to sacrifice their own interests to ensure the interests of family members. These women do not convey a strong sense of conflict between their own interests and those of the family. They do not emphasise the need for a clear division between their own interests and those of the family. In fact, as the rural female stayers in the interview showed, rural female stayers are willing to contribute to the family and do not ask for anything in return. At the same time, I have illustrated how they draw actively on their roles within the family to demonstrate their efforts to be good mothers, good wives and good daughters-in-law (or daughters). While limited by heavily gendered assumptions and practices then, and disinclined to attribute credit to themselves, the interviews illustrate that women nonetheless carve out several spaces of pride and fulfilment in the work that they do in daily life. For example, they pride themselves on being good mothers who meet 'standards'.

To sum up, in this chapter I have illustrated rural female stayers' everyday life and how by actively prioritising others, rural female stayers are able to position themselves as responsible mothers, wives and daughters (daughters-in-law). In the following chapter, I turn to consider how they interact with the people around them and how they maintain their status in relation to the community through the analytical lens of *mianzi*.

# Chapter 5 Rural female stayers and *Mianzi*—their relationships with the people around them

Rural society is a 'moral economy' with a strong collective identity (Scott, 1976). People live together in the same area and grow up in a society of acquaintances, meeting each other every day, forming a 'face-to face society', for example, a society of acquaintances, where people are bound by morality and form a friendly relationship with each other based on honesty, mutual help and charity (Wang, 2013). In China, the concept of neighbourhood and neighbourhood space in the countryside has a richer meaning, interspersed with cultural factors such as human feelings and face-saving (Ren and Yan, 2017). In the past, the neighbourhood was a very important dimension of rural society. It was made up not only of family members who are related by blood and kinship, but also of families living in close proximity (both blood and kinship families and neighbours). In other words, the neighbourhood is a continuous and intimate interaction based on geographical proximity (Ren and Yan, 2017). Villagers see their network of relationships as the foundation of society (Yan, 2003). The 'acquaintance society' exists only in groups of villagers or natural villages[1] that produce and live together in a cooperative. The sense of belonging

---

1 A natural village is different from an administrative village. It is one or more naturally formed settlements of inhabitants by family, clan or other reasons, whose origin is the spontaneous formation of a village by villagers over a long period of time in a natural environment where people naturally gather to live together.

is also higher in rural communities than in urban communities (Fei, 1998). In rural societies, these families interacted with each other in a continuous and intimate way, generating emotions and trust between neighbours, thus forming a very close community (Ren and Yan, 2017). Old conventional neighbourhood relations are based on the three principles of human kindness, face and relations (Ren and Yan, 2017). Humanity, face (*mianzi*) and relations of production are important parts of traditional Chinese culture, important aspects of farmers' daily behaviour, and the main principles of interaction between neighbours (Ren and Yan, 2017). *Mianzi* means face, and it is formed and expressed in interpersonal interactions, is contextual and variable, and a reflection of one's self-esteem and dignity as I mentioned in the Introduction.

However, urbanisation has had an impact on the rural area. Modern Chinese society has broken down the traditional geopolitical and residential structures. It has transformed from a society of acquaintances to a society of strangers, a society of anonymity (Wang, 2013). Even relationships between people and households in rural areas are gradually becoming less connected. In the village where I did my fieldwork, people divided the village into sections called '*dui*'[1], based on their geographical location. According to my understanding, each '*dui*' was originally a natural village, and these '*dui*' were then administratively planned to form what is now known as an administrative village. These administrative villages are regarded as 'semi-acquaintance societies'[2] (He, 2000, as cited by Wu, 2019b). The administrative village is a

---

1 *Dui*, a unit of measure.
2 The amalgamation of natural villages into administrative villages has broken the old social pattern of acquaintances. Although everyone in the administrative village may be familiar with each other, they do not know each other as well as they do in the natural villages. In addition, although villagers have the same administrative space, they do not live together communally in the same, shared physical space.

## Chapter 5  Rural female stayers and *Mianzi*—their relationships with the people around them

rural grassroots administrative unit set up by the state in accordance with the law, so the villagers in the 'dui' originally knew each other. It is made up of several 'dui', and the villagers in the administrative village will eventually get to know each other over a long period of time. Most of the people in the village already know each other, but the villagers in the individual 'dui' will obviously know each other better. At the same time, due to the close geographical proximity of the natural villages, young people between the different 'dui' often meet and marry each other, which in effect facilitates frequent interaction within the administrative villages. The majority of the local migrant population are women who have married into the village and it is rare for complete strangers to move in. With urbanisation, as more and more young people move to work in the city, the relationship between villagers is becoming more and more estranged. Those who remain in the village become the strings that hold together the old acquaintance society, as in Yang and Yang's (2018) research, where middle-aged and older people are the main actors in the social support network of mutual 'help', upholding social norms and the traditional mechanisms for maintaining social relations. However, according to my data, as more and more women return to the countryside, they are gradually beginning to link up with old social relations.

Since living in a community is based to some extent on acquaintances, it is hard to ignore others' views. For rural female stayers, according to my data, despite living in the countryside and being aware of the people around them, their family lives take up most of their time and they are too busy to actively care about others or talk about them. At the same time, people do not actively discuss other people in person, which is a result of the *mianzi* culture. Meanwhile, the right to make decisions within the village means, to a certain extent, gaining *mianzi*, because those who have greater voice in the village are treated with more respect by others and they can maintain their *mianzi*. It is difficult for rural women to establish new social relationships in rural communities and they have little opportunity for external contacts to strengthen their social networks (Sun, 2012). As a result, it is difficult for rural women to exercise their agency in the community and to access the corresponding responsibilities and duties. For example, according to the report from National Bureau of Statistics (2021a), in 2020, people who hold positions in the village council were mainly men, and only 24.2% of village committee members were women. In addition to this, when several families with land adjacent to each other need to decide on things together, such as the fertilisation of their farmland, even though many of the men in these families are not living in the village, their consent is needed for a decision to be made. In this situation, the women are mere 'executors' of the decision. The impact of *mianzi* on rural female stayers is multifaceted: they claim to not care about other people's lives, and yet they construct their narratives and presentations of self in the interviews by comparing themselves with others. It is important to note that this is not inconsistent with rural female stayers' reluctance to talk about other people's lives. They just don't actively talk about other people's lives in front of the person concerned. According to my findings, for rural female stayers, comparison is probably the best way to maintain their *mianzi*, so they try to highlight their positive attributes by comparing themselves with other rural women as much as possible.

As *mianzi* is an important cultural factor in the everyday lives of Chinese people (Qi, 2011), I would like to explore how rural female stayers treat and protect their *mianzi* while going about their daily activities. These women do not just passively accept others' definitions of their lives. Rather, they are actively engaged in maintaining *mianzi* as either stay-behind women or

Chapter 5 Rural female stayers and *Mianzi*—their relationships with the people around them

return women. In this chapter, I will divide the discussion around *mianzi* into three sections. The first is on *mianzi* in Chinese culture, which contains sections on the concept itself and other sayings and distinctions about *mianzi*. Secondly, I will put the accounts of return women at the centre of attention in order to discuss how they perceive other people's views of them. Thirdly, I will discuss how stay-behind women use practical examples to demonstrate their ability to maintain *mianzi*. Finally, I will discuss the topic of stay-behind women asking for help from people around them. It is about some of the practical implications of *mianzi*, including people's willingness to seek informal forms of support and the ways that they go about this.

## 5.1 Mianzi culture in China

### 5.1.1 Mianzi and lian

'Face' is formed from the dual unity of other-related *mianzi* and self-oriented *lian*, and its increase and decrease is determined by the judgement or evaluation of people's actions or behaviour by the self or others (Zhou and Zhang, 2017). *Mianzi* and *lian* are the two inseparable parts of face, which together form a value system. There is a significant degree of intersection between the value components of *mianzi* and *lian*, suggesting the coexistence and interdependence of the two forms in satisfying individual, relational and collective needs for face (Zhou and Zhang, 2017).

Previous studies have refined the definition of the concepts of '*lian*' and '*mianzi*'. According to Hu (1944), there is a distinction between *mianzi* and *lian*. Put simply, *lian* is morally oriented, while *mianzi* is socially oriented. *Lian* refers to the respect that a group has for a moral person, and *mianzi* is

143

more dependent on the self-perception of the external environment, tends towards prestige, and is used more in academia (Hu, 1944, as cited by Qi, 2011). And it is further explained that *mianzi* is provided to people by society (Qi, 2011). *Mianzi* and *lian* can also be differentiated according to the severity of the situation (Hsu, 1996). For example, if a student did poorly in an exam and only a few people knew it, it would be called a loss of *lian*. But if all the students knew about it, it would be seen as a loss of *mianzi*. There is a definite link between the ethical and the social aspects of *mianzi* (Cheng, 1986). Indeed, as Ho (1976) suggests, *mianzi* and *lian* are mutually variable in some contexts. Humanity and *mianzi* can be used interchangeably in Chinese society because they have something in common (Zhai, 2004). For example, '*diu lian*' and '*diu mianzi*' here have the same meaning, which is to lose face. In many cases, *mianzi* and *lian* describe the same situation to some extent, with only a difference in tone of voice, and in the fieldwork I conducted, the two were interchangeable in the interviewees' mouths. Therefore, in the analysis that follows I use the word *mianzi* only.

## 5.1.2 Mianzi and Chinese culture

Qi (2011) argues that *mianzi* is important across cultures, but in the Western individualistic cultures, *mianzi* is more implicit, whereas in China it is a more explicit part of social interactions. The presence of *mianzi* in Chinese society is very broad, and it is deeply involved in every aspect of Chinese social life. *Mianzi* is at the core of all social interaction in China (Chen, 2006, as cited by Zheng, 2019). In Chinese interpersonal communication, *mianzi* is often used in order to get others to meet one's needs or to gain honour for oneself and the group. At the same time, there are also many words and sayings in Chinese culture that express the concept of *mianzi*, such as 'starving to death is a small matter, but losing one's morals is a big matter' [1](Qu, 2018). For the sake of m*ianzi,* the Chinese usually make a huge effort to slowly influence the opinion of others, an effort that includes genuine self-improvement, as well as some possibly dishonest strategies (Hsu, 1996). Qi (2011) reflects on *mianzi* more critically, emphasizing its function for social control and maintaining adherence to social norms. It is a driving force for progress through mutual competition (Jiang, 2009). Relationship, as a principle of getting along, provides the Chinese with a primary reference for safeguarding feelings and maintaining *mianzi* (Luo, 1997, as cited by Zhang, Wang and Cheng, 2020). Influenced by the natural economy and the family concept, Chinese people's values are collective, so when protecting their own *mianzi,* they also have to look after the *mianzi* of everyone else (Xu, 2016). For example, the Chinese would see themselves (as individuals) as one of a group of people who have all maintained their *mianzi*, and in order to maintain their *mianzi*, the individuals in the group need to protect both their own *mianzi* and the *mianzi* of others in order to maintain the collective *mianzi*. Secondly, influenced by Confucianism, people aspire to be what the Confucian classics call a 'gentleman' and acquire people's respect in order to gain face for themselves (Xu, 2016). It is worth noting that when the term 'gentleman' was defined, it was more from a male perspective. The term 'female gentleman' was also used in later times, but it rather overemphasised the female status of the person being praised.

---

1  It is from 'Cheng's legacy'.The expression means that to die of poverty and hunger is a small matter, but to lose one's moral integrity ('jie') is a big matter. The word 'jie' in this context can also be derived from the word 'face'.

The concept of *mianzi* in Chinese culture was first introduced to the West by Hu, who argued that *mianzi* represented a socially valued reputation, which was gained through success, a step up in life experience, and a reputation accumulated through personal effort and ingenuity (Hu, 1944). *Mianzi* is the key to explaining many of the Chinese people's behaviours (Stover, 1974, as cited by Yuan, 2009) and *mianzi* and relationships are seen as core to Chinese culture (Buckley, Clegg, and Tan, 2006). A key feature of Confucianism is that everyone has a fixed position in society and must act in accordance with the rituals; if one does something or says something that is not in keeping with one's place, one will lose one's *mianzi* (Jiang, 2009). To explain further, society has customised standards of behaviour for people, and people are required to act in accordance with social standards. For example, in Confucian culture, filial piety is the first rule of being a human being and children are expected to take care of their elderly when the time comes. Shame and 'associated loss of *mianzi*' play a dominant or influential role in Chinese behaviour that cannot be ignored (Jin, 2002, as cited by Jiang, 2009). The sense of shame is dominated by what others think. In other words, what one feels things should or should not be, is determined by what others will think (Wang, 2009c).

Social orientation is a behavioural inclination that causes people to display submissiveness to others, behaviour that does not offend, that conforms to social expectations, and that incorporates the opinions of others in order to gain their approval, maintain good interpersonal relationships and protect one's *mianzi* (Jiang, 2009). Chinese social orientation refers primarily to the style and form of social interaction exhibited by individuals who integrate or cooperate with their family, other individuals, authority and non-specific others (Jiang, 2009). *Mianzi* consciousness and behaviour is a micro process

## Chapter 5  Rural female stayers and *Mianzi*—their relationships with the people around them

of interpersonal interaction, but it is in turn conditioned by the macro society (Wang, 2009c). Qi (2017) is of the same opinion, which is that individual *mianzi* may be influenced by the collective. Thus, exploring the issue of *mianzi* in the Chinese context requires a focus on the relationship between the individual and the family as well as the surrounding society.

There are both 'subjective and objective' aspects to *mianzi*. The subjective aspect of *mianzi* comes from its internalised relationship to society and is a person's self-worth in their self-evaluation, while the objective aspect of a *mianzi* is a person's social status as recognized through other people in the same society or by someone on a certain occasion (Qi, 2017). The Chinese need for *mianzi* is intrinsic to all aspects of personal and interpersonal development (Buckley et al., 2006) and may become an object of self-conscious thinking and construction (Qi, 2017). Therefore, when we showcase the life experiences of rural female stayers and how they use their agency, an analysis of their views on *mianzi* is extremely important. *Mianzi* is not a fixed standard of behaviour, as the criteria for judging *mianzi* varies from one culture to another and change with the times (Wang, 2009c). Although a certain standard of *mianzi* exists, this standard changes to some extent as society changes. Also, there are differences in the understanding and maintenance of *mianzi* in different cultural contexts. Thus, changes in society will have an impact on how people view *mianzi*, or rather, *mianzi* are created under the culture of society. As a result, different social contexts will have different perspectives on the understanding of *mianzi*, and the rural social contexts in which rural female stayers live are relatively more customary and conservative than urban areas, which explains why previous studies exploring *mianzi* among urban women may not be fully applicable to rural female stayers. In addition, because the rules about *mianzi* are influenced by

147

the current values of society and are dynamic (Qi, 2011), and as times and social circumstances have changed in rural areas too, previous studies of rural *mianzi* (Ho, 1976; Hu, 1994; Hwang,1987; Jiang, 2009) would benefit from updating. For these reasons, my exploration of *mianzi* in the accounts of rural female stayers makes an important contribution to the literature.

## 5.2 Return women and the maintenance of mianzi

Ms. He is a return woman who did not want to go back to the village at first, because her child is working in the city. Ms. He thought that even doing some retail business as a street vendor (in the urban area) by herself would be better than go back to the rural area. However, she felt she had to accompany her husband back to the rural area because he did not want to live in the city anymore. Ms. He knows some women in her village who have never lived in the urban area and when I asked her questions about them, she expressed some envy at first. However, in answering other questions, she expressed more ambivalent views on these rural women with no experience of urban life.

> Interviewer: Do you have friends who have never migrated to the urban area? And what do you think about them?
> 
> Ms. He: Women like us who can endure hardships always decide to go out to work and are able to do more work. Like those women who cannot endure hardships, they don't have any thinking of working out of the village and they only stay at the village. I want to say that not going out to work is a better choice. People like us working outside have gradually become less healthy because of the heavy work. The women who didn't work in the urban area haven't

suffered that and their bodies are better. I mainly wanted to make money, so I had no choice but to accept work in the city at that time.

Interviewer: What do you think of migrants, especially migrant women? Ms. He: More people are choosing to go to the urban area to find a job. Earning money in the village is more difficult, so for some people, there is no choice. There is no place for people in the village to earn money if they don't migrate to the urban area. Although the government can provide some subsidies that are quite good, it is still not enough. Most of these women stay in the village because they cannot not find work outside. If you don't migrate to the urban area, it means there is no hope for you. [Ms. He, return woman]

Economic reasons and children may be the main reasons why these stay-behind women cannot move to the cities, but their friends or acquaintances may have other ideas. Stay-behind women are often portrayed in the media as poor and in need of help (Liangzhou Women's Federation, 2022), though, as I mentioned in the introductory chapter, there has been some news showing the 'new' face of rural women, such as those who start their own businesses (Wu, 2018). The portrayal of stay-behind women in the news media shows how society perceives them.Unlike the descriptions given in the media, when return women talk about stay-behind women, they first express their envy. As Ms. He did at the beginning of her interview, she talked about the comforts and pleasures of staying behind. However, this actually produces a contrast. Being able to bear hardships is an excellent quality for rural women. Return women's evaluation of their behaviour of going out to work is that they can bear hardships, which means they affirm their choice. Despite what Ms. He says, there is actually an idea of looking down on women who don't have urban experience. When further elaborating her views on migrant women, she attributed the reason why others couldn't go to the city to their inability to find a job, and claimed that if people didn't go to the city, they would not have a future. Ms. He's answer highlights her pride in her urban experience, which gives her *mianzi* and a strong confidence. Ms. He didn't have to directly say that urban life had given her *mianzi*. It was enough for her to showcase her advantages by detailing the reasons why some women could not work in the city. Earning more money is often the purpose of rural people working in the city and city life can mean an increased income for many, which is rural people's universal understanding of the choice to migrate to the city. When city life is the 'better' option because of the greater financial opportunities available, return women 'have to' emphasise the superiority of city life and highlight their possessions and abilities in order to maintain their *mianzi*. In other words, return women have capabilities that other rural women do not. In addition, most people's competitive *mianzi* behaviour is to preserve *mianzi* and avoid being looked down upon (Wang, 2009b). By contrasting herself with the stay-behind women, Ms. He positions herself and the other return women in one group, and the stay-behind women in another; and as a member of the returning group, she is able to protect her *mianzi* as well as that of the group as a whole.

In the interview with return woman Ms. Zheng, she talked about the women she knew who had gone to work in the urban area, as well as those who later decided to return to the rural area. Ms. Zheng migrated to the urban area when she completed middle school. After her marriage she and her husband had been living in the city. She then returned to the rural area because her older son needed to attend middle school in their *hukou* location. That her father-in-law also needed to be taken care of was another reason for her to go back to the rural area. Ms. Zheng said:

## Chapter 5  Rural female stayers and *Mianzi*—their relationships with the people around them

'Living in the urban area costs more than in the rural area, and we also faced a lot of pressure. Going to the urban area to work is more trouble-free and worry-free, but going out means dealing with the stress of earning money. City life means you need to spend money everywhere unlike the village. Also, urban people found it hard to communicate with us. They thought we were outsiders working here and they often looked down on us. Coming and going with people in the city makes me feel a huge amount of pressure. For most migrant women who can earn money with a good job, they would not return to the rural area. Other people don't disquss these women when they migrate to the urban area or go back to the rural area, but all the people know that if they can earn money, there is no reason for them to go back home. It is better to go out (migrate to the urban area). In the village it is difficult to find work to earn money. Compared with return women, some people think that people in the city have a better life. In my opinion, I do not agree with their idea. Some migrant women come back to the village during holidays like the Spring Festival, and when they go back to the urban area, their families bring various things to them. It's normal for people to think that these individuals can't earn enough money. If you have money, you wouldn't need to take anything from your poor rural family.' [Ms. Zheng, return woman]

Ms. Zheng's words express the view that city life may not be as glamorous as it seems. She points out that there are two sides to city life, and her view tends to express more of the difficult side of city life, and she breaks down the idea that city life is better. To a certain extent, Ms. Zheng's answer somewhat disgraces the return women (thereby, herself), and her answer shatters the view that the other return women had been trying to establish for themselves

151

of living a good life in the city. Indeed, as a woman who has returned to her hometown, she is not bent on trying to elevate the superiority of city life for the sake of her own *mianzi*, and her position seems more balanced. Perhaps because I was a stranger to her, she was able to be blunt in her answers, as she did not need to be concerned about whether she would lose *mianzi* in front of me. Individuals do not care about presenting a good image to impress strangers because they have no social or interpersonal connections with strangers and the impact of the strangers' opinions on their lives is minimal (Kinnison, 2017). As with Kinnison's research, my fieldwork suggests that this can also occur in a Chinese context. Ms. Zheng implicitly addressed this view in the interview, 'I wouldn't say as much to the rest of the people who are living in our village.' In other words, she tries to avoid being judged or discussed by the village, as it would probably cause her to lose her *mianzi*. Of course, another factor is that these rural female stayers themselves lack someone to talk to, and I perhaps came across as a good listener, somebody they could talk to about their emotions and stories that they don't normally have the opportunity to tell. For many return women, the experience of urban life is not entirely positive and migrant workers are discriminated against in the city due to their status. In addition, Ms. Zheng seems to want to justify her decision to return to the rural areas in order to keep her *mianzi*. After all, returning to the countryside also left her vulnerable to discrimination by others. As Qi's research shows, *mianzi* is not only used as a means for engaging in social interaction, but also becomes an object of self-conscious consideration and intentional management (Qi, 2011). As Ms. Zheng says, 'The village people like to talk about how those who stay in the city must be living well....' Returning to the countryside thus signifies living badly or evidence of not being able to live well in the urban areas. On the one hand, return women are very eager to get '*mianzi*', but on the other hand, they are

## Chapter 5  Rural female stayers and *Mianzi*—their relationships with the people around them

very afraid of losing it. When they talk about women who go out to work, they mainly draw on their own experiences of working in the urban area, emphasising how hard it is to work outside the village and the difficulty of earning money. Return women try to construct narratives to justify their choices or distinguish themselves from others. By describing the negative aspects of urban life, they aim to preserve their *mianzi*, as they fear that they will be underestimated and therefore lose it. Showing the negative side of urban life also facilitates greater understanding from others of Ms. Zheng's choice to return to the rural areas, thus preserving her *mianzi*. What appears to be a balanced attitude is in fact arguably an effort by Ms. Zheng to keep her *mianzi* and gain the understanding of others.

Ms. Qin is a return woman who came back to the rural area because her mother needed care. Now she is living in the rural area with her mother, and her children are working in the urban area. She said:

> 'It's definitely different from the village. I could meet and interact with many strange people. In the rural area this is not possible. The village is full of people you know. I could also learn a few new ideas and have more insights when I was living in the urban area. I'm better than them (other rural women who don't have urban experience) because I've been out and seen the world. I can give my opinion when things are going on at home and my husband listens to my advice because he also feels that I am no longer ignorant. This means the family is giving me *mianzi*.' [Ms. Qin, return woman]

Although returning was not necessarily these women's intention, this may be due to a number of factors. Still, from their experience of living in the city, they have built up resources which enable them to maintain their *mianzi*. They point out that they have different contacts in the city, that there are all kinds of people in the city, and new things can happen every day. Urban life provides these low-educated rural women with a different perspective on the world and they are exposed to things they have not seen before. Their contact with urban women has enabled them to gradually discover their value, and they suggest that they have more agency in relation to family decisions. Although it is still difficult for women to make 'big' decisions, they do feel that they have gained *mianzi* in many ways, and are convinced that this is the result of living in the city. Women are active agents and they see themselves as such, but this agency can only be expressed and activated when they are not in competition with men (Judd,1990). Therefore, return women's agency is limited, yet their gains of limited decision-making power can make a big difference to their *mianzi*. As I argued in my analysis in Chapter 4, rural female stayers do not generally place a lot of emphasis on the right to be involved with family decision making. However, *mianzi*, unlike decision making, is a very important issue for them. It's more than simply gaining the attention of their families. It means being given more status. Maintaining *mianzi*, to a certain extent, helps return women to differentiate themselves from other rural women, in ways that the women themselves suggest produces new forms of agency in relation to their families. As Ortner states, agency emphasises intention (Ortner, 2001). Return women demonstrate their ability to protect *mianzi* by using agency in a limited space.

A step beyond gaining *mianzi* in the family is harvesting *mianzi* in the village. Return woman Ms. Sun expressed a great deal of pride talking about her recent past. She returned to the countryside to care for her elderly parents, while her husband worked in the city.

Her children were also in the city, but have already finished school. She said:

## Chapter 5 Rural female stayers and *Mianzi*—their relationships with the people around them

'Now I am also called in when the village discusses things. They (meaning rural people) feel that my experience of living in the city is valuable and can help make better suggestions. I am also outspoken, unlike others (meaning other rural women with no urban experience) who are too coy to speak their mind... You know that others think highly of me now.' [Ms. Sun, return woman]

In rural areas across China, local and regional government is controlled by male and patriarchal interests (Jacka, 2014). Within the family, both villagers and officials believe that men should make the decisions about agricultural production, financial investments and expenditure. As Jacka (2014) found in her research, people tend to believe that men are more competent and well informed than women. Women are not often elected to leadership positions in the village, because people think that women's 'low quality' makes them unfit for this task. They are too busy with 'internal' work. In addition, 'good' women are focused on taking care of their family, and do not deal with people outside the family, especially men (Jacka, 2014). However, many women return to the countryside with a certain degree of independence, which were different with common stayer who totally focus on family. They will actively get out of the house to socialise with others. Public space provides a place for Chinese rural women to interact with others outside of their domestic and agricultural work (Sun, 2012). For rural female stayers, public space refers both to fixed places such as the village council, as well as to non-fixed spaces in the village such as open spaces or squares, where they can interact with others. In rural areas, an important factor in judging the size of a person's *mianzi* is whether or not that person has a popular base, which depends on how good or poor the person's usual interpersonal relationships are. This is why rural people attach particular importance to their interpersonal

155

relationships (Wang, 2009b). The return women in my study suggest that their urban life has, to a certain extent, enhanced their ability to communicate with others. Their experience of the city, to some extend, helped them to speak out on family and village matters. City life has taught return women to be more confident about expressing their opinions. This in turn helps them to gain the trust of more people. With the trust of the people around them, their *mianzi* is strengthened. Return women are often categorised as women who have seen the world, set apart from other rural women. Urban life has enriched the experience of return women, and this has led to expectations being placed on them by those around them, which are not often placed on women. For example, they are expected to make suggestions that other rural women would not be able to, and to take the place of their husbands in deciding some internal family matters. According to my data, the reactions of the village towards some return women have enabled them to maintain a high level of self-confidence and *mianzi*. With this in mind, we can see that urban life shapes the possibilities for acquiring and maintaining *mianzi*. The experience of living in the city has given rural return women the courage to speak out and has also changed the way they are viewed by others. This is the village's way of acknowledging return women and a sign that they are being given *mianzi*.

To sum up, return women's descriptions of *mianzi* maintenance are somewhat contradictory. On the one hand, they talked about the difficulties of urban life to people who know about it, hoping to gain empathy to defend their *mianzi*. On the other hand, their tone changed when they were comparing themselves to stay-behind women with no experience of urban life. Return women set themselves apart from other rural women, trying to assert their own *mianzi* while demonstrating their superiority. When they return to the countryside, they suggested their vision and material wealth brought about by their urban experience allowed them to position themselves as above other rural women. The economic value they bring to the family helps them to be more affirmative of themselves, and they define their urban experience as successful. These return women who have lived in the city are then highlighted by comparisons with stay-behind women. The return women's experience fulfils the yearning for urban life in rural areas, which makes them feel they have *mianzi*. In addition, an important factor for the return women to maintain *mianzi* is that the perceived superiority of urbanity in relation to the rural society. Lian and An (2018) argued for the inequality between urban and rural areas and the imbalance between urban and rural development. This inequality is reflected in a variety of ways, such as health care, education, and income. (Zhou and et al., 2014; Wang, 2013). The urban experience of return women provides them an urban background, which they perceive to be superior to those stay-behind women. Therefore, when talking about city life, return women avoid recounting their negative experiences in the city with those who have not lived in urban areas, and they are well practised at showing the good aspects of city life in order to maintain their *mianzi*. Rural people compete, boast and compare with each other, and then gain a sense of decency or shame from it. However, rural people's pursuit of *mianzi* not only brings a sense of 'face' to the individual, but also, and more importantly, creates social stratification in the village through the act of face competition (Wang, 2009b).

While the social perception of urban tendencies provides the conditions for return women to protect their *mianzi*, it also makes it difficult for them to keep their *mianzi* in the face of migration. Return women who have experienced city life become a special presence. On the one hand, return women don't want to be compared with migrant women, as they are worried that they will come off second best. On the other hand, they hope to establish their value and show that they are different from ordinary rural women by emphasising their similar experiences to migrant women. Return women put themselves above stay-behind women, claiming that stay-behind women are less capable than they are, the losers who never made it to the city. Return women do this to emphasise the *mianzi* they have acquired from their urban sojourns, which have left them in a better position than other rural women. According to the definition of boundary consciousness, the boundary of society is established by the differences caused by the distribution of material and non-material resources and the unequal distribution of social opportunities (Lamont and Molnar, 2002). Although both stay-behind women and return women are from rural areas, the return women try to distinguish themselves from the stay-behind women using their work experience in the city, the money they earned working in the city and their value to their families. Social values, mainly referring to individuals' perceptions of others, are the meanings of human behaviour that arise from human interactions. Social values are defined by society mainly in terms of wealth, status, power, prestige, family and so on, and are a comprehensive concept whose vectors tend to change with the times (Wang, 2009a). Return women want to preserve their *mianzi* among the migrant women and stay-behind women by invoking social values such as income and family status, which are recognised and sought by the mainstream of society.

## 5.3  Stay-behind women and the maintenance of mianzi

Ms. Yang is a stay-behind woman whose husband works on a construction site in the city. His income is the family's only income, as Ms. Yang looks after the children at their rural home. She said:

## Chapter 5 Rural female stayers and *Mianzi*—their relationships with the people around them

'Rural female stayers who have lived in the city often talk about the benefits, but from my point of view, there is a feeling of discrimination; that is, the feeling that nothing is good in the village. In fact, we know they only talk about the good parts of urban life and if it is as good as they describe, why do they move back to the rural area? At the same time, they think we don't work in cities because we can't bear the hardship.' [Ms. Yang, stay-behind woman]

Stay-behind women feel like they are being discriminated against, according to Ms. Yang, especially by return women obsessed with promoting the advantages of city life in the hope of showing their superiority. They hear return women bragging about their life in the city, over-exaggerating the good aspects and deliberately omitting the hardships and stresses they faced. Although Ms. Yang is not completely unfamiliar with life in the city, she always feels herself inferior to the return women. She feels uncomfortable by their overemphasis on the 'good' aspects of their lives, which in some ways imply the 'bad' aspects of the lives of stay-behind women. As the women returning to their hometowns describe their 'exciting' city life, stay-behind women feel they have been underestimated and have lost their *mianzi*. *Mianzi* is obtained through how others perceive, as well as reflecting the respect others have for them (Qi, 2011). Stay-behind women without experience of urban life reported feeling disrespected by return women and their preoccupation with displaying the positive aspects of urban life. For even though they know less about city life, they recognize that life is never easy. And return women's blanket praise of city life makes them feel ignorant and that they are losing their *mianzi*. In addition to this, those remaining in the rural area are often seen as less capable, lazy and backward thinking. This idea also makes it difficult for stay-behind women to maintain *mianzi*. Even though they work hard at home and take care of their families, they are seen as dependent, with some media reports suggesting that stay-behind women would not be able to survive without the help of others (Liangzhou Women's Federation, 2022). In fact, although stay-behind women feel disadvantaged in comparison to return women, as expressed in their interviews, they do not agree with the idea that they are inferior to return women. They try to maintain their *mianzi* with responses to my questions that minimise the impact of their status as non-return women, so that it does not become a factor that can be used against them.

Ms. Zhao is a stay-behind woman. There are four members of Ms. Zhao's family—her husband and eldest son work in the city, while the younger son is still studying—and the family's main income comes from her husband's work plus the crops that they grow on their land. When talking about her opinion on how to deal with being discriminated against, she said:

> 'People definitely don't think the same. I can't control what other people think, so I don't usually think about what other people think about my choices. It's better to live your own life. I'm not very happy to talk about it with other people. We don't know much about other people's lives, and other people don't know much about my life.'
> [Ms. Zhao, stay-behind woman]

In the face of controversy and prejudice, some stay-behind women have shown themselves to be unconcerned. A few stay-behind women in my sample expressed the view that they are indifferent towards protecting their *mianzi* and, in fact, have given up trying to do so. Ms. Zhao does not seek to gain the approval of others in her life, nor does she appear to take

## Chapter 5   Rural female stayers and *Mianzi*—their relationships with the people around them

the issue of *mianzi* too seriously, which to some extent may be to do with the fact that she is not very integrated into rural life. Ms. Zhao came to live in her husband's village after she got married, a village where most of the young people had gone to work in the city, and she found it difficult to interact with the older people. To a certain extent she was marginalised in the village, having little interaction with other people, and this led to her not caring what other people thought of her. The more dependent those people are, the more they care about it; the more they fear collective rejection, the more the village identifies them with village norms (Wang, 2009b). However, when villagers no longer depend on the village and no longer care about what others think of them, it becomes almost impossible to maintain the village *mianzi* hierarchical structure (Wang, 2009b). Ms. Zhao is, to a certain degree, actually detached from the *mianzi* system of her village, and this detachment allows Ms. Zhao to ignore other people's opinions of her, which is a way of protecting her *mianzi*, albeit a relatively passive one. It is not so much that Ms. Zhao protected her *mianzi* but she was able to avoid losing it by living somewhat 'out of touch' with those around her. In describing their lives, some stay-behind women are able to ignore the influence of the outside world to a certain extent and focus on the microcosm of their homes.

Ms. Han is a stay-behind woman whose husband works as an electrician in the urban area and she has one child. When talking about why she did not go to the city with her husband, she said:

> 'I thought the village was good. A woman should stay at home and take care of the family, like the children and the parents. That's what is expected of women, and I think that although you can earn money by going to the city, you actually fails to do your duty as a woman.' [Ms.

Han, stay-behind woman]

Ms. Han is proud of her choice, so she has a sense of superiority when talking about return women. As discussed in Chapter 4 on the division of labour between men and women, women were asked to stay at home and look after the family, while men were asked to go out and earn money. Resonating with this ideology, stay-behind women are highly affirmative of their choices, which make them feel they have *mianzi*. During the interview, Ms. Han used the word '*shou*' several times, which is a Chinese word for duty, which by extension, also means persistence. Throughout the interview, she tried to express to me that she is persevering in her responsibilities, which is what she understands to be the biggest difference between her and the women who have returned to the rural area, and that she had always been where she was 'needed'. In her view, the experience of working in the city seems to many stay-behind women an abandonment of the rules that women should obey. Although most rural women do not work in paid employment, they pride themselves on being model wives with Chinese femininity. Hence, stay-behind women would use the comments from those who are living around them in the village to protect their *miani*. For example, Ms. Han said that 'Other people would praise my husband for taking a good wife because I stayed at home in a practical way.'

When I interviewed Ms. Feng (a stay-behind woman), she also gave her views on this question (to stay or nor to stay). Ms. Feng lives with her husband, father-in-law, and two daughters, while her eldest daughter lives on campus and returns home in the holidays. During the quiet season of the farming year, her daily routine is to pick up her little daughter from school and cook for her family. She has never lived or worked in the city. Because her husband is in poor health (he works as a community guard in the city and guards the gate),

Chapter 5   Rural female stayers and *Mianzi*—their relationships with the people around them

she is basically responsible for all the housework in the family, including farm work in the field. Ms. Feng said:

> 'I think these decisions of women who decided to return to the countryside are right. When they come back, they can farm. Besides, it is very difficult to go out (to the city) to live. The best option is to farm when they are back to living in the rural area. If they can find some odd job to do near or in the village, it is easier to support their family. It's good to live in the village. It's hard to work in the city, and migrant workers can't make much money. In fact, as I know, many people who work in cities are not as good as those in the village. When people say they have decided to live in the city and do not have any plan to return to the village, people generally think that if they make a lot of money in the city and work hard, they should be able to survive (make a living), so they live in the city (not returning to the countryside).' [Ms. Feng, stay-behind woman]

The standard of personal success is not determined by the individual, but rather it is achieved in comparison with others. Everyone has to compete and compare themselves with others and evaluate themselves through the eyes of others (Wang, 2009c). Ms. Feng affirmed her choice by speaking approvingly about women deciding to return to their hometowns. For some people, returning to the countryside means that you cannot 'Hun' in the city. If being able to eventually live in the city is regarded as a success, then even if there are sufficient reasons to return to the countryside, these people would not go back to the rural area. By analysing the reasons why return women return to their hometowns, stay-behind women highlight the superiority of her choice to never leave in the first place, therefore protecting their *mianzi*. Despite their longing for the riches of the urban areas, stay-behind women stress that rural women should be realistic and choose the right place (a rural area) to live in according to their ability. While expressing their displeasure with return women, they detailed the advantages of the life they had chosen in order to show the correctness of their decision. In my interviews with the stay-behind women, they tended to emphasise their peace of mind and willingness to work for their family. To a certain extent, they portrayed themselves as down-to-earth and hardworking, while return women were described as *'tiaoda'*. *Tiaoda*, a dialect word with a somewhat derogatory connotation, is used to describe people who are flippant and impetuous in their work.

To sum up, stay-behind women have different views and approaches when it comes to defending their *mianzi*. In some cases, they feel they have lost face due to misunderstandings and prejudices, and have therefore chosen not to pay attention to what others think as a protective measure. In others, stay-behind women try to express the negative aspects of urban life by emphasising that it results in women returning to their hometowns. At the same time, they use the social demand for a gendered division of labour to affirm their choice to stay and do women's work in the countryside. My data shows that stay-behind women are more likely to maintain their *mianzi* by putting others down than return women are. At the same time, not expressing thoughts about others is a form of self-protection for stay-behind women, and it does help them to indirectly protect each other's *mianzi*. The premise of the acquaintance community is that there are few secrets in the village, which leads to many conversations between two people or a small group of people becoming quickly known in various ways to the majority of the village. As return woman Ms. Kong said, 'It's hard for people to mention you and then compare themselves to you when you don't talk about other people.' So by not talking about other people, you are indirectly protected from being discussed by others, which also means you protect your own *mianzi*.

## 5.4 Rural female stayers and social support

The traditional 'essence of Chinese society' is that the Chinese family is a self-contained micro-state. The social unit is the family and not the individual, and it is the family that is the responsible element in local political life (Peng, 2007). Social support is defined as the quality of people's social networks and their formal or informal interactions with other people or groups; moreover, social support is a very important part of obtaining and securing one's self worth, material, informational and emotional support (Hou et al., 2015). *Guanxi* (relationships) are interpersonal in nature. As relationships involve familiarity or intimacy, trust and reciprocal obligations (Hwang, 1987), in practice they usually take place between immediate family members, relatives and friends (Nielsen et al., 2006).

Human kindness is an important bond of relationship in China and it is a sign of credit, kinship and *mianzi* (Peng, 2007). The exchange of favours is reciprocal, mutually indebted, though it may be unequal, and cannot and will not be fully repaid, so it is also continuous (Peng, 2007). There are three types of exchange of favours among Chinese people, one being when a person receives help from another person in an emergency situation, which falls under the category of 'favours' in human interaction. The second type is the more purposeful investment of favours, usually called 'giving favours', which leads to a sense of indebtedness or guilt on the part of the recipient and constitutes a 'debt of gratitude'. As a result, when the other party asks for something, they will have to return the favour. The third type is the general exchange of courtesies. It is a kind of the reciprocal visits to each other to strengthen their emotional ties, which are eventually exchanged in the form of 'giving *mianzi*' (Zhai, 2004). Social exchange usually refers to a relationship of equivalence between exchangers in terms of social resources, which is most typically expressed in the form of the so-called 'return of the favour', and is realised through the 'flow of gifts' (Yan, 2000).

*Mianzi* is socially provided to individuals and is based on social relationships or social interactions, which in turn are responsible for emotions, and the experience of these emotions becomes the basis of *mianzi* (Qi, 2011). On the one hand, rural people desire *mianzi* and compete with others in their daily lives to gain *mianzi*, but on the other hand they manage their relationships with others according to their *mianzi* position in the village (Wang, 2009c). Each person's feelings about *mianzi* are supported and encouraged by their emotions and the emotion-related behaviour of others (Qi, 2011).

Breheny and Stephens' research (2009) suggests that it is important to balance the need for help with maintaining one's dignity. Social support does not only refer to the social support that rural female stayers receive, it also includes the process by which they seek help. Whether they seek help or not, these rural female stayers' interactions with those around them show how they face life's hardships in order to protect their *mianzi* and how they show agency in their choices of support. Therefore, focusing on the topic of rural female stayers and social support helps to recognize how they exert their agency when maintaining *mianzi*. For rural female stayers, social support comes from institutions such as the government, and from relationships around rural female stayers, such as neighbours and relatives.

## 5.4.1 Support from family members and other relationships: money and people

Ms. Wu is a stay-behind woman and her husband works in the urban area for most of the year, while she lives with her little son in the rural area. She said:

> 'If I need help, I usually go to my mother (biological mother). My brothers are in Hohhot, and they are too far away to help me. And if my mother can't come to help me, I occasionally go to other relatives. I have relatives from my family in this village.' [Ms. Wu, stay-behind woman]

Ms. Wu relies on her birth family if she needs help, which was normal in the past. As mentioned in Chapter 4, married women are the mobile members of rural society, both as 'outsiders' who marry into the husband's village population and as 'outsiders' who leave their home village (Yin and Chen, 2020). With the development of Chinese society, the old adage that a married daughter is equal to 'water that has been spilled' is no longer quite as true. As time goes by and society changes, women who marry out remain close to their families and provide them with financial and emotional support, and the relationship between the family by birth and the married woman has become closer and closer, as I discussed in Chapter 4. The mother and brothers of the family of origin are usually the first people that rural female stayers turn to for help. Jacka's research found that married women's families are often combined with their biological families (2012) and my data resonates with Jacka's findings. It is easier for married women to seek help from their mothers' families, and frequent contact with them brings married women and their parents closer together. The natal family becomes the strongest support for married women. Thus, despite being seen as the *'wai'* of the natal family, this does not affect the daughters' closeness to their families of origin, and their mother becomes their first choice for help.

Ms. Wang is a stay-behind woman who lives at home alone with her young son, while her husband works in the city. Her relatives do not live in the same village as her. She said,

> 'I don't ask for help. I have no relatives in this village, nor does my husband. So there is no one to ask for help.' [Ms. Wang, stay-behind woman]

Ms. Wang's case presents a rather unique situation. For rural female stayers who have no relatives in the same village, seeking help is always a luxury. Relatives are often by default the most likely people to help, as rural communities place more value on blood ties between relatives. They are often seen as family (even if distant). In contrast, it is difficult for them to ask for help from outsiders.

Ms. Zheng is a return woman who came back to the rural area because her eldest son has reached the school age. At the same time, she has a health problem, so doing farm work is too much for her. She said:

> 'I am reluctant to ask for help, for I have a strong character and I don't want to appear weaker than others. But when I really have no choice, I will ask my relatives to help me. But it's only for small things, like taking the children to school.' [Ms. Zheng, return woman]

The interview with Ms. Zheng illustrates one aspect of rural female stayer's reluctance to seek help. For some (mostly return women), seeking help from their family is a last resort. Self-reliance was a word often used by return

## Chapter 5  Rural female stayers and *Mianzi*—their relationships with the people around them

women reluctant to seek help. The experience of living in the urban areas away from their families has improved their problem-solving skills when faced with difficulties. According to my interviews, most of the return women did not have any close friends or family to turn to during their time in the city. Even if they did have people they knew in the city, they rarely contacted each other because of their busy daily lives and the long distances involved. Therefore, it became a habit for return women to solve their difficulties on their own.

In addition, asking for help is, to a certain extent, a matter of losing one's *mianzi*, especially if it is refused. Return women tend to think that they are more capable than other rural women, which prevents them from asking for help in case they lose their *mianzi*. Ms. Qin's example highlights another reason why they are reluctant to ask people around them for help. Ms. Qin is a return woman, her husband works in the city, and she and her mother live in their rural home. Her two children live in the city and they no longer need her care.

> '(People around them) think I am capable because I can earn money in town. If I ask them for help, it makes them think that I am similar to them and it makes me feel ashamed. And if they refused, I would feel even more humiliated.' [Ms. Qin, return woman]

Return women want to be seen as capable and not seeking help is a way of affirming this. At the same time, it is difficult for return women to ask for help and maintain the illusion that they are better than women who have no experience of urban life. Asking for help could shatter this illusion and cause them to lose *mianzi*, so they carefully impression-manage the good opinion that others have of them in every way. Therefore, their requests for help are usually for small things that will not be judged, such as picking up their children from school, as Ms. Zheng said.

In addition, some rural female stayers provided a different reason for why they do not ask others for help. When Ms. Lv, a stay-behind woman, spoke of her reluctance to seek help from others, she said:

> 'When I had problems, it was really difficult; however, most of these problems were not urgent. For example, the crops in the field need to be harvested, but I won't go to my land if I'm not well. I'll take my time doing these jobs when I'm better. I don't go out and ask for help. If you ask someone for help with something, tomorrow they will certainly ask you to help them with something else. I'm not in good enough health to go if other people ask me for help. Plus, if I'm too busy, I can pay someone to help me... that's much better.' [Ms. Lv, stay-behind woman]

In rural areas, it is common to help people at sowing and harvest time (Hou et al., 2015). It is customary in rural society for favours between farmers to be unpaid and reciprocal, and they are an important bridge between villagers (Ren and Yan, 2017). In rural society, neighbourhood is a key dimension of social structure (Hou et al., 2015) and one way of maintaining interpersonal relationships with others in the neighbourhood is through the exchange of favours, which must follow two basic rules: firstly, obligation. The exchange of favours is an acknowledgement of social status, and this acknowledgement is two-way and obligatory. Secondly, there is the idea of 'payback'. The exchange of favours is a two-way process. When one party gives a gift or a favour, the other must reciprocate (Zhang and Chen, 2018). As Ms. Lv expresses, accepting help from others is an act of agreeing to return the favour in the future, since asking for help is itself an act of bowing to others. This is why some rural female stayers no longer ask for help from neighbours and others, both to avoid losing *mianzi* by asking and being forced to agree to requests in the future to maintain *mianzi*. The need to 'help' has diminished and 'favours' have become increasingly marketized in the rural area. In urbanised rural areas, relying on 'help' from acquaintances is no longer the only option. Villagers are increasingly using market mechanisms to solve their production and livelihood needs (Yang and Yang, 2018). My data, such as in the example of Ms. Lv above, showed related findings to those of Yang and Yang (2018), that more and more people are abandoning the cultural norms of human interaction in favour of the value of equal value exchange. This is due to the fact that increasing numbers of rural people are moving to the cities and returning to their hometowns, meaning that marketisation in the cities is gradually entering the countryside. When the acquaintance model is broken down, remuneration becomes the better option in order to maintain *mianzi*. This mode of payment on the one hand reduces the burden of having to deal with people in order to keep up appearances. On the other hand, it seems fairer and more acceptable for the person being hired. At the same time, it should be noted that Ms. Lv's example is still a rare case, and most people are still willing to help each other, which strengthens the exchanges between the two sides and promotes good feeling. Just as return woman Ms. Cao said, '(mutual help) is between others and me, which is much better. It doesn't feel like you're hurting your feelings over money.'

### 5.4.2 Support from government: funding and policy

Ms. Wei is a stay-behind woman. Because she has not received much education, she never thought of going to the city to work. Her husband and son both work in the city, so she is alone at home most of the time. According to her description, her family's economic situation is poor in the village. When talking about the difficulties she encountered, Ms. Wei said:

> 'No, we are mainly on our own when we encounter difficulties. I don't dare to consider seeking help. The government will help if they can. I haven't thought of taking the initiative to seek it myself. I would worry about not being able to get help and having others know about my difficulties. The others already look down on us now, and if we are turned down for help, they will look down on us even more.' [Ms. Wei, stay-behind woman]

Rural female stayers and their families are informed by the village councils and other grassroots government bodies about the relevant policies and help available to them, including financial assistance. But rural female stayers rarely go to village councils and other agencies to seek help, and many would find it difficult to go to the village hall because they are worried about their problems becoming common knowledge. What Fei calls an acquaintance society is also a 'familiar' one, in which each person knows everything about the other members of the group, nothing that happens within the group escapes the view of each member. In short, all information is shared in an acquaintance society (1998). Although the administrative village is made up of several natural villages and is a semi-acquainted society, people in the village are still familiar with others, especially those who used to live in the same natural village and know each other well. As the people in the village are more familiar with each other, information is easily shared between people, so social evaluation and face punishment of villagers are also easy to achieve (Wang, 2009b). Most of the staff serving on the village councils are local people who have been born and bred in the village, and they are well informed about the people of the village and have a good understanding

Chapter 5 Rural female stayers and *Mianzi*—their relationships with the people around them

of the rural situation. Ms. Zhao is a stay-behind woman and her response is representative: 'I don't want other people to know the state of my family. They might be able to guess some of it, but if you go to the village council (for help), you need to fill in a form and it's impossible to hide (my family's situation). I can't let my husband lose *mianzi*.' As my data shows, when information cannot be kept confidential, stay-behind women are afraid they will lose their *mianzi* if others find out about their difficulties, so they rarely seek out help. In addition, as Ms. Wei mentioned, most of the families who need help are in a disadvantaged position in the village and often face discrimination or prejudice from others. So they sometimes reluctant to seek help and risk their *mianzi*. Also, if they are refused when asking for help, rural female stayers feel that they have lost their *mianzi* and this is one reason why it is difficult for them to seek help. Especially when these families are already in a vulnerable situation in the village, they are more worried and concerned about the perception of others and want to protect their *mianzi*. This resonates with Wang's findings that as an integrated resource, *mianzi* forms a hierarchical structure within the village (Wang, 2009b). It is further explained that the hierarchical relationships that exist within the village are influenced by *mianzi*, and that villagers at the 'top' of the hierarchy need to avoid letting people find out about their deficiencies in order to protect their *mianzi*, as this may cause them to lose prestige in the village and thus lose status. At the same time, villagers at the 'lower' end of the hierarchy may work hard to gain more prestige in the village, gain more *mianzi* and then become the 'upper' end of the hierarchy. So many rural female stayers and their families are reluctant to expose the difficulties their families face, which in many cases is not just a question of losing their *mianzi*, as it is also likely they will lose their original rank in the village.

Despite her reluctance to seek help from those around her, Ms. Sun who is a return woman, takes the initiative to go to the village committee to enquire about various types of policies. She said:

> 'I have taken the initiative to find out about government policies, hoping to find one that fits my situation... Sometimes, it's hard to ask for help from other people, but asking for help from the government is much easier.' [Ms. Sun, return woman]

The interesting finding here is that the return women in my study have been more active in seeking help from the government than the stay-behind women, and Ms. Sun's answer serves as a representative example. Most of the return women interviewed admitted to going to the village council to ask about government policies and seek help. As return woman Ms. Qian says, 'I often go to the village hall to see if there are any new policies that apply to my situation and I would like to get some help. The help is practical and I don't worry about other people laughing at me.' Return women do not seem to be as worried as stay-behind women about the possibility of losing their *mianzi* when finding a solution to their problems proves their competence. From Ms. Chu's point of view, she was 'able to get help and it shows my ability. My family as well as my neighbours feel that I am the one who has the ability.' Return women refuse to make the connection between losing their *mianzi* and being able to get help. At the same time, this shows that they are more interested in gaining recognition for their help than in losing their *mianzi* because of rejection. Besides, return women's urban work experience gave them the opportunity to meet and interact with more strangers, as Ms. Chu notes: 'When I was working in the city, even if someone helped introduce me to a job, I had to negotiate my own salary and the employers were strangers... But after a few times, I got braver.... Now in the village, all I have to do is go to the village council and ask (the council is full of people I know) and I have no trepidation.' The experience of living in the city has helped to open the eyes of rural female stayers and has also changed their minds to a certain extent, enhancing their ability to interact with others. In addition, when dealing with other farmers, farmers often act differently depending on the position they hold in the village in relation to the other part, and 'they have to do things differently according to who he/she faces, as there is a disparity of power and obligations between different classes (Wang, 2009b). As Wang points out, rural people make decisions about their own behaviour based on what others see, which is also a way for them to protect their *mianzi* (2009c). Ms. Chen's interview corroborates Wang's view: 'People in the village feel that people who work in the city have seen the world, so even though I am now back living in the village, they still look at me with that impression and are more polite to me when I go to the village council to ask questions. They are polite to me and I feel I have *mianzi* and act more confident.' The experience of living in the city has, to some extent, given return women more recognition and the village people are happy to give them *mianzi*, so they are more positive about seeking help and are not worried about losing their *mianzi* due to asking for help.

Most of the return women spoke about their experience of going to the village council to ask about policies and seek help on their own initiative. Moreover, their experience of living in the city played a positive role in their searching for help. Meanwhile, rural female stayers who have relatives or parents in the village were less proactive in accessing policies, though. Most of the rural female stayers' families have benefited from government policies. For example, they received subsidies, were contacted by village government staff about the policies and accepted the welfare on offer. On the one hand, asking their parents or relatives for help does not bring about a loss of *mianzi*, as these people fall under the category of family members. On the other hand, seeking help from the government may lead to a situation of being looked down upon. In relationships between families, such as husband and wife, parents and children, there is no problem of losing or increasing *mianzi*. However, when social distance expands from the family to the community and the village, the problem of *mianzi* begins to come to the fore (Kinnison, 2017). Many basic rural matters, including the distribution of benefits and subsidies, are decided by the grassroots village council. Due to the fact that everyone in the village is familiar with each other, many people who go to the village council for help are quickly made aware of their situation by the whole village, and the rejection of their request for help can make them feel ashamed. Furthermore, return women exhibit an ambivalence: they emphasise that they do not want to seek help from their families because it might affect other people's opinions of them and thus cause a loss of *mianzi*; but they see getting help from the village council as confirmation of their own capabilities. Return women do not agree that there is an inverse correlation between asking for help and *mianzi*, and they see their urban experience as giving them *mianzi* in the village. Being able to get help by asking for it demonstrates their competence. Therefore, they were more positive about seeking help from the village council than the stay-behind women.

## 5.5 Conclusion

As a very important part of Chinese culture, *mianzi* is thoroughly integrated into the daily lives of rural female stayers and influences them in many ways. Rural people are very concerned with the issue of '*mianzi*' in their daily lives and when they talk about other people, they tend to protect their *mianzi* by

## Chapter 5   Rural female stayers and *Mianzi*—their relationships with the people around them

finding more appropriate reasons for their choices in order to get the listener to acknowledge the validity of these choices. Rural female stayers protect their *mianzi* by countering the prejudices of others and by emphasising self-choice in order to construct their positive approach to life as well as show their agency to make decisions for the family and even the village. Through the analysis of how rural female stayers maintain their *mianzi*, it is easy to find that in a situation where stay-behind and return women do not know each other well, they tend be positive about their lives and choices in order to preserve their *mianzi*, while trying to find better reasons for their choices. In the process of maintaining their *mianzi*, rural female stayers attempt to break down prejudices. When they are able to gain or retain *mianzi*, their status is enhanced and this provides them with additional resources in facing life and its various difficulties.

At the same time, it is worth noting that the experience of living in the city has had a greater impact on rural female stayers than might have been expected. On the one hand, society does not have enough tolerance and understanding for return women, and has created a 'loser' image for them. On the other hand, it's difficult for stay-behind women who have never lived in the urban areas to understand the migration experiences of return women. Indeed, given that the Confucianism ideology of women's roles and responsibilities within the family is paramount, return women who leave their families are already initially in a position of incomprehension. To some rural people, migrant workers look like second-class citizens of the city. Under the impact of these two ideas, return women who decide to go back to the rural area have certain difficulties in breaking these prejudices and misconceptions. However, it is the experience of migration that creates new possibilities for return women and allows them to gain more recognition and a voice from those around them, which in turn shapes their possibilities to gain and retain *mianzi*. As a result, return women express more certainty about their status and right to be involved in making decisions.

In addition, the role of agency in the protection of *mianzi* is important. If we think of 'agency' as a kind of right, it is the ability we have to control our own destiny and influence the development of other people and things (Man, 2016). On the one hand, in order to protect *mianzi*, rural female stayers emphasise how they exercise their agency by showing their lives, in terms of decision-making power and so on. On the other hand, as I have elaborated in the literature review, agency is constrained by the limited space in which women's efforts of protecting the *mianzi* are displayed, as well as by the cultural context. Thus, return women may have more space to mobilise their agency, in contrast to stay-behind women, given their experience of urban life.

Through exploring how rural female stayers face prejudice and protect their *mianzi*, we gain further understanding of how they try to use the limited resources available to them to shore up their social status. In the next chapter, I would like to continue this focus on the ways that rural female stayers are able to emphasise the positive aspects of their lives, and turn to explore what they have to say on the subject of happiness and its meaning in daily life.

# Chapter 6 A 'happy life' for rural female stayers?

In previous studies of rural female stayers (Li, 2010; Wang and Wu, 2020; Ju and Wang, 2022), the main emphasis has often been on the negative aspects of their lives, such as their misfortunes. As I mentioned in the previous chapter, rural female stayers often struggle with these negative views and social misconceptions as they attempt to maintain their *mianzi*. With this in mind, the key question I explore in this chapter is what constitutes a 'good' or 'happy' life for these rural female stayers, and in what ways they claim that happiness is (and is not) relevant to their lives. I argue that it is important to focus on how rural female stayers understand happiness, as this counteracts some of the ways in which others define their lives. We can see how they themselves define or describe their own lives and with what views, as well as the way they approach this life. Furthermore, from a more critical perspective, the possibility of happiness as described by rural female stayers helps us to understand social conventions about the way life 'should' be lived as a woman in rural China, as the happiness they describe is articulated in relation to these norms. I suggest that these assumptions about how life should be lived as a stay-behind Chinese woman in turn limit the parameters of their lives in particular ways.

In much of the existing literature pertaining to people living in rural China, happiness has been measured quantitatively as part of the construct of subjective happiness (Shui et al., 2020; Zhou et al., 2018). Whilst these studies have been helpful in highlighting various factors that correlate with subjective happiness, I wanted to prioritise my participants' own understandings of happiness. In exploring these ideas, I draw on sociological approaches to happiness that have explored what the idea of happiness does, and how it organises social life. In particular, Ahmed, in writing about happiness in Western contexts suggests that happiness can be something we wish for, on the one hand a way of getting what we want, and on the other a symbol that we have got what we want (Ahmed, 2010). Ahmed attempts to guide us to think about what really makes us happy, what makes us unhappy and what happiness is if we can achieve it (2010). Ahmed bases her interpretation of happiness directly on a sociological theory of emotions, for example, by examining the things that are influenced by happiness. In this, she critically suggests that happiness does not come from 'good things' (p20), but rather that nice things are the product of our happiness being repeated over and over again. At the same time, she talks about how family is both something that affects us and something that we are led by (2010). Although many people think of happiness as the feeling of good things in life, in reality happiness is a balance of good and bad experiences (Cieslik, 2015).

While Ahmed's arguments provide a useful critical lens for thinking about happiness, they are developed in relation to the way in which happiness works in Western contexts. In this chapter, I am concerned with what happiness means in the lives of rural female stayers in rural China. This requires an understanding of the cultural meanings and possibilities of happiness in China. Through my data I will show how the Chinese rural female stayers in my study understand or illustrate a happy life through their own reflections on their lives. Retaining a critical perspective, I also consider what these versions of a happy life could be said to 'do', i.e. how they also define the parameters of a normal life.

Chapter 6 A 'happy life' for rural female stayers?

In this chapter, I will analyse the possibilities of happiness for rural female stayers from their own accounts. I begin by exploring what a happy life is like as described by rural female stayers. In the second section I turn to consider how happiness was often described in relation to understandings of the future and I will highlight the issue of '*bentou*', as a specific set of relations to the future. Finally, I will discuss some unusual cases encountered during the data collection—rural female stayers for whom happiness was not a topic that can be talked about.

## 6.1. Happiness for rural female stayers (both stay-behind women and return women)

It is important to note that when I talked to stay-behind women about happiness, they also referred to it in terms of a satisfying life. Sometimes, they used the word satisfied to replace the word happiness. This is because in Chinese, the word 'satisfaction' means to feel happy because of fulfilling one's wishes and conforming to one's own mind. Although we Chinese people do talk about happiness a lot in our daily lives, happiness is often seen as a big concept and is not an 'everyday' topic. During the interviews, I found that participants were relatively subtle in their expressions of emotion, so they often used less emotive words instead of strong ones. For example, they often used the phrase 'okay' or 'indifferent' rather than stating clearly that something is good or bad, and they rarely expressed their extreme pleasure or disgust at anything.

### 6.1.1 What makes a happy life for rural female stayers?

Due to their need of taking care of their families, when rural female stayers described their happy lives for me, it often revolved around family life. Just as it is impossible to avoid children, parents and husbands when talking about the everyday life of rural female stayers, in fact, when the conversation revolved around happiness, these are the parts that were at the heart of the conversation. Taking good care of their children and family is usually the benchmark for defining successful women in Chinese society. So, when rural female stayers believe that what they are doing is in line with social values, they gain a sense of satisfaction and pride. Therefore, they always emphasised their fulfilment of society's demands on women when they described what it means to live happily.

First, for rural female stayers, children often dominated these accounts. Ms. Zhou is a return woman, and she has a daughter who is studying in high school. She said:

> 'My life is mainly focused on taking care of my child... She is still doing well in her studies and this is because I have insisted that she develops good study habits from the time she started school. Even now, I still accompany her to do her homework every day. I am always worried that she isn't able to learn on her own. Because I try to accompany her when she is studying, I have to do most of the housework late at night or early in the morning. But when she gets praise from her teachers or gets good grades, I feel that my effort is worth it. The fact that she is good makes me happy.' [Ms. Zhou, return woman]

As I illustrated in Chapter 4, motherhood is a very important part of rural female stayers' lives. Children are a key focus, and rural female stayers' descriptions of happiness often revolve around the topic of their children. Just as parents should teach their children as a matter of course, the family-centred rural female stayers in my study see their children's success as their own happiness, while they focus on their children's education and life. During the interviews, rural female stayers mentioned that parents, especially stay-behind mothers, gain a great sense of happiness and achievement through the success of their children when they achieve the goals set by their parents. They rely on their children to achieve their own happiness. The stay-behind mothers I interviewed took great pride in talking about their children's good qualities, especially when they are developing in the way they want them to, and the needs and wants of the child are sometimes ignored in this process. For example, when her child clashes with her own ideas, Ms. Qian's response is straightforward. Ms. Qian is a return woman who only has one son. Because of her son's poor school record, she sent her son to the army as a soldier two years ago.

> 'My son is not good at school and he didn't want to study in his first year in junior high school. I disagreed, so he didn't drop out of school. I asked him to at least graduate from junior high school... I had hoped he would go to university, but now I have to change my mind and find another road for him. It will be easier for him to find a job when he returns from the army in the future.' [Ms. Qian, return woman]

Growing up is often treated as a generational conflict by both parents and their child. The child wants what the parents do not want (Zhang, 2008). In a Western context, Ahmed (2010) suggests that reconciling the respective needs is the main pillar of a happy family: either the child understands the wisdom of the parents and then aligns her needs with what the parents want for her, or the parents understand the child and align their wishes for the child with the child's needs; or, of course, it is most often the case that both parties reach relative agreement through some kind of compromise (Ahmed,

2010). Although this is true of some Chinese families to some extent, for most families in my research, it is not so much that the children understand their parents' decisions as that the children mostly lose the right to choose. As my participant expressed, within the Chinese happiness story, it is the choices and growing up that meet the parents' standards that are seen as right, or as making a happy life. Children are prescribed a life and are entrusted with the hopes of their parents. If they fail to achieve their parents' initial plans, then their parents change their goals and plan their children's lives for a second time. The child will rarely contradict the parent's decision, which is in effect a compromise on their part. Ms. Qian's choice to 'find another road for him' is similar to that of the majority of the rural female stayers I interviewed. When children themselves have difficulty reaching the goals initially set for them, rural female stayers have to compromise on the reality of the situation and choose another path that fits their values and allows them to achieve a 'good' life goal for their children. Even if it is a compromise, when this goal is eventually reached, rural female stayers see it as the right choice and are happy that it has been achieved. Despite the compromise made by rural female stayers, we cannot say that this is a victory for the child. As Ms. Zhou kept stressing, 'They are too young to understand society. So how can they make their own decisions? The parents' [plans] are for their own good, and this they will know when they grow up.' It is therefore important to note that the happiness of rural female stayers has little to do with whether their children actually feel happy or not. Their understanding of happiness is based more on their own values. Rather than seeking happiness through the happiness experienced by their children, they express happiness when their children grow up in accordance with their plans. This is qualitatively different from what happens with Western parents, whose desire for the child's happiness may be providing some freedom (Ahmed, 2010). My participants saw their children's success as their own happiness and the paths they choose for their children are mostly in line with popular values. In fact, they position growing up in a way that meets the public's expectations, which is deemed the most important thing, as they just want their children to grow up in a way that fits with the prevailing social norms, for example, to leave the countryside to go to university and then to work and stay in the city, or to learn skills that can help them get a job more easily. Ahmed argues that when a parent says 'I just want you to be happy', they are indicating that it is easy to be happy, that it is something good for a parent to want, and so the child should want it too (2010). This means it is harder for a child to pursue different outcomes. Rural female stayers impose their own values on their children while deriving their own happiness from them. Thus, the child is asked to fulfil the mother's wishes, and rural female stayers only describe that condition as happiness if their children fulfil their expectations.

In addition to children, the presence of parents as the people being cared for by the rural female stayers are also a feature of their accounts of the meanings and possibilities of happiness. Ms. Feng has to look after her husband's father and her youngest daughter on her own during the periods when her husband goes to the urban area. Her daughter is in town for school, and only returns home at weekends.

She said:

> 'My parents-in-law were very good to me, and now I take good care of the elderly [meaning her husband's father] as well. It is my duty to do so, too. They often praise me to their relatives and I feel happy even if I have to work more. I got on well with my parents-in-law, which made my life comfortable and happy. Since my mother-in-law passed

away, I think looking after my father-in-law is my responsibility. He is my husband's parent, which means he is also my parent... I am quite happy with my life now. My father-in-law is in good health. In fact I just help to cook for him. He is able to do most things by himself. On the other hand, he has some government-issued benefits which also help my family live better. I'm quite content now.' [Ms. Feng, stay-behind woman]

When the husbands of stay-behind families go out to work, the main responsibility for caring for parents will be taken on by rural female stayers, as mentioned in Chapter 4. Because of her ability to take care of her children and her husband's parents, Ms. Feng felt happy with her life. For Ms. Feng, her main responsibility during the week was to take care of her husband's father. But it was not a 'difficult job' as her husband's father can do most of the work himself and she had to do very little and there is not a lot of heavy lifting involved. At the same time, her husband's father received some financial assistance from the government. This money was also considered to be the family's income and will be managed by Ms. Feng's husband. This income had gone some way to reducing the financial stress suffered by the family and has improved their quality of life. In her account, the chores she needed to do were within her reach and were seen as work that was meant to be hers, so she felt happy when she finished. Also, the praise she received was an aspect of her life that she rated as happy, which was seen as an added 'bonus'.

Ms. Zhu is a return woman and now lives with her mother-in-law in the rural area. Her husband works in the city. Her children are away at school and are only home during the school holidays. Therefore, she and her mother-in-law are usually the only two people in the house. She said:

'My husband usually works in the city, so it's usually just me and my mother-in-law at home. She (meaning her mother-in-law) is mainly taken care of by me, and that's the way it should be. If her daughter is willing to come and help me take care of her together, I am of course happy, but I don't care if she doesn't come; it is supposed to be my duty. My mother-in-law often praises me to my neighbours. Although I sometimes feel like it is hard work, I also feel that this hard work is deserved. All in all, my days are very happy every day.' [Ms. Zhu, return woman]

In the context of filial culture, rural female stayers are naturally regarded as the people who should take on of the responsibility of caring for their parents (mainly meaning their husband's parents). When rural female stayers take on this 'required' responsibility, they feel that they are doing the right thing. At the same time, if family members praise rural female stayers for taking care of their parents, they feel that they have been recognized by others, and this recognition is experienced as happiness. Meanwhile, rural female stayers barely mention the husband's responsibility when it comes to caring for the in-laws. This is partly due to the fact that most of their husbands work outside the home and do not live with their parents for long periods of time, and partly due to the fact that, as I mentioned in Chapter 4, the responsibility for caring for parents is often taken up by women, and thus reflects gendered expectations.

Ms. Sun previously worked in the city with her husband and returned to the countryside a few years ago to care for her father. She is proud of her choice when she talks about this:

'My father is very old and it is difficult for him to take care of himself.

After my mother became ill, there was no one else who could take care of him. I then decided that I would take care of them. I couldn't let my parents live badly, and even though I have a lot less income since I came back, I feel happy because I did what I was supposed to do. I didn't think about sending them to a nursing home. You know, there was no other way to do it. I can afford it. It's just a bit of hard work, I can't have people saying I don't look after the elderly.' [Ms. Sun, return woman]

Ms. Sun's interview indicates that choosing to care for her parents will result in a sense of happiness, even though it may reduce her income and lower her standard of living. Rural female stayers' contribution to the family is recognized by their families as a source of happiness. For most rural female stayers, their contributions to the family or children are expected by other family members and society, and they regard these as the source of their value to the family. Although financial pressure for the whole family has always been an area that cannot be ignored, it is more often placed on men. Rural female stayers in my study often need to deal with matters from within the family, so they do not tend to hesitate when faced with caring for the elderly. At the same time, rural female stayers do not think that they are inferior to other people because they care for their children or the elderly alone. On the contrary, in their view, this reflects their quality of a good wife and mother in line with historical Chinese culture.

Rural female stayers always take care of their parents-in-law at home. This is because children are expected to take care of their parents, which is in line with the Chinese culture of filial piety, and women are seen as the implementers of parental care.

Ochiai (2008a) argues that in China, one of the reasons why the elderly need to be cared for by their children is due to the lack of institutions or systems in society to care for them. My research showed differences with Ochiai's research findings, indicating that in rural areas, taking care of their parents is more a matter of inheriting traditional living habits. As Ms. Sun said, sending an elderly person to an institution can be gossiped about by others and seen as unfilial. Whether or not to send the elderly to an institution is a controversial issue in Chinese society. It is not in line with the Chinese culture of filial piety, which sees it as filial for children to have to take care of their parents, but to take care of them through an institution, even if it may cost money of the children, is still seen as somewhat unfilial. Moreover, many elderly people are reluctant to go to an institution and they feel they are being abandoned (Wu, 2017). Historically, Chinese culture has placed high demands on filial piety, which is seen as a way for children to reciprocate the kindness of their parents, as mentioned in Chapter 4. The Chinese saying *'bai shan xiao wei xian'*[1] expresses the extremely high status of filial piety. Thus, from the perspective of children, it is their duty to take care of their parents; from the perspective of parents, being taken care of is a reward for having raised children in the past. In my study, I found that these normative ideas of filial piety were evident in rural female stayers' accounts of their happiness and satisfaction in caring for elderly relatives. They did not refer to the availability of institutional elder care.

Ms. Han is a stay-behind woman, and her husband works in the urban area most of the year. She lives with her parents-in-law and her son in the parents-in-law's home. She said:

---

1  It means that of all the virtues, filiality comes first.

> 'Since I got married, I have live with my parents-in-law. They have taken good care of me and treated me like a daughter. Therefore, I have lived a very comfortable and happy life at my in-law's home.' [Ms. Han, stay-behind woman]

Because rural female stayers live with their parents-in-law, it is not just the satisfaction and status that women gain from caring for them that facilitates the description of this experience as a happy life, but also the relationships among them. According to my participants, like Ms. Han, for rural female stayers in rural China, family happiness is not only reflected in their relationship with their children, but also in their relationship with their parents-in-law (e.g. being treated 'like a daughter'). How well they get along with their parents-in-laws has a significant impact on their daily lives. Although taking care of elders may increase the workload of rural female stayers, rural female stayers describe having a harmonious relationship with their parents-in-law as helping them to achieve a greater sense of well-being. This is supported by Ms. Han's story about her neighbour who lives with her mother-in-law, too.

> 'Her mother-in-law didn't like her when she got married and disliked that her natal family was poor... She hadn't gone out to work before, but her mother-in-law always scolded her. She had no choice but to go to work with her husband. She came back to the village a few years ago because she was looking after her children who were school-age. Her mother-in-law said she could not take the children to school and asked her to come back and bring them up herself (my mother-in-law helped me bring up the children all those years). But she has earned some money from her part-time job, so her mother-in-law is now treating her better than before.' [Ms. Han, stay-behind woman]

The story of Ms. Han's neighbour also proves that maintaining a good relationship with your mother-in-law is important for a happy life. Although it is not necessarily the responsibility of a mother-in-law to help her daughter-in-law take care of the children, it is a default custom in China. Ms. Han only mentions her neighbour being scolded by her mother-in-law and the need to bring up her children herself; however, this is a small thing in daily life. The small thing that shows the impact of a bad relationship with her mother-in law is actually felt in all aspects of daily life. The inconvenience of everyday life is only one part of the equation, but there is also the emotional stress that can affect the happiness of rural female stayers.

As noted in Chapter 4, the topic of husbands was a concern for my participants in their descriptions of daily life. Husbands also featured in discussions of happiness. Rural female stayers generally talked about not being decision-makers in the family, but the context of being rural female stayers impacted on this. For example, Ms. Wu, who is a stay-behind woman said:

> 'I used to listen to my husband, but he's away from home so much. Now that I can't wait for him to decide on a lot of things... I occasionally worry if he'll object to my decisions... But since I started deciding on things around the house, I feel like life has gotten a little easier. The conditions at home now definitely don't meet everyone's needs. The children have to be satisfied first, the parents have to be taken care of, I can suffer and it's okay [if my demands are not met]...It's the feeling that I have the initiative, even though my needs are still not being met, but that was the one I gave up voluntarily. This life where I can make decisions makes me feel happy.' [Ms. Wu, stay-behind woman]

The rural female stayers who I interviewed do not generally seek the right to make decisions in family matters, as Ms. Wu said, 'I never hope for the right to make the decision, and it is normal to follow the husband'. Most of the women who I interviewed showed indifference towards the right to speak their mind or they agreed with the traditional family relations, where the husband is the main decision maker in the family. But when the husband left the family to work outside the home, this traditional pattern of division of labour was broken, giving women more power to decide on family matters. As they gradually have greater voice, rural female stayers find themselves able to make more decisions for the family. Although this is often accompanied by stress, happiness goes hand in hand with the stress and the power to decide brings them satisfaction with themselves. Ms. Wu's face was full of pride when she talked about making decisions for her family. She has gained recognition of her place in the family by having a voice and thus feels more satisfied with her life. Ms. Wu was happy that she could have more influence on decision making. In fact, although rural female stayers still prioritise their families in their decisions, it is the subjective 'sacrifice' which they are happy and proud to make. This also demonstrates that the approach to a happy life is passive and stoic, a passive way of coping that appears to emphasise self-restraint. It also demonstrates the Chinese mentality of *'zhi zu chang le'* (Matthyssen, 2018). Rural female stayers themselves do not express a strong desire for family power, but if they do gain some, they are very aware that they have a lot or more than they did before, giving an account of themselves feeling satisfied through gaining power, and thus happy.

Ms. Zhu's family has just moved into a newly built house. She used to work in the city with her husband. Then she returned to the countryside for the birth of her second child, and has since stayed there to look after the elderly and children. Ms. Zhu said:

> 'He knows that he can't take care of the family without me. We're getting better now, and in addition to his (husband's) income from working, the government also subsidises the children's schooling. In the past, I wouldn't have thought we could live in a house like this.' [Ms. Zhu, return woman]

On the one hand, Ms. Zhu affirms her indispensability to the family, and on the other hand, she indirectly expresses her contented views towards life. A happy life is one of gaining recognition, especially for rural female stayers who cannot earn money for the household. Compared to her previous living situation, Ms. Zhu's family's material conditions have improved significantly, which has given her a clear sense of happiness and achievement, as shown by 'living in a house like this'.

Ms. Zhang is a return woman, and she lives with her father-in-law and two children in the rural area. Her husband is employed in the city as a construction site worker. She said:

> 'The biggest thing I expect from my husband is that he earns money to come back home... this determines how happy or unhappy we are with our family's life. I don't need him to worry about things at home and I can take care of the elderly and children. When he was working on the previous construction site he earned a good income and I found the days relaxing; recently, he has been doing all the temporary work so his income is very unstable and I often worry about the money...' [Ms. Zhang, return woman]

In addition, as I have highlighted several times in my analysis, the focus of rural female stayers' discussion often centred on household income. When it comes to happiness, a stable and adequate income is the foundation. For rural female stayers, only when the lowest physical needs are met can they talk about other needs. Many rural female stayers believe that as long as their husband works hard to earn money and they look after their families at home, they can have a happy family and marriage, and further, that the happiness of the family becomes rural female stayers' own happiness. Therefore, it is inevitable that rural female stayers will be worried and stressed about the financial situation of the family. The husband chooses to work in the city so that his family can get a better life and improve their economic conditions. According to Ms. Zhang's story, there is a positive correlation between economic income and happiness. Despite the fact that a family without a husband lacks someone to share the stresses, chores and labour with, the rural female stayers do not mind sacrificing their own interests; they gain their own happiness through the happiness of their family. As Ms. Zhang says, 'When the family is feeling happy, I am feeling happy.'

To sum up, the lives of rural female stayers revolve around family, and their descriptions of their happy lives revolve around their family members. When rural female stayers talk about this, their accounts are mostly based on the inherent idea of *'nan zhu wai, nv zhu nei'* which I mentioned in Chapter 4. The idea emphasises the fact that women focus on the internal affairs of the family and men focus on the external aspects. In their accounts of their present lives, my participants placed their family's happiness ahead of their own, for example, suggesting that they did not mind hard work as long as their family members were happy. As I have illustrated throughout this section, rural female stayers' descriptions of happiness are completely in line with social norms and social values concerning the role of a 'good' wife, mother and daughter-in-law. Thus, it is important to recognize how gendered norms are implicated in a template for a so-called 'good life' for rural female stayers, potentially hindering other possibilities for a 'happy' life.

When discussing the issue of happiness with my participants, a large part of their attention was focused on talking about income and consumption. They often connected their happiness to being in a good economic situation (and conversely, as I consider further later in this chapter, accounts of the absence of happiness were often connected to difficult economic circumstances). As I talked about in Chapter 4, the reason why many people leave the rural area is so that they can earn more money in the urban area. Given the relatively poor living conditions in rural areas, and the low and limited income levels, it is unsurprising that the participants' narratives of happiness are connected to economic prosperity. For example, Ms. Zhang talked about how '(our family) didn't have a house before thinking about having a house of our own, but now that we have built a house after earning money, we feel quite good and have extra peace of mind every day.' For many families with rural female stayers, most of them are faced with caring for the elderly as well as children. So income has a big impact on them and many families have a heavy financial burden as they need to cover the education costs of their younger children as well as saving up for a house for their older children (especially their sons) to get married in the future. Notably though, echoing many other aspects of their narratives, the financial requirements of rural female stayers are basically centred around family or children. In contrast to research concerning gender in urban China (e.g., Tao and Li, 2015; Qian and Qian, 2014), my participants do not generally give accounts of happiness as connected to their own individual financial security. However, as I go on to explore in the next section, women who have migrated to cities and have returned, do position their own self-development and (to some extent) pleasure as an important source of satisfaction.

### 6.1.2 The specific circumstances of return women

Urban life not only increases the income of rural families, but it opens the eyes of the women who have experienced urban life. This urban life has changed the mindset of return women and their experience of urban life has brought them new perspectives and aspirations. As a result, when they talk about happiness, they emerge with multiple perspectives.

Ms. Chu is a return woman. After finishing looking after her children's schooling in the urban area, Ms. Chu returned to the rural area under her husband's request, and when she talked about the changes to her life, she said,

> 'One has to be satisfied with oneself. Urban living experience is actually an upgrade for me. I feel more confident than before because I have a wider perspective now. I feel that doing housework at home is actually making a contribution... (In the past) I felt that earning money was the most important thing for the family and so my husband contributed a lot to the family. Now I feel that I can also make a big contribution to the family. The exposure to people in the city is a unique experience and my own ability has improved... and I'm pursuing different things. I originally went out for my children to accompany them to school, but now although my life still revolves around the children, I occasionally spend a little money for my own amusement.' [Ms. Chu, return woman]

Return women who had experienced the city were more able to acknowledge their value and contribution to their families. As described in Chapters 4 and 5, experiences gained through living in the city for a period of time seemed to impact return women's accounts of themselves. In fact, city life seems to have provided a chance for them to develop a new understanding of what they contribute. This change is also an expression of how they define their lives. As return women come to realise their contribution and value to their families, the way they express their satisfaction is often through economic consumption. This seems to be a reward, showing that they are worthy of this 'non-essential' unplanned spending.

In the interview, Ms. Chu also talked about how her life and thoughts have changed since she returned to the countryside as a return woman. After she came back to the rural area, she did not want to just stay at home. So, she used her experience of working in the urban areas to find some temporary work in the surrounding areas of the village. She also talked about the changing of her husband's attitude, and the impact on the gendered division of labour within the home. She said:

> 'Because I earn money, my husband can't complain that I'm only idle at home... My husband and I are the same now. We both have income outside. So when we are at home, he has to do the housework too, like washing clothes and so on...I'm glad I'm bringing in an income for the family as well.' [Ms. Chu, return woman]

As vital as the income return women bring home is the change in their families' attitudes, which is also crucial. And while return women express how city life has changed their thinking, they are also excited to express the changes in their family's view of them. Although many return women still acknowledge that their husbands' income remains the main source of household income, the fact that they can earn their own money helps them regard themselves on the same level as their husbands. In other words, for these return women, having an income is much more important than how much they earn when it comes to measuring their household contribution. In addition, when the husband becomes more involved in the household work, return women are relieved from the workload on the one hand and feel that they have gained a more equal status on the other. For example, Ms. Zhao said, 'We are all the same now, we all take on part of the housework at home'. Ms. Zhang also talked about this issue, 'I have less work to do now so I have time to go out a bit and do things I want to do, like playing poker.'

Then there is the example of Ms. Cao who after returning to the countryside, is now a housewife and has no financial income. She expressed during the interview that she found life in the city more comfortable and happy. She said of the time when she had her own income that, 'When I was in the city, my husband always discussed with me if I had an opposing view to his, but now if I object to him, he will say I don't earn money and use that to silence me.'

While Ms. Cao continues to contribute heavy and time-consuming labour to her household (through unpaid domestic labour), her husband only values her paid income. As a consequence, she describes her life satisfaction as higher in the city, where she also had an income and was treated as an equal participant in discussions. Her interview shows how the contributory nature of domestic work can in fact be easily overlooked.

Those around these return women also confirm that they seem different compared with the past. Ms. Wu's neighbour is a woman who has returned to her village. Her husband did not return to the countryside with her, so she became a stay-behind woman after returning to the rural area. Ms. Wu said about her neighbour:

> 'She returned to the countryside because she was pregnant with her second child... It is definitely better to go out to work and earn more... But she is now also working in a factory around the village. I think she used to live in the city and that's why she was thinking of getting a job to earn money. She has a busy life, but she feels happier working hard than staying at home... I think my neighbour's life has more bentou than people like us.' [Ms. Wu, stay-behind woman]

*Bentou*, in this case, means 'hopes for the future'. The urban experience has given rise to a change in the values of return women, which has led, as Ms. Wu said, to return women trying to find work opportunities in rural areas as well. The experience of living in the city has, to a certain extent, changed return women's view of themselves and they have developed a sense of relative independence. They also realise that their contribution to the family can be focused on more than just family matters. The financial income return women receive from their work gives them a greater sense of their own worth, and they describe this as satisfaction with life.

Ms. Chu also expressed the fact that she had more rights in the family:

> 'I myself feel that I have contributed to the family, and I speak more forcefully than before, such as when discussing things I can also express my opinion, although the big things still have to follow my husband's decision. But when I speak out my opinion, he will listen now. So I am satisfied with my life. As I often say, I have a position in my family. I feel similar to women in the city... My children also think I am not the kind of housewife his father says... I have a strong personality, and now

I am very respectable at home and outside. So I feel that life is very hopeful and happy every day. That is, I am quite satisfied with myself and my life.' [Ms. Chu, return woman]

It is interesting to see the way in which return women attributed decision-making power to having a happy, or satisfied life. Unlike stay-behind women, the return women are less content with patriarchal modes of decision-making after their experience of urban life. They present a different picture of a happy life in which they emphasise the idea of obtaining more equality with men. Although they still recognize their husbands as the 'authority' of the family, they are satisfied that they have been given a voice. This demonstrates that the migrant experience helps rural female stayers to gain more space to exercise their agency. They form their narratives. The increase in their agency is associated with more happiness.

However, while many return women narrated migration as a journey of self-transformation that led to a happier (and more individually powerful) life through skills acquired in the city, others suggested that happiness could be found through pursuing a more conventional rural life. The urban population is becoming more and more mobile, and living spaces become more and more isolated and cramped. As Ms. Chu said, 'When I lived in the city, the neighbours didn't know each other. Because most people moved around a lot, they didn't have time to get to know each other.' For rural female stayers, life in this environment seems even more difficult to adjust to. Unlike men who work outside the home, they have relatively limited access to people, especially mothers who are accompanying their children, which can make their lives very narrow. Ms. Jiang, who was a return woman, said, 'I can't go out to work because I need to look after my children. My daily life is basically staying at home and my main opportunity to go out is to buy food.

Because I don't know anyone, I often feel alone when my children go to school.' Besides, one of the things that makes these return women feel even more isolated is that they find it difficult to talk to others even when they feel overwhelmed. 'I rarely talk to my friends or my mother (who are living in the countryside) about my life in the city. They are too far away from me, ' Ms. Zhu said in a conversation with me. Although city life may bring income, it is not a happy life for some return women, especially those who are not able to work while in the city. The reason they cannot work outside the home may be because they have difficulty finding work, or because they cannot work as they need to look after their children. City life is more of a compromise they make for their families.

In addition, the pressures of city life are also a reason for return women to describe rural life as a happy life. Ms. Zhu previously ran a snack shop in the city with her husband, but then her husband did not like life in the city, so they returned to the countryside together. Ms. Zhu said:

> 'The reason for me migrating to the urban area to work at the very beginning is to earn money... in the city every day is very tiring and very busy. I was always thinking about going back to the rural area at that time, and I feel the rural life can be a little easier... although going out to earn money is quite good, the city people are ultimately not the same as rural people. There are differences in doing things and even talking. For example, people in the city are not used to going to other people's homes to chat. You can go there, but they feel inconvenienced. So the pressure is also quite big. I wasn't sure if going back to the countryside was a good choice before I went back to the rural area. Then, when I returned to the rural area, I felt that life was much easier and less stressful. I am much happier now.' [Ms. Zhu, return woman]

In this account, urban dwelling is described as difficult for migrant women. For the rural-urban migrant family, the gap between urban and rural living habits is the first thing to emerge, followed by the enormous pressure brought on by the economic stress of trying to survive in the city. Research has likewise demonstrated that the intense pace of life in the urban area is very different from the countryside. The inconvenience of not having a *hukou* and the frequent discrimination they encounter make it difficult for migrant workers to integrate into the city (Li, 2014; Zhu and Wu, 2007). This is partly an indication that although city life provides space for return women to exercise their financial and decision-making agency, it does not follow that they will feel happy when they have the space to do so. Like Ms. Zhu, many of the return women expressed, to varying degrees, the stress of urban life and the relief they felt upon returning to the rural area. They often emphasised that the stress of urban living was compounded by having to deal with concerns for their husbands. For example, Ms. Zhou repeatedly stressed in the interview that the pressure of city life is 'the pressure of having to worry about money every day when you open your eyes, and whether he (her husband) will be able to find a job'. At the same time, this example illustrates that when life circumstances change, the gendered division of labour in the household may remain the same—men are still seen as the breadwinners, even if many return women are also given the opportunity to work. It is therefore worth exploring the extent of the impact of urban life experience on return women, and whether a happy life is still predicated on the husbands to provide sufficient financial income to secure a living. It is further explained that return women's own income is overlooked in their measure of happiness in life, although they may emphasise the good changes that income brings to their lives. This will therefore be a topic for in-depth discussion in future research.

In general, rural women want to work in the city because working in the urban area brings in a bigger income, but on the other hand, many recognize the difficulties of integration and the huge mental stress that urban life causes. So when return women talk about happiness, two rather contradictory descriptions emerge due to their different experiences and understandings of urban life. This contradictory account of the experience of urban life appeared in the mouths of almost every return woman who participated in my interviews: they emphasised the advantages of urban life and the wages they could earn, but at the same time, they tried to rationalise the 'objective' influences on their return to the countryside by comparing urban life with their life in the countryside now. On the one hand, urban life can be narrated as a catalyst for self-change and self-development, which enables women to live a happier life through realising (and having others' recognition of) their worth. On the other hand, it was sometimes presented as a situation of great hardship and unfamiliarity, making the experience of returning to rural dwelling as one of relief and satisfaction with the carefree and familiar life in the countryside.

## 6.2  Rural female stayers and future happiness

In this section, I will explore how rural female stayers describe their futures. In doing so, I consider the temporal aspects of happiness. I do this by addressing two quite different contexts in which women talked about the future. The first was introduced by me as an interviewer, asking women to comment on their childhood dreams. As I go on to illustrate below, the notion of 'dreaming' about the future was dismissed as impractical by my participants, who emphasised the importance of the circumstances of their present lives as shaping both the possibilities of dreaming, and of acquiring happiness. In contrast, I suggest that they became much more animated when talking about having *bentou*, i.e. concrete possibilities for making future happiness.

### 6.2.1 The gap between childhood dreams and reality

When I interviewed rural female stayers, two of the key questions I asked were about their childhood dreams and their ideas about what the future holds for them. When they were confronted with questions about their childhood dreams, the answers of rural female stayers are strikingly similar.

Firstly, there is the answer of not having thought about the future. In other words, they suggested that they didn't have dreams when they were young. As Ms. Wu explained:

> 'My father and mother's old family had bad land so their income was low. I was just cooking at home and stuff. There were too many children at home, and then I got married at a young age... I didn't think much about the future at that time.' [Ms. Wu, stay-behind woman]

Anticipation is emotional, an orientation towards the future, an expectation of something to come (Ahmed, 2010). What Ms. Wu describes is the opposite of anticipation. Never thinking about dreams, to a certain extent, is not looking forward to the future. In fact, for most of the women I interviewed, describing childhood yearnings or dreams for the future is a relatively difficult question. When interviewing the rural female stayers, their first reaction talking about childhood dreams was strangeness, followed by shyness. Actually, during my interviews, most of them were too shy to talk about their dreams, and Ms. Zhao's words were straightforward, 'We are not like you city people, we don't understand these (dreams).' From Ms. Zhao's and Ms. Wu's answers, it is clear that the family environment of some rural female stayers when they were young was a difficult one, and this family situation actually exposed them to the idea that the material conditions of their lives did not facilitate dreaming, which to a certain extent erased their illusions about the future. At the same time, Ms. Zhao's and Ms. Wu's examples here show that dreaming and anticipation of the future may require specific life circumstances to be created.

Secondly, there is the minority of rural female stayers, represented by Ms. He, who described having a clear plan for the future in her answer about childhood dreams. Ms. He, a return woman, gave a clear answer about her childhood dream, which reflects the views of one type of rural female stayers who participated in my interview. Ms. He said:

> 'At that time, I was very young and I wanted to marry someone who has the urban *hukou*, in order not to have to suffer. I felt sorry for my mother's generation, seeing them suffer. But (she eventually married a village man), there is no big difference in life (compared with my mother).' Afterwards, she added, 'No life is perfect.' [Ms. He, return woman]

Some rural women used to wish they could get out of the countryside when they were children. Like Ms. He, they have now given up on their original ideas and put more focus on their families, especially their children. To some extent, the dreams they failed to realise didn't bother them too much. In one way, as they look forward to the future, they have recognized the possibility of their dreams not coming true. In addition, the conditions of the people living around them and the social milieu they belong to also affect their dreams. In fact, these rural female stayers' childhood dreams are very practical and concrete. What happens to those around them affects not only their thoughts of dreams but also their judgments about the possibility of achieving them. At the same time, they are not averse to accepting reality. When Ms. Zhou, a return woman, talked about her childhood dream, she said, 'At that time, I was also thinking of living like a city dweller, but it didn't work out. It was all just a child's imagination.' In fact, in the interview, Ms. Zhou's opinion towards not realising her childhood dream was expressed more as shyness regarding her childish ideas than regret for failed hopes. Ms. Zhou explicitly stated her childhood dreams. Her awkwardness towards talking about them is that she may not be using the right words. This is mainly due to the gap between her childhood dreams and her life now. Dreams that fail to start from reality lack the possibility of realisation. She is well aware that she was not able to realise the future she imagined as a child. Therefore, she constantly emphasises in her interviews her young age and the limitations of her life at the time.

Ms. Qian's interview expresses her opinion towards those unfulfilled childhood dreams, while showing how to balance dreams with the present. Ms. Qian returned to the countryside because it was difficult for her to earn money in the city. In her interview, she took her views on childhood dreams one step further. She said:

> 'When I was a child, I thought that I could earn money and live well in the city, so I was envious at that time and wanted to go to the city. At that time, I was too young to know that what I thought was unrealistic. Now we are just being practical and looking at the present moment to live our lives. For example, I am trying to save money in the hope of fixing up our house next year. And looking at the present moment would bring a good future.' [Ms. Qian, return woman]

During the interview, Ms. Qian tried to distance herself from her childhood by avoiding talking too much about her childhood dreams. To some extent, a focus on the present has strengthened her confidence in the possibility of a better life in the future. The implication that a childhood dream is not a realistic expectation is intended to increase confidence in the achievability of her present dream (in other words—*bentou*). Real life situations and childhood dreams that are far removed from each other are contradictory. The acknowledgement of reality makes the participants look more at the realities of life and less at their hopes for the future. Even if they are not dissatisfied with their current situation, it may be difficult to define their current life situation in terms of happiness, because they give quite specific descriptions of what they think a good life is. Although being in the present is never a pejorative term in Chinese culture, it is partly an expression of indifference to the future. When rural female stayers put too much emphasis on their current lives, they are to some extent refusing to think about the future. On the one hand, this is because the unfulfilled future of their childhood has reduced their confidence in their expectations of the future. On the other hand, living in the present means being grounded. Rural female stayers do not doubt that their efforts will be rewarded.

To sum up, for those rural female stayers who have not been able to name their childhood dreams, the topic of childhood dreams may be a 'luxury' only available to urbanites, as imagining the future may require certain prerequisites, such as an affluent upbringing. On the other hand, other rural female stayers who participated in the interviews see childhood dreams as the unrealizable imagination of their childish selves. What makes them feel embarrassed about their childhood dreams is not that they have not been realised, but that they seem too unrealistic to them as adults. At the same time, they try to use their understanding of life in the present to show their thoughts on the present and the way they deal with things, as a way to look forward to the future. The idea of focusing on the present as a means of realistically realising the future is captured by the notion of *bentou*[1]. And *bentou* is more emphatic in having achievability. I will discuss rural female stayers and *bentou* in the next section.

## 6.2.2 Bentou—A practical route to a happy future

In northern China, *bentou* is often used as a colloquialism instead of the word for hope. Although it has a similar meaning to hope, *bentou* is more often used to describe a future that can be pursued. What is the specific meaning of the term '*bentou*'? According to Liu's (2014) research, during the interviews he conducted, the farmers' verbal responses focused on one or more of the following: having a son, in particular, passing on the family name to the next generation; having a good life, for example, a decent house, being well fed and clothed; some views emphasised the need for harmony in the family, and furthermore, harmony in the relationships between family members, such as a loving husband and wife; while others emphasised achievements in career, etc. (Liu, 2014). Overall, *bentou* basically covers the specifics of every aspect of a person's life, and it is largely in line with what the Confucian tradition requires of most ordinary people. In fact, although *bentou* and hope have relatively similar meanings, we use them with a difference in tone. Simply explained, *bentou* tends to be more about the subjective perception of a good and achievable future. Research on the topic of *bentou* explicitly has been relatively rare in recent years in academia. However, *bentou* was used by a high percentage of rural female stayers in the interviews, so I decided to use

---

[1] *Bentou* originally belonged to the dialect of northern China, but with the media, movement of people and other factors, it gradually became known and used in more and more areas.

*bentou* in order to better explore rural female stayers' understanding of their future dreams.

In contrast to their reticence to engage with the topic of childhood dreams, rural female stayers became quite talkative when it came to their future plans and aspirations for life. For most of them, what they imagine for their future lives is not an unrealistic fantasy, but more of a plan of action. Most of the descriptions of their future lives are based on their children, especially if they have a son.

### 6.3.3.1. Dreaming of the future through one's children

Ms. Wu, a stay-behind woman, has some clear aims for the future. When talking about plans, she smiled and said:

> 'I don't care what others like to say. Children and family are important. I feel very happy now, and I don't have a lot of pressure in my own life. My plans (are) all for my children... I don't think about myself. I want to provide for my child (young son) to study. I studied less myself, so I hope that my child will study more. In the future, if I can work, I will go out and do some work... actually for the sake of the children. I think about earning some money for my children, and I don't need this for my own life. I don't think about myself.' [Ms. Wu, stay-behind woman]

When rural female stayers plan or imagine their future, they normatively put their children first. Rural female stayers who become mothers place their children at the centre of their plans for the future. They map out their future according to the direction they have planned for their children. This is partly due to the fact that many rural female stayers neglect their own needs and partly due to hitting a plateau in their own life situation. This so-called reaching a plateau situation is hard to overcome and nobody knows how long it will take to overcome it. This plateau period is often described as a time when life does not seem to see the slightest noticeable change despite much hard work. As Ms. Wu says, 'My life as a whole will just be the way it is now and not change much more.' So when planning for the future, rural female stayers tend to put their hopes in their children, who are not yet set in their lives, and hope that their plans will lead to a better life for their children. Rural female stayers hope to enable their children to have a 'successful' life and then make their family's lives better.

In addition, planning for rural female stayers' future with their children in mind also gives those rural female stayers who are not happy with their current situation an extra dimension of expectation. Ms. Zhou, on her return to the rural areas, worked in her brother's agricultural cooperative. And Ms. Zhou's interview offers a new perspective:

> 'My husband is away from home so I have a lot of work to do, and it causes me to often feel exhausted... I don't have enough time to rest. But when I think about my child and plan for them, I feel a bit more relaxed and feel that my life has *bentou*.' [Ms. Zhou, return woman]

Taking care of parents-in-laws as well as children, doing housework and even working on the land—rural female stayers' daily lives are not only physically tiring, but also mentally taxing. When rural female stayers are under stress, children are part of the source of their stress, but they are also a factor in relieving it. As I have explained in Chapter 4, Chinese families are child-centred and therefore children have become a spiritual support for rural female stayers. The expectations they have of their children's future also make their own lives seem more promising. With this child-centred approach,

Chapter 6 A 'happy life' for rural female stayers?

rural female stayers' *bentou* is actually completed through their children and they are able to achieve a higher level of happiness through their imagination of the future by placing their happiness in their children. Having expectations for their children's future not only makes rural female stayers feel happy now, but also gives them confidence in the future. *Bentou* expresses the possibility of a realisable future, so it is focused on future good results, not the present situation, which can be improved and overcome by hard work and planning.

Ms. Wu's husband works in the city for most of the year, and she has to take care of her youngest son in the rural area. Her eldest son works in the city and plans to stay there. When I asked Ms. Wu what she thought of life and whether she was happy, she replied:

> 'It's good, he (her husband) earns a salary every month; the main pressure for me is the apartment my family bought for my son in the urban area and it left us in debt, but we have enough money to live in the rural area. (The oldest son) has a lot of expenses in the city, and now that we have bought the apartment, we can prepare for his marriage. We have made something of it.'

And she added that:

> 'I am just trying to save as much money as I can with my husband, even though my son is not thinking of getting married for the time being, but I have to think about it as a mother and have to prepare him for the *Caili*[1] and the amount of money he will need in the future.' [Ms. Wu, stay-behind woman]

---
1   *Caili*: this refers to the money and goods given by the man and his relatives to the woman and her relatives, mainly in accordance with custom, when the marriage is formed.

Ms. Wu's dreams revolve around her son and she demonstrates the common phenomenon of being a mother who needs to plan for the long-term future of her son. In the case of a child-centred approach to their own future, the sex of the child also determines how long the parents will plan for their child. It is interesting to note that if the child of a rural female woman is a boy, even after he has finished school, the mother will still try to plan everything for them and place his needs at the top of her own goals for the future. When young couples are ready to get married, preparing the house is the responsibility of the groom (and his family) (Hu, 2013). Owning one's own house is a commonly pursued goal and dream in China (Hu, 2013). Buying an apartment has put Ms. Wu under a lot of pressure, but it has also brought her *bentou*. Under the influence of Chinese culture, the man needs to provide a house for the marriage (Lian and Zhao, 2017). As marriage is highly normative in China, it is a step in life that parents can plan ahead for their children, and buying a house has always been on Ms. Wu's wish list. When the event actually came to fruition, the happiness she gained was greater, far more than the stress of carrying a mortgage. The family will prepare everything their son needs, and this is due to the deep-rooted cultural practice of men being able to pass on the family name under the influence of patriarchy (Li, 2012). As I have elaborated earlier, one of the meanings of *bentou* is to have a son, and these rural female stayers consider it normal, as much as a duty, to take on all the future needs of their sons as their own. On the one hand, this is because the male child will inherit the family, but on the other hand, there is an implicit expression of the cultural phenomenon of old age. Sons will typically assume the task of supporting their parents. Ms. Chu's expression is more direct, 'I can only live well if my son lives well.' This expresses the mother's emotions for her children, but also illustrates the fact that her own future depends on her own son. Therefore, to a certain extent, when rural female stayers regard

Chapter 6　A 'happy life' for rural female stayers?

their sons' future as a key factor in their plans, they are also planning for their own future and old age, their own *bentou*.

### 6.2.2.2 Other future plans of rural female stayers

Ms. Zhou is a return woman who lives with her daughter and whose husband works in the urban area. Ms. Zhou's face was still full of longing when she talked about her dreams for the future. She said:

> 'I am always full of dreams about the future of life. As an example, I wanted to live in a building where at least I don't need to make a fire by myself or suffer the cold weather. I also want to save some money, I hope that I can have a stable salary without worrying about money, and there will be someone at my home who can help me with housework. My illness is also mainly due to mental stress, and my health is not good. I think it's good to have a workplace—where people are not idle—some sources of income... all aspects can be better. I hope that every day there is a place I can go to for support... to show my own value.' [Ms. Zhou, return woman]

It is easy to see that Ms. Zhou's imagining of the future is extremely specific and comprehensive, an inevitable aspect of everyday life. However, when we analyse Ms. Zhou's dream word by word, it is actually based on two main factors: income and health. Ms. Zhou mentioned her friend who is working in the urban area: 'My friend was able to work in the city with her husband, and her family had built a new house (in the countryside), because two people earned money. You should know that if I could earn money, my life would be the same as my friend's.' Ms. Zhou tried to use her friend's example to show how much this income would have helped her family if she had had it. She does not specify how much she wants to earn, but she can imagine

213

that a second income would greatly enhance the quality of her family's life. This imagination makes her feel satisfied and happy, to the extent of ignoring the work stress that can lead to health conditions. Ms. Zhou's descriptions paint a picture of what she imagines her future life to be like, and they are more specific. Despite Ms. Zhou's clear statement that this is unrealistic and a fantasy, part of it does serve as a *bentou* for rural female stayers to work towards.

For the sake of *bentou*, some return women did present new options for future plans in which they try to make plans for themselves. Ms. He who is a return woman, said:

> 'I'm still thinking of going to the city to find a job. But in the future, I will always have to go back to the rural area. We are rural people and we are more adapted to rural life.' [Ms. He, return woman]

Many return women want to go back to the city to earn money and then return to the countryside for their old age. It is worth noting that Ms. He does not mention her children in her future plans, as she has only one daughter who is no longer studying. Because of patriarchal traditions, daughters often leaves their birth families to join their husbands' families. As a result, these rural parents rarely put their daughters' futures in the context of their own *bentou*. Therefore, for rural female stayers with only daughters, this may be seen as good news, as they can put their own needs more at the centre of their future planning. For example, Ms. Xu, who only has three daughters, also talks about this:'When my daughters finish their study, my responsibility for them ends. And it's time to plan my rest life.' Despite of such plans, they will still not hesitate to offer help when their daughters need it, for example, by taking care of their children. As was seen in Ochiai's (2008a) study,

Chapter 6  A 'happy life' for rural female stayers?

Chinese parents are by default expected to help their children take care of their children, especially the parents of their daughters. However, this help is mostly considered temporary and does not interfere with the rural female stayers' long term plans, as their daughters are not taken into account when they plan their future. In addition, although rural female stayers acknowledge that the quality of life in the city is better, they invariably choose to return to the countryside to retire after abandoning their quest for higher wages. This is partly because it is difficult to earn money in old age, but also because they recognize that life in the countryside is more comfortable, with familiar surroundings and long-term, and that if they have savings from a part-time job, life in the countryside can be extremely happy.

Rural female stayers achieve happiness by imagining their future lives in quite concrete ways. Even if only through their imagination, rural female stayers get to feel hope about what future could be. Their future is described as relatively concrete, which gives them a direction to work towards, known as *bentou*. In addition, their *bentou* also appears to be more practicable because it is specific.

## 6.3   The impossibility of happiness talk

Although, for many rural female stayers, happiness is a distant topic and not on their radar, most are not averse to talking about it. They may not use happiness to evaluate their present lives or imagine their future lives, but they still maintain a positive view and imagination of the direction of their lives. However, among the rural female stayers I have interviewed, there are a small number of them who think they do not have the chance of happiness.

Ms. Wang is a stay-behind woman, with two sons, the youngest of which is studying in the primary school in her village. Neither her parents nor her parents-in-law live with her, and they do not even live in the same village. She said of her daily life:

> 'Every day, I mainly take care of my children (second son), but I can't do anything else. I am not in good health, I have a heart condition. I can't do any other work. I mainly rely on medication to maintain my health. I am young, but I can only cook at home... not like others who are my age. Others would go out to work and earn money. I not only can't work, but also have to spend money on medication. My husband doesn't have any training, so he is only doing manual labour, which doesn't bring in a lot of money. I am the one who wants to show my strong and positive energy to others, but now under this condition, I can only be barely alive.' [Ms. Wang, stay-behind woman]

It is financial and physical factors like these that literally make talking about happiness irrelevant to some rural female stayers. As Ms. Wang, who is in poor health and under financial pressure, put it: 'My life is barely living... can't talk about happiness.' The rural female stayers' husbands are the breadwinners of the family and they are responsible for the upbringing of their children. For these rural female stayers, planning the family's income and expenditure is their greatest responsibility. Survival is still their main problem, making it very difficult for them to think and talk about happiness.

Ms. Jiang has two daughters and has returned home to care for her eldest daughter due to her daughter's bad health. When talking about her life, she said:

> 'My daughter is chronically ill and this puts a lot of pressure on me. Even though the government gives us subsidies, we are still not financially well off. But the most important thing is my daughter's

## Chapter 6　A 'happy life' for rural female stayers?

health. I don't know if she will get well and I feel like I can't see a future. It's stressing me out.' [Ms. Jiang, return woman]

The sense of powerlessness brought on by her daughter's medical condition has left Ms. Jiang tied up in knots, and the burden caused by her anxiety about the future makes it difficult for her to evaluate how her life is going. Before the interview ended, Ms. Jiang said: 'The truth is that if my daughter is able to regain her health, then I will feel a lot more relaxed.' The powerlessness of feeling bound by circumstances beyond control was expressed in the interview with Ms. Jiang. When rural female stayers who put their children first encounter a situation that is detrimental to their children, hope for happiness seems to disappear when the reality of the situation hits. Ms. Jiang's story illustrates another factor that makes it impossible to discuss happiness, the health of a child. When the health of the child becomes an unpredictable and unknown situation, rural female stayers as mothers are under enormous pressure. To a certain extent, their expectations of their own and their children's future lives are shattered and the present situation is distanced from their own expectations. It is also difficult to discuss happiness when rural female stayers are too far away from what they expect. Especially when rural female stayers feel powerless to improve their life circumstances.

Although the examples of Ms. Wang and Ms. Jiang are not common, I do not want to ignore the existence of these rural female stayers. Their descriptions reflect circumstances that cannot be ignored: both are in a more difficult financial situation than the other participants and have relatively poor health to deal with, either their own or that of their families. Regarding the health factor, although the government provides benefits[1] to alleviate the financial

---

1　The government provides medical benefits to residents, such as reimbursement of medical expenses. However, access to these benefits is limited to public hospitals.

burden on the family, this may not fully cover the full cost of treatment due to other factors[1]. Both Ms. Wang and Ms. Jiang face high levels of psychological stress due to their own or other family members' health problems, which makes it difficult for them to think about happiness or discuss what it means to live a happy life. Secondly, there is the financial pressure. Whether it is a lack of income for the family or a difficult financial situation due to health reasons, the fact is that it is difficult for these rural female stayers to talk about happiness in this situation. Therefore, for rural female stayers, there are certain prerequisites for discussing happiness, such as having a financial income that can support their daily lives or being in good health. Throughout my interviews, these two things do not need to be established at the same time. To explain further, if the financial situation is good, then happiness is not seen as completely hopeless. On the other hand, good health can be a key factor. What is meant here is not only the health of the rural female stayers themselves, but also the health of their families, mainly the health of their children. As I have explained above, rural female stayers see their children as their own *bentou*, and therefore the children become an important indicator of how they measure their lives. If their own health is an indicator of their ability to create a better living environment for their children, their children's health is an indicator of their hopes for the future. It is often the case that the health of the children is valued far more than their own health.

Ms. Zheng's story is one of the more common situations. Ms. Zheng, who is a return woman, looks after her large family in the countryside. She lives with her youngest daughter, her father-in-law, her son, her daughter-in-law and

---

1 For example, Ms. Jiang's daughter began to visit private hospitals regularly after she had been ill for some time. The expenses incurred at the private hospital are not reimbursed, and this also places a greater financial burden on Ms. Jiang's family.

their child. Her husband works outside the rural area and the family income comes mainly from her husband. Ms. Zheng is in poor health, but still needs to look after both the land and the household chores. Her assessment of her happiness in life is straightforward. She said:

> 'I can't say whether I'm satisfied or not. I'm too busy to think about satisfaction. There's nothing I can change if I'm not satisfied. When I'm having a hard time, I just know it in my heart and don't say it out loud, and I don't tell my children. I don't want them to feel the pressure. All I do is think about the life in front of me and try to overcome those difficulties.' [Ms. Zheng, return warrior]

The choice for many is to live in the present. The future is an excessively distant topic, as the reality of life is an inescapable part of it. At the same time, the difficulties of real life have left some rural female stayers with no time to focus on the topic of happiness. These rural female stayers are more concerned with their own lives; whether they are happy with their lives is not on their mind. For this group of rural female stayers, living in the moment may be the true meaning of life. They believe that the difficulties and pleasures of life will pass, but living each day with care will certainly make their lives better and better. The approach of most rural female stayers when faced with a situation in their lives that is not as good as they would like it to be, is that they will persevere for a little while longer and that the difficulties will be overcome. These rural female stayers' insistence seems not to have a very clear goal. They try to ignore the uneasiness caused by the good or bad outcome of the future by focusing on the current situation. To a certain extent, this allows them to express happiness about their lives. But this is not enough to give them the confidence to recognize that they have a chance to be happy. Ms. Zheng's response also shows another aspect, like I analysed earlier, that rural female stayers see their family's happiness as their own and that they achieve happiness through others. They also refuse to tell their children about the stress because they fear that this will cause their children to feel the same difficulties that will make it difficult for them to be happy. At the same time, this concealment is an act to protect themselves and their children's *mianzi*, as the loss of it puts their children at a disadvantage in comparison with others, which may become a burden for their children and make them feel unhappy. This demonstrates once again that rural female stayers are putting the interests of their families ahead of their own.

## 6.4 Conclusion

Rural female stayers are often able to fulfil the expected gender roles at the centre of their descriptions when talking about the possibilities of a happy life. As rural female stayers are more dependent on their families, rural female stayers' happiness is reflected in their relationships with family members. They are more willing to give of themselves and have a more sacrificial spirit. When there is a conflict of interest, family members often come first. Rural female stayers thought that such dedication also leads to a sense of happiness. In other words, they see the happiness of other family members as their own. Moreover, hand, being able to make their own decisions about family matters and being recognized for them makes them feel happier. Rural female stayers' happiness is closely related to their daily life. Income, children and marriage are often mentioned as priorities.

As I have illustrated throughout the thesis, the experience of living in the city makes the return women unique and they have a different perception of happiness. Some return women suggest that a happy life could involve more emphasis on self-fulfilment and autonomy, which highlights the ways in which

Chapter 6  A 'happy life' for rural female stayers?

migration can lead women to embrace the disruption of gender norms. On the one hand, the experience of living in the city boosts the self-confidence of return women and helps them to recognize their contribution to their families, thus enhancing their sense of happiness. On the other hand, the enormous stress of life in the city challenges them physically and mentally, so returning to their homeland becomes the first step towards a happy life for them. It is important to highlight how these effects might in some cases be temporary, for example, if return women lose their status as economic contributors when they return to the rural area.

As well as looking at these depictions of a happy life, I have considered some of the temporal dimensions of happiness in these women's accounts. For rural female stayers, childhood dreams are a scarce resource. As children, some of them did not imagine the future and did not have a clear idea of their own future. For others, clear dreams and unfulfilled realities are part of their daily life. On the one hand, they are happy to remember their childhood dreams; on the other hand, they are not depressed by the gap between their dreams and reality. In particular, I have demonstrated how rural female stayers relate to the future most in terms of concrete plans or realism (*bentou*). The children are most often mobilised as the key resource for achieving *bentou*. Their imagination of a better future for their children is a source of happiness that does not dry up. *Bentou* is the future direction of the lives of rural female stayers. It is not about their thoughts and satisfaction with their current lives. As Matthyssen's (2018) research shows, the Chinese understanding of life is characterised by a culture of patience and a belief in destiny. Rural female stayers believe that if they can persevere, happiness will be within their reach. This description of life gives the rural female stayers hope for the future, and is seen as a way forward for them. For most of the rural female stayers who

221

participated in my interviews, a 'happy' future is foreseeable; in the present, even by imagining the future, their happiness is increased. These rural female stayers in fact anticipate that they will encounter a happy future; their efforts day are a promise of future happiness.

Finally, I have emphasised throughout the chapter the centrality of material circumstances in rural female stayers' accounts of the possibilities of happiness. This is perhaps shown most starkly through the accounts of women who rejected the language of 'happiness' as irrelevant to their current lives due to the difficult material circumstances in which they lived.

In this chapter I have explored how rural female stayers discuss the idea of 'happiness' in the context of their own lives. Overall, I have demonstrated that paying attention to what rural female stayers say about happiness has the potential to both illuminate the rules of being a good woman in this context, as well as to illustrate ways in which these rules might be disrupted, for example, when return women start talking about seeking out pleasure more individually and at the same time realise that paying for something 'non-essential' for themselves is worth it. Their descriptions subvert the stereotypes of how we used to describe happy lives, and in their descriptions of their understanding of happiness, they show their own understanding of what a happy life is, while counteracting other people's definitions of their lives. They try to describe their understanding of happiness by showing their own state of life. For example, when talking about *bentou*, their faces are often full of hope, and their language is positive and energetic. At the same time, the happiness described by rural female stayers is more a template for happiness that conforms to social norms, and their descriptions of these happy lives articulate social norms that, in turn, limit their possibilities for happiness. To explain further, for example, one of society's stereotypical criteria for a happy

Chapter 6 A 'happy life' for rural female stayers?

life is for the child to be 'successful', so they may be obsessed with 'directing' the child's life, thus neglecting other possibilities for their happiness, because it is difficult for them to escape these rules. Furthermore, we cannot ignore the weight and influence that economic aspects have on the way they talk about happiness. Their expressions offer new insights into the academic study of happiness. For example, that the experience of living in the city may have influenced rural female stayers' perceptions of happiness. At the same time, their understanding of happiness may also break with past stereotypes, especially in the description of *bentou*, which shows a more positive outlook on their future lives. This is because *bentou* shows the possibility of future happiness.

223

# Chapter 7  Conclusion

## 7.1  Overview

The thesis began with an introduction describing my reasons for undertaking this research quest to explore the issue of rural female stayers' life experience. I interpret this journey of research as the logical outcome of the collision of a new perspective that intruded into my humdrum life and my own perceptions. Having lived a life surrounded by media news, I have noticed many negative portrayals or speculations about the lives of rural female stayers in the media, and these were an important reason for me to begin this research. The urban-rural dichotomy has led to inequalities between urban and rural areas in many ways, such as income, educational resources and health services (Zhou et al., 2014). These inequalities have influenced rural people to aspire to living in the city. The superiority of the city has influenced society to discriminate against rural areas, and this discrimination has caused people living in rural areas to suffer prejudice (Zhang and Lin, 2019). Although I did not set out to disrupt the socially constructed image of the rural female, I did want to find out whether the experiences of rural female stayers differed from society's perceptions in the face of social change. For example, with the promulgation of a number of poverty alleviation policies in rural areas by the government, and social changes such as more rural women having access to urban jobs in the process of urbanisation, the living conditions of rural women have also been affected by these changes. So it was possible for them to have options that were not available before. Throughout this project these collisions have always led me to reflect on my own academic approach to researching rural female stayers and my concern for their everyday lives. I wanted to explore how rural female stayers make sense of their everyday experiences and how they understand the good life or happiness.

Rural areas in China are often an important topic of sociological research and have attracted the attention of many sociologists (Ye, 2018; Christiansen, 2007; Ye and Wu, 2008; Murphy, 2021; Jacka, 2014). Some of these studies have focused on so called stay-behind women and have illuminated some of the difficulties they face (Jacka, 2014; Huang, 2018). For example, Jacka's research (2014) focuses on the agency and well-being of elderly left-behind women; others have emphasised the emotional experiences of rural female stayers and gender relations (Xu, 2010; Ye and Wu, 2009). For example, Xu's study (2010) used the survey data of more than 1,000 rural women to study the marital stability of rural left-behind women. In addition, for return women, much of the research has focused on their husbands (Bai and He, 2002; Tian, 2012), with rural female stayers themselves often receiving less attention. In contrast to these previous studies, my thesis builds on previous research by focusing more on the experiences of rural female stayers, and by presenting their accounts of their experiences from different perspectives inside and outside the home. Furthermore, although past research has provided insightful analysis into the domestic lives of rural women, there are still some unanswered questions, among which is the lack of detailed information on rural women's family roles. Given the developments and changes in China's social environment and economic conditions over the years, I have suggested that it is valuable to understand the contemporary lives of rural female stayers and analyse how they understand their daily experience. In addition, past studies focusing on rural women have mostly focused on the southern regions of China, with just a few focusing on the northern regions, such as Shanxi Province (Ma, 2018) or Gansu Province (Niu and Kang, 2018). I also want to try to illustrate how I have engaged with this in my thesis. For example, I have explored what it tells us about the future plans of rural women in northern China. Since southern China have a different social environment from the northern region, it's worth analysising.

Before starting my research, I read a lot of literature, including media news reports about rural areas, and I watched some documentaries about rural areas. My previous preparation enriched my understanding of rural female stayers, and this project builds on that understanding. In writing about the methodology and research process of this study, I presented the planned and expected parts of my research process as well as the unexpected and unanticipated ones. The original proposal and design of this study underwent constant revision and refinement both before and after the fieldwork. Both the conceptualization of research ethics and the relationship between the participants and the researcher became fundamental pillars in the revision process. Indeed, this process of interaction was a challenge for me at every turn, starting from the recruitment of participants through to the conduct of the interviews. For example, I needed to keep an open mind about what these women are talking about and give them the space to tell their stories. And I also needed to ensure that my thought did not influence the interviewees' thinking during my conversations with them. At the same time, the unpredictable and unexpected situations encountered during the interviews highlighted time and again the complexity of ethical issues and individual differences, for example, the unexpected situation of a respondent crying, which I talked about in the methodology chapter. Although I used the

Chapter 7   Conclusion

same interview outline for the same group of people, the uniqueness of the participants reminded me of the uniqueness of each interview, and that while there were clear themes across the interviews, every woman had her own story to tell.

In my conversations with these participants, in addition to verbal communication, I was able to harvest information such as expressions and gestures, which became part of my research data. At the same time, given that my interviews were conducted in Chinese and my thesis would be written in English, I also went through the ponderous task of converting the audio recordings to text and translating them after completing the data collection. I thus have multiple identities in my research, as a collector of data, a translator, and a researcher. This made me more attentive to my own identity as an urban woman and 'outsider', careful about my position, and also strengthened my reflective spirit towards the data. In addition, in the course of the fieldwork, I tended to first draw closer to the interviewees in order to put them at ease, and through this effective method I was able to obtain a great deal of vivid and detailed data. The fieldwork was conducted in the context of my relationship with the respondents and my reflection on the data, which also became the initial stage of my data analysis.

**Analytic chapter summaries**

My discussion of data analysis in this thesis has been divided into three chapters. First, I analysed how rural female stayers perceive themselves in terms of their roles within the family in Chapter 4. Through the participants' descriptions of their daily lives, I have argued that rural female stayers are given responsibilities that the family requires of them, often because of their femininity. The patriarchal and social environment requires women to take on more of the work within the family. For example, the responsibility of caring for children or the elderly is often taken on by rural female stayers, as men are often asked to take on the 'outside' things. However, the standard of measuring contribution within the family (e.g. in financial terms) means rural female stayers' contribution to the family is often not recognized. In this case, rural female stayers have limited chances to acquire financial resources, and they have to face the disadvantage that gender limits their choices in the division of labour. However, according to the descriptions of my participants, rural female stayers maintain a positive view of this and try to show their enthusiasm and efforts in life by explaining their roles as mothers, daughters or wives and the responsibilities that come with those roles. At the same time, the participants also expressed their own definition of what a 'good' mother, daughter or wife is, and how they gained status by doing these various forms of work well.

In Chapter 5, I discussed *mianzi* culture, which reaches into all aspects of everyday life and affects the daily lives of rural female stayers in a number of ways. Through the participants' accounts, my research illustrates the ways in which rural female stayers actively protect their *mianzi* and resist others' prejudices. For rural female stayers, the main way to protect their *mianzi* is to show the positive side of their lives. For example, stay-behind women emphasise that their contribution to caring for their families at home is in line with the demands of society and the family, and that this is the right thing for them to do. While defending their own *mianzi*, rural female stayers also implicitly express their views about other rural women whose life experiences are different from their own, often in the context of defending their *mianzi*. In my analysis of return women, I found the experience of city living to be a point worth noting. The experience of urban life has created more life choices and possibilities for return women, and their recognition by the people around them also makes it easier for them to maintain their *mianzi*. In addition, I further discuss the issue of *mianzi* and decision-making power. My returning interviewees also talked about having a stronger voice in family affairs as they gain more recognition in the process of maintaining *mianzi*.

In the final part of my data analysis, Chapter 6, I shifted the topic of discussion to the question of happiness. I have analysed how rural female stayers describe their happiness; their responses demonstrate their own understanding of happiness, often placing the fulfilment of the desired gender roles at the centre of their descriptions, and they also attempt to show how their future happiness will be attained (*bentou*). At the same time, their descriptions of a happy life fit into a socially constructed template of happiness, which to some extent limits their possibilities for an 'alternative' happy life, for example, by recognizing the priority of children and the elderly and therefore tending to neglect their own needs. Rural female stayers also break down some of the ways in which others define their lives by demonstrating their understanding of what it means to be happy. For example, they try to negate the prejudices of others about stay-behind women by showing that their husbands who work in the city bring more income to the family and thus improve their living conditions. At the same time, my participants also provided a new perspective that urban life experience enables return women to better recognize their own contribution, which also provides them with a new perspective on how to describe their happiness. For example, some return women recognize their contribution to the family and think that they deserve additional expenses, and such affirmation of their own value is portrayed as happiness by them. Finally, based on the descriptions of rural female stayers, it is worth noting that the description of happiness is conditional and that economic status and health conditions has an intuitive impact on the way they describe their happy lives and their opinions. It is further explained that a certain economic basis may be a condition for them to associate their life with happiness, because the impact of economics on family life is clear and direct.

## 7.2 Contribution of the research

This study utilised a snowballing method to recruit participants. The semi-structured interviews were conducted with 25 rural female stayers, thus providing a new and rich source of data for the research field. This thesis explores a gap in the sociology of rural life in China, looking at the daily lives of rural female stayers and how they view themselves in relation to the people around them. The analysis illustrates how they understand their life experience, and highlights their resourcefulness and their courage to overcome difficulties that they face.

Firstly, my study develops research concerning rural female stayers, which has tended to focus on their problems or difficulties. This thesis is novel. It includes a discussion of happiness in relation to rural female stayers' lives. I demonstrate the value of beginning from rural female stayers' own accounts of happiness, and how they can actually provide concepts for sociologists to think about happiness differently. In particular, the idea of *bentou* suggests different ways of orienting to the future (in comparison to Western and urban Chinese accounts of happiness). The rural female stayers' depiction of *bentou* expresses a different way of thinking about the future and shows a new perspective on a type of happiness that is rooted in practicalities, or realisable goals. The rural female stayers also expressed their understanding of happiness as something that can be attained through supporting the lives of others, for example, by planning the future for their children and thus trying to attain their own happiness. My discussion about what some rural female stayers couldn't say or understand about happiness illuminates the problems involved in imposing particular cultural understandings of happiness even when both participants are speaking the same language. For example, as I am an urban woman, my interviewees and I have different understandings and descriptions of happiness.

Secondly, my study counters the negative depictions of female rural stayers in a lot of media discourse (Xinhua, 2019; Huang, 2006; SoHo, 2019) and in some academic literature (Li, 2018; Qiao, 2009; Jiang, 2011), by beginning from the perspective of female rural stayers themselves and conducting an in-depth qualitative analysis of how they make meaning about their lives. Rural female stayers show their characteristic of hard-working in the process of discussing their daily life. At the same time they show how they can use their agency to face the difficulties of life. These analyses refute the stereotype of people in need of help expressed by rural female stayers in the past media. Throughout the thesis I have shown both how women's lives are shaped by dominant ideas about gender and also the active ways that they are involved in making meaning about themselves and their lives. For example, they try to gain the approval of others and protect their *mianzi*, and they show how they describe their *bentou* through planning their children's future. Also, they showed the versions of agency that are available to them. While they try to do their best to service their family on their own, they also sometimes negotiate seeking outside help.

Thirdly, while there has been relatively limited research on return women in previous studies, this study highlights the return women's perspective while demonstrating how to include rural female stayers and return women in the analysis, illustrating aspects and differences between the two experiences through comparison. For example, I analyse separately how return women and rural female stayers maintain *mianzi*. Through the comparison, the impact of urban living experiences on rural female stayers is highlighted, which offers new insights into the phenomenon. At the same time, I show how people's experiences of gender and the discourse of filial piety in daily life are intertwined with migration histories. Qi's (2015) research shows that women in urban China are dealing with tensions between Western individualism and more traditional gendered notions of filial piety. In my research, I show the return women who have had contact with urban areas are importing (in a sense) more individualised notions into daily life when they return, and I suggest that the experience of living in the city has enriched the daily life experience of return women and provided them with a new perspective on their self-worth and contribution. For example, return women acknowledge that it is their responsibility to make personal sacrifices for their parents, but they also acknowledge their contribution and value to their families, and some say they are worth the 'unnecessary' expenditures that they choose to make just for themselves (such as buying a dress that they 'don't need' just because they like it).

Fourthly, my research extends the focus of previous research which, in considering women's daily experience and agency, has tended to focus on urban women. This study breaks this pattern by taking female rural stayers as the subject of the study and revealing the daily lives of women in rural households through the presentation of their everyday concerns and activities, while understanding how they exercise their own agency. Although a heavily agricultural and patriarchal culture still exists in the context of rural life, this study avoids the male-dominated, male-centred narrative and allows women to emerge as individuals. The advantage of this is that the perspective of women is highlighted, and they are placed at the centre of the environment as storytellers, thereby helping to show their connections to other aspects. By examining how rural female stayers present their daily life, I am placing women at the heart of analysis at a time of social change. Rural female stayers are also interacting frequently with their matriarchal families. For example, daughters may also be the primary caregiver for their parents. Given that the impact of these changes on rural female stayers is also of great interest, my research shows these new changes provide new and up-to-date information on the field.

Fifthly, my research offers new perspectives for understanding women and agency in rural China. Within the context of a patriarchal cultural environment, my research demonstrates that rural female stayers exert agency within the household and with those around them, for example, by gaining decision-making power over household matters, given the limited space available to them. This suggests that rural female stayers have a certain amount of space for expanding ways of doing gender. It is important to note, however, that agency is adapted to the cultural context; in other words, the existing social and cultural structures are not broken by these expansive acts. Rural female stayers still need to follow the gender expectations given to them by society, although agency does provide them with a certain amount of space to do gender in slightly expanded ways.

Finally, my research offers empirically novel qualitative research about northern China's rural areas. Most of the existing sociological research on rural women has been conducted with data from southern China (Murphy, 2021; Wang and Ye, 2020). Due to the large size of China, there are large differences between the north and the south.¹ Firstly, taking the example of Inner Mongolia where I conducted my fieldwork, this area is relatively sparsely populated², and because it is located in the northern part of China. This area has long winters and is therefore not suitable for growing crops all year round despite the vast land. Secondly, there are fewer factories or companies that need a lot of workers in the north than in the south, so it can be more difficult for migrant workers in the north to find relatively stable jobs in the city. In my interviews, some of the interviewees mentioned that one of the reasons for not considering working in the city is that it is difficult to find a job. Digging into the reasons why it is difficult for them to find a job, although the educational level is an influencing factor, the lack of large, personnel-intensive factories around is also a major reason. Meanwhile, the use of the phrase *bentou* is another northern regional feature. My study adds the use of the dialect *bentou* as a concept through which to understand the meaning of future happiness in northern China. In fact, through my respondents' accounts, the use of *bentou* provides a template for our understanding of how rural female stayers understand happiness. Although knowledge of the term is not restricted to the northern region, it is indeed used mainly by the northern region. Therefore, if the fieldwork had been conducted in the southern region, the description of a happy life might have made use of different linguistic concepts. A valuable

---

1 The geographical divide between the north and the south of China: there are differences between these two regions but the nature of them partly depends on the different ways in which the divide is made. In this case, I use the geographical boundary between the north and the south, which is the line along the Qinling Mountains and the Huaihe River, i.e. the 800mm equivalent precipitation line. The northern area is north of the Qinling Mountains-Huanghe River Line, while the southern area is south of the Qinling-Huaihe Line.

2 The rural population of Inner Mongolia is 7.63 million in 2021, accounting for 1.5% of the country's rural population (National Bureau of Statistics, 2022).

direction for future research would be to explore to how happiness is described in the southern regions of China, and what understandings of both happiness and the future are produced through alternative forms of language. Given these differences between the northern and southern regions, it is important to use the rural areas of the north within fieldwork.

## 7.3 Limitations of my research

I am aware that the findings of this study do not provide a clear or complete answer to how rural female stayers understand themselves. My sample was quite small, although this is common in qualitative research. At the same time, I recruited candidates from several rural women with whom I was initially familiar, and with their help, the snowballing recruitment method allowed me to reach out to more potential participants. I contacted and recruited all the potential participants directly and identified the final sample. By investigating the backgrounds of my participants, I was able to find some of the same key factors influencing them. The fact that my participants came from villages in the same area, the environment in which they lived and their educational status meant they had similar backgrounds and faced similar life situations, which in turn led them to have similar perspectives. This could mean my data is too concentrated on the same angle, ignoring the existence of potential other angles. Therefore, the stories shared could not be used as data to study the full range of rural female stayers' everyday experiences.

In addition, I divided the participants into two groups based on whether they had experience living in the city: return women and stay-behind women. When recruiting participants I found it relatively difficult to recruit rural women who had no experience of urban life at all, and although I tried to keep the ratio of these two at one to one, the end result was that nearly two-thirds of my data consisted of return women. As I explain in the methodology chapter, this is due to the fact that the area is near the city as well as the age limitation. Since the villages where I did fieldwork are close to the city, most rural women are actively trying to find work in the city, and they also have more chances to go to the urban area. At the same time, I wanted my interviewees to be in the age group that has more choice, not too young (and therefore limited by their family of origin), and not too old (as this group may find it more difficult to get work in the cities and may have more health problems than the young). This also became a limitation in the research; however, it is also worth considering whether this means that the number of so-called stay-behind women in the area is declining as urbanisation takes place.

While I acknowledge the limitations of this study in terms of representation, I believe that it nevertheless offers a limited but specific scope of exploration, and this is its strength. My participants shared their everyday lives, and these stories not only vividly illustrate their life experiences, but also describe the dilemmas in their lives and how they have faced them. My participants are kind-hearted, unassuming rural women, and despite their direct way of speaking, it is their detailed and vivid descriptions that in fact reveal the subtle details that are easily overlooked. My main role as a researcher is to discuss these stories analytically. However, this could not have been done without the help of my participants. At the same time, it is not my intention to generalise the whole of the lived experience of rural female stayers and this means that I agree that women's experiences are potentially more diverse than those considered here. Although the scope of this study is very limited, it is also specific. In other words, this study may be just a splash of colour in a large painting, but it is also an important and meaningful part of the viewer's understanding of the whole picture.

I would like to emphasise that the lived experiences shared by my participants should not be taken as a timeless testimony of their lives. The analysis for this study is based on interview data generated from the interactions between me and my participants. The fieldwork done under the influence of space and time created the conditions under which I collected the data. The daily lives of my participants and their understanding of themselves will continue after my interviews are completed. There is reason to believe that as the social environment and their living conditions change, they will have new thoughts and develop new understandings of their lives. In fact, several of them kept in touch with me after I had finished the interviews. In my interactions with them, they would tell me about the new changes in their lives and how these new changes had affected them. Through these conversations, as time passes and more research is done with rural female stayers, I need to recognize that my research is one of many that focus on rural women and what I have here is a snapshot of these rural female stayers' lives, and in future research it might be nice to do more longitudinal work.

## 7.4 Research themes with potential for the future

Although this thesis presents some new ideas and fills in the gaps of previous research, there are still some issues related to rural female stayers that have not been fully explored. Therefore, I have proposed a number of possible future research themes below.

### 7.4.1 Future plans and back to the urban area

According to the answers of my interviewees, staying in or returning to rural areas is not their only option and if they have returned, this does not mean the end of their urban lives. Some of my respondents indicated that their children would be living in the city, and would implicitly express the possibility that they might also return or go to live in the city as a result. Their aim was to take better care of their children. One of the focuses of this study was to explore the everyday experience of rural female stayers living in rural areas, hence my participants are women who are currently living in rural areas and have no plans to relocate to urban areas in the near future. Therefore, I excluded women who were moving to urban areas from the selection of respondents. When future researchers wish to focus on the lives of rural female stayers, it is possible that women who are moving to the city again would be a good subject to study, which would fill a gap in the current research. In the literature on migrant women, future researchers could focus on the changes in the lives of rural female stayers after re-entering the city and the comparison of the two urban lives. Also, the impact of these different choices on other women in the rural areas deserves to be discussed in future research.

## 7.4.2 Rural female stayers and their mothers-in-law

Although I have discussed the role of rural female stayers as daughters-in-law in my analysis in Chapter 4, I have also analysed how rural female stayers understand what it means to be a good daughter-in-law and how this understanding is reflected in their daily lives. In fact, rural female stayers' understanding of their role as daughters-in-law leads them to follow the decisions of the male members of the family, or in some cases the decisions of the female elders, and consequently there is less room for them to exercise their agency. This finding reflects that such unequal female relations within the family are also worth discussing. Given that my study focuses more on how rural female stayers understand their own lives, I have not considered how the lives of the two adult women within the family are related in depth.

In fact, the relationship between mother-in-law and daughter-in-law is very subtle under the influence of patriarchy and filial culture. Both the rural female stayers and their mothers-in-law have a low level of decision-making power in the family, while the mothers-in-law consciously emphasises the need for their daughters-in-law to be subservient to them. Therefore, future researchers could try to explore the perceptions of agency of daughters in law's relationship with their mothers-in-law and how these perceptions are reflected in their family life.

### 7.4.1 The impact of the relaxation of the one child policy on daughters

I have talked about the importance of children to the family and the relationship between rural female stayers and their children in Chapters 4 and 6. I have also talked about the reluctance of young rural female stayers to have a second child in order to be a 'good' mother. Much of the existing research shows that under the one-child policy, daughters are receiving more family resources, such as increased investment in education, as a result of having fewer children in the home, and daughters also have stronger relationships with their families of origin. However, with the gradual liberalisation of the one-child policy, the willingness of rural families to have children may also change. How young rural female stayers cope with this change will in fact become an interesting new issue. For example, whether they will be given sufficient space to follow their idea of having only one child, and secondly, whether the status of daughters in the family will revert to that of the past when there is more than one child in the family. As my research focuses more on the lives of rural female stayers themselves, I have not explored the topic of contact and communication between stay-behind mothers and their daughters in any great detail. Neither have I explored whether there is a conflict between parents influenced by patriarchy and young rural female stayers who have been exposed to new ideas and have experienced urban life. Future research could therefore attempt to establish whether the lives of these rural female stayers will change when the one-child policy is abolished and whether this causes changes in their perceptions of the gender division of labour.

## 7.5 Final reflections

During the first year of my PhD, I was often asked about my research by friends and acquaintances. I tried to present my research simply and easily so that they would find it at least interesting to listen to. From the feedback of my listeners, I have to admit that my descriptions were probably so common that they found it difficult to separate the research from everyday life. It was only then that I realised that perhaps 'ordinary' was the right word to define my research. This is not to say that my research is ordinary or bland in value, but rather that our everyday lives hold a thin veil of what is called the ordinary, and it is the theorization of social interaction that helps us lift that veil.

This PhD will probably be my first step on the academic path, a path that loops around the need to keep lifting the veil of the ordinary, and I am keen to find a word to define or guide me on my way. I have realised that actually 'not knowing' might be very appropriate. This phrase came up several times in my interviews and was used by different participants to answer different questions. When my participants found my questions difficult to understand or when they were unsure whether the answers they thought matched the questions, they often started their responses with a 'not knowing'. In fact, in the chat that prompted me to start this research, my grandmother's housekeeper also answered 'not knowing' several times, and although I didn't have a lot of experience at the time, I thought her attempt to use not knowing to emphasise that her next words might not be the same as mine. Looking back on my research's interviews, when the answer began with 'not knowing', what these questions had in common was that rural female stayers would more or less lift a little of the veil that had been placed over their faces. The so-called 'not knowing' maybe a key word to the researchers. It reminds us as researchers to pay attention to knowledge that is unknown to us in the midst of interaction, and it shows that our knowledge is generated in collaboration with participants. These were the points that led me to question my own assumptions as a researcher, and their presence prompted me to be careful about what the participants said later. Because when this phrase comes up, the answers that follow tend to be more cautious, and I need to be more focused and cautious about possible follow-up questions. At the same time, academic research is also a process of 'not knowing', a word that can also remind me of the fact that I don't know enough. So 'not knowing' is the perfect keyword, and I would like to make this word the motto of my academic career in order to maintain a spirit of reflection and curiosity about existing research.

# Appendices

## Appendix 1　Check list for personal information（个人信息检查表）

| Items（项目） | Check（检查） |
|---|---|
| Age and marriage time<br>年龄和结婚时间 | |
| Education level<br>教育程度 | |
| Migration experience<br>迁移经验 | |
| The situation of the children in the family (age, sex, education level, marriage)<br>家庭中孩子的状况（年龄、性别、教育程度、婚姻状况） | |
| The living conditions of now and past (self/family/--)<br>现在和过去的生活条件（自我/家庭/--） | |
| The main occupations currently engaged in (agriculture/pure household/non-agricultural/other)<br>目前从事的主要职业（农业/纯家庭/非农业/其他） | |
| Health condition<br>健康状况 | |
| Sources of family income (husband-migrant workers/agriculture/other)<br>家庭收入来源（丈夫－农民工/农业/其他） | |
| Husband's situation (physical condition, income, work etc.)<br>丈夫的情况（身体状况、收入、工作等） | |
| Relatives (like parents-in-laws)<br>亲戚（如公婆） | |
| Elderly support (number of elderly individuals and whether they need to be take care of)<br>赡养老人（几个老人，是否需要照顾） | |

# Appendix 2  Outline of interview questions (English Version)

## Questions for return women

1. What is a typical day like (What is your daily life)?

And the follow-up questions:

(1) Are there parts of your daily life that you particularly enjoy?

(2) Is there anything you find difficult about your daily life?

(3) What is the most stressful thing in your daily life?

(4) What is the most enjoyable thing in your daily life?

2. Could you tell me a bit about how you decided to come back to the rural area and how you feel about coming back here?

3. Which place do you prefer, rural or urban? And why?

If the answer is urban, I would like to ask them if there is a plan to migrate to urban areas.

4. Can you tell me something about the impact of your experience in the urban area on your current life?

And the follow-up questions:

(1) What do you think about these experience?

(2) Comparing your current life with life before migration, are there any changes?

5.. Does your husband return to the rural area with you? How do you feel about this?

If the answer is no, ask them:

(1) Are there any influences on you when your husband decide not to return rural area with you?

(2) How does long-term separation from your husband affect your life?

(3) How do you keep the relationship between husband and wife?

6. How do other people (your family members) regard your decision to return the rural area?

P.S. Family members refer to people who are living together with them.

7. Do you have friends who have never migrated to the urban area?
And the follow-up questions:
   (1) And what do you think about them?
   (2) How do other people think about them? For example, do people talk about them? Do their families approve? Please tell me some examples and stories about them.

8. What do you think of migrants, especially the migrant women?

9. Do you know people who have returned to the rural area?
And the follow-up questions:
   (1) And what do you think about their decision of return?
   (2) How do other people think about them? For example, do people talk about them? Do their families approve? Please tell me some examples and stories about them.

10. Generally speaking, who is the person who makes the decisions in your family?

11. Can you talk about the issue of family contributions (your value for your own family)?
   (1) What do you think you have contributed to your own family?
   (2) And what contribution do the other members of your family have?

P.S. Family members refer to people who are living together with her.

12. Are you satisfied with your current life?

If their answer is no, the follow-up question is: which part do you think needs improvement?

13. What did you imagine your life to be like when you were a child? Did you have any dreams and aspiration about your future?

14. Has your mother migrated to the urban area and worked there?

15. Have you heard any news from TV or newspapers about women who are in similar situation as you?

If their answer is yes, the follow-up questions are:

    (1) What is the content of the news? Do you agree with the content of it?

    (2) What do you think after hearing the news?

16. If you have ever seen news about left-behind women, what kind of news is it? What are your thoughts or attitude after hearing the news?

17. Do you ask for help when you are in trouble (for example, when your child gets ill or there is too much farm work to do)?

If their answer is yes, the follow-up questions are:

    (1) Who do you usually ask for help?

    (2) Why that person?

**Questions for stay-behind women**

1. What is a typical day like (What is your daily life)?

And the follow-up questions:

    (1) Are there parts of your daily life that you particularly enjoy?

    (2) Is there anything you find difficult about your daily life?

    (3) What is the most stressful thing in your daily life?

    (4) What is the most enjoyable thing in your daily life?

2. Can you tell me something about your husband's migration?

And the follow-up questions:

   (1) Can you tell me how you're feeling about your husband's migration?

   (2) And how do you feel about staying in the rural area?

3. What do your friends/relatives say about your husband's migration?

4. Does long-term separation from your husband affect your life?

5. How do you keep the relationship between husband and wife?

6. Do you have any plans to migrate to the urban area and live with your husband in the future? Why or why not?

7. Do you have any friends who are living separately from their husband like you?

And if the answer is yes, the follow-up questions are: Do you keep in touch with them? Why or why not?

8. Do you know anyone who is living in the countryside with her husband?

And the follow-up questions:

   (1) What do you think of them?

   (2) Is there any difference in your life, compared with theirs?

9. Do you know anyone who is a return woman?

And the follow-up questions:

   (1) What do you think of them?

   (2) How do other people think about them? For example, do people talk about them? Do their families approve? Please tell me some examples and stories about them.

   (3) Is there any difference in your life, compared with theirs?

Appendices

10. Do you have friends who have migrated to the urban area?
And the follow-up questions:
   (1) What do you think about them?
   (2) What do other people think about them? For example, do people talk about them? Do their families approve? Please tell me some examples and stories about them.

11. Can you talk about the issue of family contributions (your value for your own family)?
And the follow-up questions:
   (1) What do you think you have contributed to your own family?
   (2) And what contribution do the other members of your family have?
P.S. Family members refer to the people she lives with.

12. Generally speaking, who is the person who makes the decisions in your family?

13. Are you satisfied with your current life?
If their answer is no, the follow-up question is: which part do you think needs improvement?

14. What did you imagine your life to be like? When you were a child? Did you have any dreams and aspiration about your future?

15. Have you know some news from TV or newspapers about women who are in same situation with you?
If their answer is yes, the follow-up questions are:
   (1) What is the content of news? Do you agree with the content of it?
   (2) What are your thoughts or attitude after hearing the news?

16. If you have ever seen some news about return women, what kind of news is it? What do you think after reading the news?

17. Do you ask for help when you are in trouble (for example, when your child gets ill or there is too much farm work to do)?

If their answer is yes, the follow-up questions are:

    (1) Who do you usually ask for help?

    (2) Why that person?

# Appendix 3　Outline of interview questions (Chinese Version )

返乡妇女——采访问题大纲

1. 你生活中典型的一天是什么样的（你的日常生活是什么）？

以及后续问题：

　　（1）你的日常生活中是否有你特别喜欢的部分？
　　（2）你觉得日常生活中有什么困难吗？
　　（3）你日常生活中最紧张的是什么？
　　（4）你日常生活中最愉快的事情是什么？

2. 你能告诉我你是怎么决定回到农村的吗？你觉得回到这里怎么样？

3. 你喜欢农村还是城市？为什么呢？

如果答案是城市，我想问他们是否有计划迁移到城市。

4. 你能告诉我你在市区的经历对你现在生活的影响吗？

以及后续问题：

　　（1）你觉得这些经历怎么样？
　　（2）与移居城市前相比，你现在的生活有什么变化吗？

5. 你丈夫和你一起回到农村了吗？你对此是怎么想的？

如果答案是否定的，问他们：

　　（1）丈夫决定不和你们回农村，是否对你们有影响？
　　（2）与丈夫长期分居对你的生活有何影响？
　　（3）如何维护夫妻关系？

6. 其他人（你的家人、朋友等）如何看待你返回农村的决定？

7. 你有没有从未到城市打过工的朋友？
以及后续问题：
（1）你觉得他们的生活怎么样？
（2）别人怎么看他们？例如，人们谈论他们吗？他们的家人赞成吗？请给我讲一些例子和故事。

8. 你怎么看城市移民，尤其是移民妇女？

9. 你认识返回农村的人吗？
以及后续问题：
（1）你认为他们的返回决定如何？
（2）别人怎么看他们？例如，人们谈论他们吗？他们的家人赞成吗？请给我讲一些例子和故事。

10. 一般来说，在你的家庭里谁是做决定的人？

11. 你能谈谈家庭贡献（你对自己家庭的价值）的问题吗？
（1）你认为你为自己的家庭做出了什么贡献？
（2）你的其他家庭成员有什么贡献？
附：家庭成员包括与她生活在一起的人。

12. 你对现在的生活满意吗？
如果他们的答案是否定的，那么接下来的问题是：你认为哪些方面需要改进？

13. 当你还是个孩子的时候,你是怎么想象你的生活的?你对自己的未来有什么梦想和抱负吗?

14. 你的妈妈去过城市打工并且生活过吗?

15. 你从电视或报纸上听说过关于和你处境相同的妇女的新闻吗?
如果他们的回答是肯定的,那么接下来的问题是:
    (1)新闻内容是什么?你同意它的内容吗?
    (2)听到这个消息后你觉得怎么样?

16. 如果你看过一些关于留守妇女的新闻,那是什么样的新闻?听到这个消息后,你认为(或你的态度)如何?

17. 当你有困难的时候(例如你的孩子生病或有太多的农活要做),你会寻求帮助吗?
如果他们的回答是肯定的,那么接下来的问题是:
    (1)你通常向谁求助?
    (2)为什么会这样?

**留守妇女—采访问题大纲**

1. 你生活中典型的一天是什么样的(你的日常生活是什么)?
以及后续问题:
    (1)你的日常生活中是否有你特别喜欢的部分?
    (2)你觉得日常生活中有什么困难吗?
    (3)你日常生活中最紧张的是什么?
    (4)你日常生活中最愉快的事情是什么?

2. 你能告诉我一些关于你丈夫移民到城市的事情吗？
以及后续问题：
（1）你能告诉我你对丈夫移居城市的感觉吗？
（2）你觉得留在农村怎么样？

3. 你的朋友/亲戚对于你丈夫移民城市怎么看？

4. 与丈夫长期分居会影响你的生活吗？

5. 你如何维护夫妻关系？

6. 你有没有计划将来移居市区和你丈夫住在一起？为什么或者为什么不？

7. 你有没有像你这样和丈夫分开生活的朋友？
如果答案是肯定的，那么接下来的问题是：你和他们保持联系吗？
为什么或者为什么不？

8. 你认识和丈夫住在乡下的人吗？
以及后续问题：
（1）你觉得他们的生活怎么样？
（2）与他们相比，你的生活有什么不同吗？

9. 你认识归乡妇女吗？
以及后续问题：
（1）你觉得她们怎么样？
（2）别人怎么看她们？例如，人们谈论她们吗？她们的家人赞成吗？

请给我讲一些例子和故事。
（3）与她们相比，你的生活有什么不同吗？

10. 你有移居到市区的朋友吗？
以及后续问题：
（1）你觉得他们怎么样？
（2）别人怎么看他们？例如，人们谈论他们吗？他们的家人赞成吗？请给我讲一些例子和故事。

11. 你能谈谈家庭贡献（你对自己家庭的价值）的问题吗？
以及后续问题：
（1）你认为你为自己的家庭做出了什么贡献？
（2）你的其他家庭成员有什么贡献？
附：家庭成员包括与她生活在一起的人。

12. 一般来说，在你的家庭里，谁是做决定的人？

13. 你对现在的生活满意吗？
如果他们的答案是否定的，那么接下来的问题是：你认为哪些方面需要改进？

14. 当你还是个孩子的时候，你是怎么想象你的生活的？你对自己的未来有什么梦想和抱负吗？

15. 你从电视或报纸上听说过关于和你处境相同的妇女的新闻吗？
如果他们的回答是肯定的，那么接下来的问题是：
（1）新闻内容是什么？你同意它的内容吗？

（2）你听到这个消息后有什么想法（或态度）？

16. 如果你看过一些关于返乡妇女的新闻，那是什么样的新闻？你看了新闻后觉得怎么样？

17. 当你有困难的时候（例如你的孩子生病或有太多的农活要做），你会寻求帮助吗？
如果他们的回答是肯定的，那么接下来的问题是：
    （1）你通常向谁求助？
    （2）为什么会这样？

# Reference

Afridi, F., Li, S. and Ren, Y. (2015). Social identity and inequality: The Impact of China's *Hukou* System. *Journal of Public Economics*, 123, 17–29.

Ahmed, S. (2010). *The Promise of Happiness*. Durham [NC]: Duke University Press.

Back, L. (2007). *The Art of Listening*. Oxford, Berg.

Bai, N. and Li, J. (2008). Migrant Workers in China: A General Survey. *Social Sciences in China*, 29(3), 85–103.

Benston, M. (1997). The Politics of Women's Liberation. In Rosemary Hennessey and Chrys Ingraham (Eds.). *Materialist Feminism—A Reader in Class, Difference, and Women's Lives*. New York: Routledge, pp.17–23.

Berger, R. (2015). Now I See It, Now I Don't: Researcher's Position and Reflexivity in Qualitative Research. *Qualitative Research*. 15(2), 219–234.

Bi, C. and Oyserman, D. (2015). Left-Behind or Moving Forward? Effects of Possible Selves and Strategies to Attain Them Among Rural Chinese Children. *Journal of Adolescence*, 44, 245–258.

Bi, H. (2006). The Women's Employment in the Process of Urbanization in China. *Journal of Yunnan Nationalities University,* 23(4), 62–66.

Bi, S. (2019). 'Parents and Parents In-Laws' in the New Era: Pressure Transfer Under the Imbalance of Gender Ratio (xin shi qi de'niang jia yu po jia' xing bie bi li shi heng xia de ya li zhuan yi). *China Youth Study*, (09), 63–70.

Biao, X. (2007). How Far Are the Left-behind Left Behind? A Preliminary Study in Rural China. *Population, Space and Place*, 13(3), 179–191.

Breheny, M. and Stephens, C. (2009). I Sort of Pay Back in My Own Little Way: Managing Independence and Social Connectedness Through Reciprocity, *Ageing and Society,* 29 (8), 1295–1313.

Bryman, A. (2012). *Social Research Methods*. Fourth edition. Oxford: Oxford University Press.

Buckley, P., Clegg, J. and Tan, H. . (2006). Cultural Awareness in Knowledge Transfer to China—the Role of Guanxi and *Mianzi, Journal of World Business,* 41, 275–88.

Budig, M. and England, P. (2001). The Wage Penalty for Motherhood. *American Sociological Review*, 66(2), 204–225.

Cain, C. (2012). Emotions and the Research Interview: What Hospice Workers Can Teach Us. *Health Sociology Review*, 21(4), 396–405.

Cao, Y. and Hu, C. (2007). Gender and Job Mobility in Postsocialist China: A Longitudinal Study of Job Changes in Six Coastal Cities. *Social Forces*, 85(4), 1535–1560.

Chan, K. (2013). Women's Property Rights in a Chinese Lineage Village. *Modern China*, 39(1), 101–128.

Chan, K. and Wei, Y. (2019). Two Systems in One Country: the Origin, Functions, and Mechanisms of the Rural-urban Dual System in

China. *Eurasian Geography and Economics*, 60(4), 422–454.

Chang, H. (2013). *Survey Report: Nearly 40% of Parents with only Children, Mothers Have the Most Influence on Children.* [online] People. cn. Available at: http://politics.people.com.cn/n/2013/0915/c1001-22926312.html [Accessed 13 May 2019].

Chang, H., Dong, X. and MacPhail, F. (2011). Labor Migration and Time Use Patterns of the Left-behind Children and Elderly in Rural China. *World Development,* 39(12), 1–12.

Chang, L., McBride-Chang, C., Stewart, S. and Au, E. (2003). Life Satisfaction, Self-concept, and Family Relations in Chinese Adolescents and Children. *International Journal of Behavioral Development*, 27(2), 182–189.

Chang, W. (2017). Research Ethics in Rural Survey: A Discussion Based on Methodological Meaning (nong cun diao cha zhong de lun li: ji yu fang fa lun de tao lun). *Statistics & Information Forum*, 32(11), 21–28.

Chen, C. and Fan, C. (2018). Rural-urban Circularity in China: Analysis of Longitudinal Surveys in Anhui, 1980–2009. *Geoforum*, 93, 97–104.

Chen, F. (2014). Impacts of Living Strategies on the Marital Satisfaction of the Rural Married Women Staying Home Alone: A Perspective of Sexual Life Quality. *South China Population,* 29(6), 10–20, 32.

Chen, J. and Hu, M. (2021). City-level *Hukou*-based Labor Market Discrimination and Migrant Entrepreneurship in China. *Technological and Economic Development of Economy*, 27(5), 1095–1118.

Chen, M. (2018a). Does Marrying Well Count More Than Career? Personal

Achievement, Marriage, and Happiness of Married Women in Urban China, *Chinese Sociological Review,* 50(3), 240–274.

Chen, M. (2018b). Understanding Ideal Motherhood from the Perspective of Urban Middle-Class Mothers: A Case Study of Families in Shanghai (cheng shi zhong chan jie ceng nv xing de li xiang mu zhi xu shi—yi xiang ji yu shang hai jia ting de zhi xing yan jiu). *Journal of Chinese Women's Studies*, 146(2), 55–66.

Chen, P. and Wang, X. (2012). A Review of 'Family and In-law's Family: The Living Space and Backstage Power of Rural Women in North China' (niang jia yu po jia—hua bei nong cun fu nv sheng huo kong jian he hou tai quan li de ping jia). *Collection of Women's Studies*, 111(3), 113–115.

Chen, R. (2015). Weaving Individualism into Collectivism: Chinese Adults' Evolving Relationship and Family Values. *Journal of Comparative Family Studies*, 46(2), 167–179.

Chen, X. (2017). Influence of Social Welfare on the Fertility Intentions for a Second Child among Urban Women (ying xiang cheng shi nv xing er hai sheng yu yi yuan de she hui fu li yin su zhi kao cha). *Journal of Chinese Women's Studies*, 139(1), 30–39.

Chen, Y. and Xu, J.(2016). How Urbanization Affects Balanced Growth Urban-rural Area in China (Zhong guo cheng shi hua dui cheng xiang ping heng zeng zhang de ying xiang). *Economic Theory and Business Management,* 3, 72–85.

China Women's News, (2018). *How to Promote Women's Empowerment and Development in Rural Revitalization—New Perspectives of the Symposium on Rural Revitalization and Women's Development (ru he zai xiang cun zhen xing zhong zhu tui fu nv fu qian yu fa zhan—xiang cun zhen xing yu fu nv fa zhan xue shu yan tao hui zhi xin shi dian).* [online] China Agricultural University. Available at: <https://news.cau.edu.cn/art/2018/6/13/art_8779_573581.html> [Accessed 17 June 2022].

China Women's News (2021). *Key Data from the Fourth Survey on the Social Status of Women in China (di si qi zhong guo fu nv she hui di wei diao cha zhu yao shu ju qing kuang).* [online] China Women's News. Available at: <http://paper.cnwomen.com.cn/html/2021-12/27/nw.D110000zgfnb_20211227_1-4.htm> [Accessed 26 February 2022].

China Women's News (2022). *From Poor Mountainous Areas to the Capital of E-commerce, 'Her Power' Holds Up 'Half the Sky'.* [online] All-China Women's Federation. Available at: <https://www.women.org.cn/art/2022/4/27/art_822_169211.html> [Accessed 17 July 2022].

Chou, X., Feng, Q., Lu, J., Liang, J. and Yu, B. (2020). Transformation of Rural China Under the Commodity Economy: Culture and Society (shang pin jing ji xia de xiang tu zhong guo bian qian:wen hua yu she hui). *China Economic and Trade Herald*, (5), 144–145.

Cieslik, M. (2015). Not Smiling but Frowning: Sociology and the Problem of Happiness. *Sociology*, *49*(3), 422–437.

Clarke, V. and Braun, V. (2017). Thematic Analysis. *The Journal of Positive Psychology*, 12(3), 297–298.

Clough, P. and Nutbrown, C. (2012). *A Student's Guide to Methodology.* 3rd ed. London: SAGE Publication, pp.49–172.

Connelly, R., Roberts, K. and Zheng, Z. (2012). The Role of Children in the Migration Decisions of Rural Chinese Women. *Journal of Contemporary China,* 21(73), 93–111.

Conway, M. and Vartanian, L.R. (2000). A Status Account of Gender Stereotypes: Beyond Communality and Agency. *Sex Roles*, 43(3/4), 181–199.

Cooke, F. (2005). Women's Managerial Careers in China in a Period of Reform. *Asia Pacific Business Review*, 11(2), 149–162.

Croll, E. (1983). *Chinese Women since Mao.* London: Zed Books.

Curasi, C. (2001). A Critical Exploration of Face-to-Face Interviewing vs. Computer-Mediated Interviewing. *International Journal of Market Research*, 43(4), 1–13.

De Bruin, A. and Liu, N. (2020). The Urbanization-household Gender Inequality Nexus: Evidence from Time Allocation in China. *China Economic Review*, 60, 101301.

Dearnley, C. (2005). A Reflection on the Use of Semi-Structured Interviews. *Nurse Researcher.* 13(1), 19–28.

Ding, J. and Xu, N. (2018). The Impact of Parents Going Out to Work on the Health and Education of Left-behind Children (fu mu wai chu wu gong dui liu shou er tong jian kang yu jiao yu de ying xiang). *Population Research*, (1), 76–89.

Ding, Q., and Sun, J.(2019). The Spatial Effect of China's Urbanization on Urban-rural Income Gap (zhong guo cheng shi hua dui cheng xiang shou ru cha ju de kong jian xiao ying). *Journal of Dongbei University of Finance and Economics,*(3), 46–54.

Ding, S., Dong, X. and Li, S. (2009). Women's Employment and Family Income Inequality during China's Economic Transition. *Feminist Economics*, 15(3), 163–190.

Doody, O. and Noonan, M. (2013). Preparing and Conducting Interviews to Collect Data. *Nurse Researcher*. 20, 5, 28–32.

Du, F. (2001). Modernization and Patriarchy: A Gender Perspective—Review of The Decline of Patriarchy: A Study of Gender in the Modernization Process in Rural Jiangnan (xian dai hua yu fu quan zhi:xing bie shi jiao de shen shi—"fu quan de shi wei:jiang nan nong cun xian dai hua jin cheng zhong de xing bie yan jiu"ping jie). *Collection of Women's Studies*, 42(5), 13–17.

Duncan, S. and Fiske, D. (2015). *Face-to-Face Interaction: Research, Methods, and Theory*. London: Routledge.

Emerson, R. M., Fretz, R. I., & Shaw, L. L. (1995). *Writing ethnographic fieldnotes*. Chicago: University of Chicago Press.

Etikan, I., Alkassim, R. and Abubakar, S. (2016). Comparison of Snowball Sampling and Sequential Sampling Technique. *Biometrics & Biostatistics International Journal*, 3(1), 00055.

Evans, H. (1995) L. Defining Difference: The 'Scientific' Construction of Sexuality and Gender in the People's Republic of China. *Signs: Journal of Women in Culture and Society*, 20(2), 357–394.

Evans, H. (2008). Sexed Bodies, Sexualised Identities and the Limits of Gender. *China Information*, 361–386.

Evans, H. and Strauss, J. C. (2010). Gender, Agency and Social Change. *The*

*China Quarterly*, 204, 817–826.

Ezzy, D. (2010). Qualitative Interviewing as an Embodied Emotional Performance. *Qualitative Inquiry*, 16(3), 163–170.

Fan, C. and Chen, C. (2020). Left Behind? Migration Stories of Two Women in Rural China. *Social Inclusion*, 8(2), 47–57.

Fan, C. C.(2004). Out to the City and Back to the Village: The Experiences and Contributions of Rural Women Migrating from Sichuan and Anhui. In Gaetano, A. and Jacka, T. (eds.). *On the Move: Women and Rural-to-Urban Migration in Contemporary China*. Columbia University Press, pp.177–206.

Fang, Y. and Walker, A. (2015). 'Full-time Wife' and the Change of Gender Order in the Chinese City. *The Journal of Chinese Sociology*, 2(1), 1–19.

Fei, X. (1998). *Earthbound China*. Beijing: Peking University Press.

Feng, X. (2013). *Social Research Methods (she hui yan jiu fang fa)*, Fourth edition. Beijing: China Renmin University Press(CRUP).

Fincher, L.H. (2016). *Leftover Women: The Resurgence of Gender Inequality in China*. London: NBN International.

Flick, U. (2009). *An Introduction to Qualitative Research*, 4th ed. London: Sage Publication.

Fong, V. L. (2002). 'China's One-Child Policy and the Empowerment of Urban Daughters', *American Anthropologist*, 104(4), 1098–1109.

Gaetano, A. (2015). *Out to Work—Migration, Gender, and the Changing Lives of Rural Women in Contemporary China*. University of Hawai'i Press, pp.130–136.

Gao, H. and Ye, W. (2009). Analysis on the Construction of Patriarchal Culture on the Femininity (qian xi fu quan zhi wen hua dui nv xing qi zhi de jian gou)). *Journal of Jinling Institute of Technology*, 24(4), 80–83.

Gao, M. (2020). The Connection and Integration of Market, Ecology and Public Welfare: A Study on the Female Entrepreneurship after Returning to the Countryside (shi chang, sheng tai yu gong yi de lian jie rong he—fan xiang nv xing chuang ye yan jiu ). *Journal of Chinese Women's Studies*, 161(5), 97–109.

Geng, L. (2010). Analysis of the Snowball Sampling Method (gun xue qiu chou yang fang fa man tan). *China Statiscits*, 08, 57–58.

Goffman, E. 1972 . 'On Face-Work: An Analysis of Ritual Elements in Social Interaction', in Goffman, E. (ed.) *Interaction Ritual: Essays on Face-to-Face Behaviour*. London: Penguin, pp5–46.

Gooch, A. and Vavreck, L. (2016). How Face-to-Face Interviews and Cognitive Skill Affect Item Non-Response: A Randomized Experiment Assigning Mode of Interview. *Political Science Research and Methods*, 1–20.

Griffee, D.T. (2005). Research Tips: Interview Data Collection. *Journal of Developmental Education*, 28(3), 36–37.

Grunow, D. (2019). Comparative Analyses of Housework and Its Relation to Paid Work: Institutional Contexts and Individual Agency. *KZfSS Kölner Zeitschrift für Soziologie und Sozialpsychologie*, 71(S1), 247–284.

Gu, H. (2020). Return to Tradition or Value Pluralism: Switching Perspectives in Current Research on Gender Perspectives (hui gui chuan tong hai shi jia zhi duo yuan:dang qian she hui xing bie guan nian yan jiu de shi jiao qie huan). *ACADEMICS*, (3), 123–129.

Han, L., Wang, S. and Liu, C. (2019). China's Rural Development Progress and Regional Comparison: A Study Based on Assessment of China's Rural Development Index from 2011 to 2017 (zhong guo nong cun fa zhan jin cheng ji di qu bi jiao). *Chinese Rural Economy*, 07, 1–19.

Hancock, D. and Algozzine, B. (2016). *Doing Case Study Research: A Practical Guide for Beginning Researchers*. 3rd ed. New York: Teachers College Press.

Hand, H. (2003). The Mentor's Tale: a Reflexive Account of Semi-Structured Interviews. *Nurse Researcher*, 10(3), 15–27.

Hao, Y. & Feng, X. (2002). The Influence of Parent-Child Relations on the Growth of the Only Child. *Journal of Huazhong University of Science and Technology (Social Sciences)*, 16(6), 109–112.

He, C. and Ye, J. (2014). Lonely Sunsets: Impacts of Rural-urban Migration on the Left-behind Elderly in Rural China. *Population, Space and Place*, 20(4), 352–369.

Hitlin, S. and Elder, G.H. (2007). 'Time, Self, and the Curiously Abstract Concept of Agency', *Sociological Theory*, 25(2), 170–191.

Ho, D. (1976). On the Concept of Face. *American Journal of Sociology*, 81(4), 867–884.

Hoepfl, M. (1997). Choosing Qualitative Research: A Primer for Technology

Education Researchers. *Journal of Technology Education*, 9(1), 47–63.

Hollway, W. and Jefferson, T. (1997). Eliciting Narrative Through the In-depth Interview. *Qualitative Inquiry*, 3(1), 53–70.

Hopkins, B. (2007). Western Cosmetics in the Gendered Development of Consumer Culture in China. *Feminist Economics*, 13(3–4), 287–306.

Hou, F., Cerulli, C., Wittink, M., Caine, E. and Qiu, P. (2015). Depression, Social Support and Associated Factors Among Women Living in Rural China: A Cross-Sectional Study. *BMC Women's Health*, 15(1), 1–9.

Hsu, C. (1996). *'Face': An Ethnographic Study of Chinese Social Behavior*. Ph.D. Yale University.

Hu, H. (1944). The Chinese Concepts of 'Face.' *American Anthropologist*, 46(1), 45–64.

Hu, J. (2015). The Welfare Effect of Time Allocation of Housework in Chinese Families—A Comparative Analysis Based on Gender Differences and Urban and Rural Backgrounds (zhong guo jia ting jia wu shi jian pei zhi de fu li xiao ying—ji yu xing bie cha yi he cheng xiang bei jing de bi jiao fen xi). *Journal of Shanghai University of Finance and Economics*, (06), 35–46.

Hu, M. (2019). *Why left-behind women are so crucial to solving the "three left-behind" problem in rural areas (po ju nong cun san liu shou nan ti, liu shou fu nv wei he ru ci guan jian)*. [online] Sohu News. Available at: <https://www.sohu.com/a/352868845_161795> [Accessed 26 April 2022].

Hu, Y. and Scott, J. (2014). Family and Gender Values in China. *Journal of*

*Family Issues*, 37(9), 1267–1293.

Huang, Y. (2006). Female Migrant Workers' Fertility Desire and Its Environmental Impact Factors. *Contemporary Manager*, 01, 214–215.

Huang, Y. and Pan, S. (2009). Research Ethics in Social Surveys in China: Methodological Reflections (zhong guo she hui diao cha zhong de yan jiu lun li:fang fa lun ceng ci de fan si). *Social Sciences in China*, (02), 149–162.

Hwang, K. (1987). Face and Favor: the Chinese Power Game, American Journal of Sociology, 92, 944–974.

Jacka, T. (2012). Migration, Householding and the Well-being of Left-behind Women in Rural Ningxia. *The China Journal*, 67, 1–22.

Jacka, T. (2014). Left-behind and Vulnerable? Conceptualizing Development and Older Women's Agency in Rural China. *Asian Studies Review*, 38(2), 186–204.

Jacka, T. (2015). *Rural Women in Urban China*. London: Routledge, pp. 165–244.

Jackson, S. and Scott, S. (2002). Introduction: The Gendering of Sociology. In Jackson, S. and Scott, S (eds) *Gender: A Sociological Reader*. London: Routledge, pp1–26.

Jackson, S., Ho, P. S. Y. and Na, J. N. (2013). Reshaping tradition? Women Negotiating the Boundaries of Tradition and Modernity in Hong Kong and British families. *The Sociological Review,* 61(4), 667–687.

Jaschok, M. and Miers, S. (1994). *Women and Chinese Patriarchy*. Hong

Kong: Hong Kong University Press.

Ji, Y., Wu, X., Sun, S. and He, G. (2017). Unequal Care, Unequal Work: Toward A More Comprehensive Understanding of Gender Inequality in Post-Reform Urban China. *Sex Roles*, 77(11–12), 765–778.

Jiang, C. (2009). The Roots of Face Culture and Its Social Functions (*mianzi wen hua chan sheng gen yuan ji she hui gong neng*). *Guangxi shehui kexue (social sicence)*, 165(3), 116–120.

Jiang, Y. (2011). Reflections and Suggestions on the Issue of Left-behind Women in Rural Areas (nong cun liu shou fu nv wen ti de si kao yu jian yi). *Chinese Women's Moment*, (8), 44–46.

Jin, Y. (2001). Urbanization—Another Opportunity and Challenge for the Development of Women (cheng shi hua—fu nv fa zhan de you yi ji yu yu tiao zhan). *Collection of Women's Studies*, 43(6), 4–10.

Jin, Y. (2010). Mobile Paternal Authority: Changes in Migrant Farmer Families (liu dong de fu quan:liu dong nong min jia ting de bian qian). *Social Sciences in China*, (4), 151–165.

Jin, Y. (2011). Mobile Patriarchy: Changes in the Mobile Rural Family. *Social Sciences in China*, 32(1), 26–43.

Ju, L. and Wang, Y. (2022). The 'Changes' and 'Difficulties' of Women Left Behind in Gansu Province Under the Vision of Rural Revitalization (xiang cun zhen xing shi ye xia gan su sheng liu shou fu nv de 'bian' yu 'nan'). *Gansu Agriculture*, (2), 81–85.

Judd, E.R. (1990). 'Men are More Able': Rural Chinese Women's Conceptions of Gender and Agency. *Pacific Affairs*, 63(1), 40–61.

Kabeer, N. (2015). Gender equality, Economic Growth, and Women's Agency: The 'Endless Variety' and 'Monotonous Similarity' of Patriarchal Constraints. *Feminist Economics*, 22(1), 295–321.

Kan, M. and He, G. (2018). Resource Bargaining and Gender Display in Housework and Care Work in Modern China. *Chinese Sociological Review*, 50(2), 188–230.

Kinnison, L. (2017). Power, Integrity, and Mask – An Attempt to Disentangle the Chinese Face Concept. *Journal of Pragmatics*, 114, 32–48.

Lamont, M. and Molnar, V. (2002). 'The Study of Boundaries in the Social Science.' *Annual Review of Sociology*, (28), 167–195.

Leung, A. (2003). Feminism in Transition: Chinese Culture, Ideology and the Development of the Women's Movement in China. *Asia Pacific Journal of Management*, 20, 359–374.

Li, D. and Tsang, M.C. (2003). Household Decisions and Gender Inequality in Education in Rural China. *China: An International Journal*, 1(02), 224–248.

Li, H.(2001). Examining Public Policy from a New Perspective—'Social Gender and Public Policy' (cong yi zhong xin de shi jiao shen shi gong gong zheng ce—'she hui xing bie he gong gong zheng ce'). *Collection of Women's Studies*, 5, 4–13.

Li, H. (2012). Son Preference and Patriarchal Systems: Empirical and Gender Analysis of the Imbalance in Sex Ratio at Birth in China (nan hai pian hao yu fu quan zhi de zhi du an pai—zhong guo chu sheng xing bie bi shi heng de xing bie fen xi). *Collection of Women's Studies*, 110(2),

59–66.

Li, J. (2005). Women's Status in a Rural Chinese Setting. *Rural Sociology*, 70(2), 229–252.

Li, M. and Zhang, X. (2018). Research on the Migrant Husband's Substitute Support to the Left-behind Wife —Taking City C in Inner Mongola as An Example(liu dong zhang fu dui liu shou qi zi de bu wei xing zhi chi—yi nei meng gu C shi wei li). *Journal of China Women's University*, (5), 47–55.

Li, Q. and Long, W. (2009). Analysis on the Influencing Factors of Migrant Workers' Intention to Stay in City and Return Home (nong min gong liu cheng yu fan xiang yi yuan de ying xiang yin su fen xi). *Chinese Rural Economy*, (2), 46–54, 66.

Li, W. (2014). A Review of Research on the Urban Integration of Migrant Workers (nong min gong cheng shi rong ru wen ti yan jiu zong shu). *Review of Economic Research*, (30), 38–49.

Li, X. and Zhang, J. (2008). The Influence of Confucian Doctrine on the Process of Socialising Gender Equality (ru jia xue shuo dui xing bie ping deng she hui hua guo cheng de ying xiang). *Journal of Dali University*, (1), 53–57.

Li, X., and Wang, H. (2008). The Present Situation and Function of Chinese Dialects (han yu fang yan de xian zhuang ji qi zuo yong). *Journal of Adult Education of Hebei University,* 10(2), 96–97.

Li, Y. (2018). The Status Quo of Rural Left-behind Women's Happiness and analysis of influencing factors—Taking Nanchong City, Sichuan

Province as an example (nong cun liu shou fu nv xing fu gan de xian zhuang ji ying xiang yin su fen xi). *Labor Security World*, 11.

Li, Y. (2010). The Issue of Left-behind Women (liu shou fu nv wen ti qian xi). *Agricultural Science-Technology and Information*, (24), 3–4.

Li, Y., Liu, L., Lv, Y., Xu, L., Wang, Y. and Huntsinger, C. (2015). Mother–Child and Teacher–Child Relationships and Their Influences on Chinese Only and Non-only Children's Early Social Behaviors: The Moderator Role of Urban–rural Status. *Children and Youth Services Review*, 51, 108–116.

Li, Z. (2016). *Ye Jingzhong: The Problem of Left-behind Women Is A Cost of Social Development (Ye Jingzhong: liu shou fu nv wen ti shi she hui fa zhan de yi zhong dai jia)*. [online] China Agricultural University News. Available at: <http://news.cau.edu.cn/art/2016/12/11/art_8779_489611.html> [Accessed 24 June 2022].

Li, Z., Fu, H. and Wang, G. (2022). *Helping Left-behind Women Broaden Their Employment Channels (bang liu shou fu nv tuo kuan jiu ye qu dao)*. [online] Souhu News. Available at: <https://www.sohu.com/a/567200517_121434694?scm=1019.e000a.v1.0&spm=smpc.csrpage.news-list.7.1658114317689xzAw4Uv> [Accessed 10 June 2022].

Lian, S. and Zhao, J. (2017). Do You Have to Buy A House to Get Married—A Study of the Impact of Youth Housing on Marriage (jie hun shi fo yi ding yao mai fang—qing nian zhu fang dui hun yin de ying xiang yan jiu). *China Youth Study*, 61–67.

Liang, D. and Wu, H. (2017). Research on the Dynamic Mechanism of Agricultural Feminization and Its Impact on Rural Gender Relations—

Based on the Field Survey of Villages in Jiangsu, Sichuan and Shanxi Provinces (nong ye nv xing hua de dong li ji zhi ji qi dui nong cun xing bie guan xi de ying xiang yan jiu—ji yu Jiangsu, Sichuan,Ji Shanxi san sheng de cun zhuang shi di diao yan). *Journal of Chinese Women and Studies*, (6), 85–97.

Liang, H., Tang, Y. and Huo, X. (2014). Liushou Women's Happiness and Its Influencing Factors in Rural China. *Social Indicators Research,* 117(3), 907–918.

Lingshan Women's Evaluation (2022) '*Women in Action on Mother's Day*'—Care for Poor Left-behind Women.(*wen qing mu qin jie jiu guo zai xing dong: guan ai pin kun liu shou fu nv huo dong*)[online] The Paper. Available at: <https://www.thepaper.cn/newsDetail_forward_17979365> [Accessed 2 July 2022].

Liu, J. and Cook, J. (2018). Ageing and Intergenerational Care in Rural China: A Qualitative Study of Policy Development. *Contemporary Social Science*, 15(3), 378–391.

Liu, J. (2014). Aging, Migration and Familial Support in Rural China. *Geoforum*, 51, 305–312.

Liu, J. (2016). Ageing in Rural China: Migration and Care Circulation. *The Journal of Chinese Sociology*, 3(1), 1–19.

Liu, J. (2017). Patriarchy-Modernization-Individualization: Changes in Studies of Niangjia.(*fu quan zhi—xian dai hua—ge ti hua: niang jia de yan bian shu li*) *Journal of Chinese Women's Studies*, 143(5), 98–105.

Liu, S. (2011). As Mothers, As Wives: Women in Patrilineal Nuosu Society. In: S. Du and C. Ya, (eds.), *Women and Gender in Contemporary Chinese Societies*. Lexington books, pp.149–170.

Liu, X., Yang, C., and Jiang, Y. (2015). Research on the Differences in Social Evaluation of Successful People of Different Genders—Based on the Perspective of 'Strong Women' Alienation (She hui dui bu tong xing bei cheng gong ren shi ping jia cha yi yan jiu—ji yu "nv qiang ren" yi hua shi jiao). *Modern Business Trade Industry*, (19), 110–111.

Liu, Y. (2014). Living a Fortune Life for Hope and Value: A Local Chinese Concept to Understand Peasant's Suicide in Ji Village (lun *Bentou*—li jie ji cun nong min zi sha de yi ge ben tu gai nian). *Sociological Review of China*, 2(5), 68–86.

Lu, D. (2002). The Prominence of Human Subjectivity and Initiative (ren de zhu ti xing he neng dong xing de tu xian). *Proceedings of the Congress of the Members of the Chinese Society of Anthropology and the Fourth National Symposium on Anthropology*, 331–334.

Lu, S. and Chen, W. (2021). Differential Acceptance in Village Participation: Women Married out of Their Villages Returning Home Together in Jiangxi Province (cun zhuang can yu zhong de cha bie hua jie na—jiang xi sheng nong cun wai jia nv ji ti hui niang jia huo dong yan jiu). *Journal of Chinese Women's Studies*, 163(1), 42–54.

Luo, C. (2017). The Effect of Couples' Income Gap and Age Gap on The Subjective Well-being of the Couples: Analysis based on Microdata (hun yin guan xi, sheng ji ce le lüe dui nong cun liu shou fu nv zhu guan xing fu gan de ying xiang yan jiu). *South China Population*, 32(139),

24; 36–47.

Luo, C., Yang, X., Li, S. and Feldman, M. (2017). Love or Bread? What Determines Subjective Wellbeing Among Left-Behind Women in Rural China? *Gender Issues*, 34(1), 23–43.

Luo, M. and Chui, E. (2018). Gender Division of Household Labor in China: Cohort Analysis in Life Course Patterns. *Journal of Family Issues*, 39(12), 3153–3176.

Luo, M. and Chui, E. (2019). Moving from Rural to Urban China: How Urbanization Affects Women's Housework. *Sex Roles*, 81(3–4), 127–139.

Ma, H. and Guo, P. (2020). Summary of Research on Left-behind Women in Rural China in Recent Ten Years (jin shi nian wo guo nong cun liu shou fu nv yan jiu zong shu). *Journal of Inner Mongolia Agricultural University (Social Science Edition)*, 22(2), 7–12.

Ma, H. (2018). Reflections on the Development Dilemma of Rural Left-behind Women—Taking Northern Shaanxi as an Example (nong cun liu shou fu nv fa zhan kun jing zhi si kao). *Journal of Yan'an University (Social Sciences Edition)*, 40(4), 66–69.

Ma, Y., Liu, Z. and Song, X. (2019). A Study on the Early Exploration Stage of the Reform of Socialist Market Economy System with Chinese Characteristics (zhong guo te se she hui zhu yi shi chang jing ji ti zhi gai ge de zao qi tan suo yan jiu). *Journal of Shanghai University of Finance and Economics*, 21(4), 4–15.

Ma, J. (2018). Research on the Renewal of Children's Educational Concepts of Rural Mothers (nong cun mu qin de er tong jiao yu guan nian geng xin wen ti yan jiu). *Think Tank Era*, (44),149–157.

Mahfoud, Z., Ghandour, L., Ghandour, B., Mokdad, A. and Sibai, A. (2014). Cell Phone and Face-to-face Interview Responses in Population-based Surveys. *Field Methods*, 27(1), 39–54.

Man, K. (2016). Agency Theory and the Development of Female Anthropology (neng dong xing li lun yu nv xing ren lei xue de fa zhan yan jiu). *Journal of Beifang University of Nationalities*, (3), 63–67.

Matthyssen, M. (2018). Chinese Happiness: A Proverbial Approach to Popular Philosophies of Life. In. Hird, D. and Wielander, G(eds.). *Chinese Discourses on Happiness*. Hong Kong: Hong Kong University Press, pp. 189–207.

McNay, L. (2004). Agency and Experience: Gender As A Lived Relation. *The Sociological Review*, 52(2_suppl), 175–190.

McIntosh, M. and Morse, J. (2015). Situating and Constructing Diversity in Semi-Structured Interviews. *Global Qualitative Nursing Research*, 2, 1–12.

Mi, C. and Nie, R. (2016). Thoughts on the Application of Non-probabilistic Sampling Method in Large Data. *Statistics and Management*, 04, 11–12.

Murphy, R. (2021). The Gendered Reflections of Stayers in China's Migrant Sending Villages. *Journal of Rural Studies*, 88, 317–325.

Murphy, R., Tao, R. and Lu, X. (2011). Son Preference in Rural China: Patrilineal Families and Socioeconomic Change. *Population and Development Review*, 37(4), 665–690.

National Bureau of Statistics. (2017). *Survey Report on Migrant Workers in 2016*. [online]. Available at: http://www.stats.gov.cn/tjsj/zxfb/201704/t20170428_1489334.html [Accessed 16 Oct. 2021].

National Bureau of Statistics. (2018). *Statistical Bulletin for National Economic and Social Development in 2017*. [online]. Available at: http://www.stats.gov.cn/tjsj/zxfb/201802/t20180228_1585631.html [Accessed 17 Oct. 2021].

National Bureau of Statistics. (2021a). *Final Statistical Monitoring Report on the Programme for the Development of Chinese Women (2011–2020) (zhong guo fu nv fa zhan gang yao 2011–2020 zhong qi tong ji jian ce bao gao)*. [online] National Bureau of Statistics. Available at: <http://www.stats.gov.cn/xxgk/sjfb/zxfb2020/202112/t20211221_1825526.html> [Accessed 23 May 2022].

National Bureau of Statistics. (2020). *The Data of People's Life*. [online] Available at: <http://data.stats.gov.cn/easyquery.htm?cn=C01> [Accessed 18 May 2020].

National Bureau of Statistics. (2021b). *GDP of Inner Mongolia*. [online] Available at: <https://data.stats.gov.cn/search.htm?s=内蒙古%20GDP> [Accessed 23 February 2022].

National Bureau of Statistics. (2022). *Migrant Workers Monitoring Survey Report 2021(2021 nian nong min gong jian ce diao cha bao gao)*. [online] Available at: <http://www.stats.gov.cn/tjsj/zxfb/202204/t20220429_1830126.html> [Accessed 17 June 2022].

Navarro, V. (2012). Graduate Women's Beliefs about Gender Roles in China. *Asian Women*, 28(2), 55–79.

Nielsen, I., Nyland, C., Smyth, R., Zhang, M. and Zhu, C. (2006). Effects of Intergroup Contact on Attitudes of Chinese Urban Residents to Migrant Workers. *Urban Studies*, 43, 475–490.

Niu, F. and Kang, C. (2018). A Study on the Composition and Characteristics of Northwest Rural Minority Left-behind Women's Social Support Networks (xi bei di qu shao shu min zu liu shou fu nv she hui zhi chi wang luo gou cheng ji qi te zheng yan jiu). *North West Ethno-national Studies*, (3), 33–44.

Noy, C. (2008). Sampling Knowledge: The Hermeneutics of Snowball Sampling in Qualitative Research. *International Journal of Social Research Methodology*, 11(4), 327–344.

Oakley, A. (1972). *Sex, Gender and Society*. Routledge.

Ochiai, E. (2008a). Researching Gender and Childcare in Contemporary Asia. In E. Ochiai and B. Molony (eds.) *Asia's New Mothers: Crafting Gender Roles and Childcare Networks in East and Southeast Asian Societies,* Kent: Global Oriental Ltd, pp. 1–30.

Ochiai, E. (2008b). The Birth of the Housewife in Contemporary Asia: New Mothers in the Era of Globalization. In E. Ochiai and B. Molony (eds.) *Asia's New Mothers: Crafting Gender Roles and Childcare Networks in East and Southeast Asian Societies,* Kent: Global Oriental Ltd., pp. 157–180.

Ochiai, E. Mari, Y., Yasuko, M., Zhou, W., Onode, S., Kiwaki, N., Fujita, M., & Hong, S. (2008). Gender Roles and Childcare Networks in East and Southeast Asian Societies. In E. Ochiai and B. Molony (eds.) *Asia's New Mothers: Crafting Gender Roles and Childcare Networks in East and Southeast Asian Societies,* Kent: Global Oriental Ltd.

Ortner, S. (2001). Specifying Agency: The Comaroffs and Their Critics. *Interventions,* 3(1), 76–84.

Pang, B. (2022). *The Person in Charge of the National Development and Reform Commission Answers Reporters' Questions on 'Key Tasks of New Urbanization and Integrated Urban-Rural Development in 2022' (guo jia fa zhan gai ge wei you guan fu ze ren jiu '2022 nian xin xing cheng zhen hua he cheng xiang rong he fa zhan zhong dian ren wu' da ji zhe wen).* [online] www.gov.cn. Available at: <http://www.gov.cn/zhengce/2022-03/22/content_5680367.htm> [Accessed 17 May 2022].

Pearson, V. (1995). Goods on which One Loses: Women and Mental Health in China. *Social Science & Medicine,* 41(8), 1159–1173.

Peng, Y. (2007). An Examination of Social Mobility in Rural Areas—Education in Perspective (nong cun she hui liu dong de kao cha—jiao yu de shi jiao). *Social Sciences in Nanjing,* (6), 129–135.

Pessoa, L.(2008). On the Relationship Between Emotion and Cognition. *Nature Reviews Neuroscience,* 9(2), 148–158.

Peters, K., Kashima, Y. and Clark, A. (2009). Talking about Others: Emotionality and the Dissemination of Social Information. *European Journal of Social Psychology,* 39, 207–222.

Photo of Huaihua. (2022). *Employment and Entrepreneurship for Women Left-behind in Rural Areas(nong cun liu shou fu nv jiu ye chuang ye).* [online] Sohu News. Available at: <https://www.sohu.com/a/565927512_113696?scm=1019.e000a.v1.0&spm=smpc.csrpage.

news-list.1.1658114317689xzAw4Uv> [Accessed 17 June 2022].

Qi, X. (2011). Face: A Chinese Concept in a Global Sociology. *Journal of Sociology,* 47(3), 279–295.

Qi, X. (2014). Filial Obligation in Contemporary China: Evolution of the Culture-System. *Journal for the Theory of Social Behaviour*, 45(1), 141–161.

Qi, X. (2017). Reconstructing the Concept of Face in Cultural Sociology: in Goffman's Footsteps, Following the Chinese Case. *The Journal of Chinese Sociology,* 4(1), 1–17.

Qian, Y. and Qian, Z. (2014). Work, Family, and Gendered Happiness Among Married People in Urban China. *Social Indicators Research*, 121(1), 61–74.

Qiao, X. (2019). Study on the Current Situation of the : Lives of Rural Left-behind Women and Countermeasures (nong cun liu shou fu nv sheng huo xian zhuang yu dui ce yan jiu). *Journal of Chongqing City Management Vocational College*, (4), 19–21.

Qiu, S. (2022). Family Practices in Non-cohabiting Intimate Relationships in China: Doing Mobile Intimacy, Emotion and Intergenerational Caring Practices. *Families, Relationships and Societies*, 11(2), 175–191.

Qu, X. (2018). Research on the Concept of Face Subcategory with Chinese Characteristics (zhong guo te se hua de mian zi ci fan chou gai nian de yan jiu). *Journal of Heilongjiang College of Education*, 37(9), 120–122.

Reinharz, S. and Chase, S. (2011). Interviewing Women. In Gubrium. J, and Holstein. J, (Eds.). *Handbook of Interview Research.* London: SAGE

Publications, pp.220–238.

Ren, Y. and Yan, M. (2017). Drifting apart: Increasingly Alienated Neighbourhoods in A Changing Village—An Observation of LSZ Village (jian xing jian yuan:xiang cun bian qian zhong ri yi mo sheng hua de lin li guan xi:yi xiang dui LSZ cun de diao cha). *THEORETICAL INVESTIGATION*, 194(1), 154–158.

Renmin. (2013). *Survey Report on the Current Situation of Family Education Guidance Services in China(wo guo jia ting jiao yu zhi dao fu wu xian zhuang diao cha bao gao).* [online] Renmin. Available at: <http://politics.people.com.cn/n/2013/0915/c1001-22926323.html> [Accessed 3 June 2022].

Rowley, J. (2012). Conducting Research Interviews. *Management Research Review*, 35(3/4), 260–271.

Sappleton, N. and Lourenço, F. (2015). Email Subject Lines and Response Rates to Invitations to Participate in a Web Survey and A Face-to-Face Interview: the Sound of Silence. *International Journal of Social Research Methodology*, 19(5), 611–622.

Schultze, U. and Avital, M. (2011). Designing Interviews to Generate Rich Data for Information Systems Research. *Information and Organization*, 21(1), 1–16.

Scott, James. (1976). *The Moral Economy of the Peasant: Rebellion and Subsistence in Southeast Asia.* New Haven and London: Yale University Press.

Shan, H., Liu, Z. and Li, L. (2015). Vocational Training for Liushou Women in

Rural China: development by design. *Journal of Vocational Education & Training,* 67(1), 11–25.

Shen, Y. (2016). Filial Daughters? Agency and Subjectivity of Rural Migrant Women in Shanghai. *The China Quarterly*, 226, 519–537.

Shen, Y. (2019). Post-patriarchal China: An Analysis of the Changing Power Relations and Gender Inequalities within Urban Families (hou fu quan zhi shi dai de zhong guo—cheng shi jia ting nei bu quan li guan xi bian qian yu she hui xing bie bu ping deng li cheng fen xi). [online] Available at: <https://www.chinathinktanks.org.cn/content/detail/id/n9c6qb65> [Accessed 16 October 2021].

Shi, L. (2009). Little Quilted Vests to Warm Parents' Hearts: Redefining the Gendered Practice of Filial Piety in Rural North-eastern China. *The China Quarterly*, 198, 348–363.

Shi, X. and Zheng, Y. (2020). Feminist Active Commitment and Sexual Harassment Perception among Chinese Women: The Moderating Roles of Targets' Gender Stereotypicality and Type of Harassment. *Sex Roles*, 84(7), 477–490.

Shu, X., Zhu, Y. and Zhang, Z. (2007). Global Economy and Gender Inequalities: The Case of the Urban Chinese Labor Market. *Social Science Quarterly*, 88(5), 1307–1332.

Shui, Y. *et al.* (2020). Work-family Balance and the Subjective Well-being of Rural Women in Sichuan, China. *BMC Women's Health*, 20(1).

Singh, P. and Pattanaik, F. ( 2020). Unfolding Unpaid Domestic Work in India: Women's Constraints, Choices, and Career. *Palgrave Communications*,

6(1), 1–13.

Song, Y., Zheng, J. and Qian, W. (2009). To Be, or Not to Be: Rural Women's Migration Decisions—A Case Study of the Yangtze River Delta. *The Chinese Economy,* 42(4), 63–74.

Spencer-Oatey, H. (2007). Theories of Identity and the Analysis of Face. *Journal of Pragmatics*, 39(4), 639–659.

Stake, R. (1978). The Case Study Method in Social Inquiry. *Educational Researcher*, 7(2), 5–8.

Su, H. and Wei, Q. (2020). Research on the Left-behind Women's Marital Well-Being from the Perspective of Life Course—Based on the Field Interview in Laiyuan County(sheng ming li cheng shi jiao xia nong cun liu shou fu nv hun yin xing fu gan yan jiu—ji yu Laiyuan xian de shi di fang tan). *Modern Business Trade Industry,*(7), 83–83.

Su, H. (2004). (eds.) *The View Of Social Gender from Multiple Perspectives (duo chong shi jiao xia de she hui xing bie guan)*. 1st ed. Shanghai: Shanghai University Press.

Sun, J. (2019). Study on Building Advanced Rural Gender Culture in the Context of Rural Revitalization—A Perspective on Safeguarding Women's Land Rights and Interests (nong cun zhen xing bei jing xia gou jian xian jin xiang cun xing bie wen hua yan jiu). *Theory Research*, (7), 80–81.

Sun, J.Y., Li, J. (2017). Women in Leadership in China: Past, Present, and Future. In: Cho, Y., Ghosh, R., Sun, J., McLean, G. (eds.) *Current Perspectives on Asian Women in Leadership.* Palgrave Macmillan,

Cham, 19–35.

Sun, L. (2012). Women, Public Space, and Mutual Aid in Rural China: A Case Study in H Village. Asian Women, 28 (3). 75–102.

Sun, M. (2020). 'Gender' Revolution and Two Forms of Gender Constructivism ('gender' ge ming yu xing bie jian gou lun de liang zhong xing tai). *Zhejiang Social Science*, 12, 88–94.

Sun, W. and Cheng, J. (2013). The Predicament of Chinese Rural Women's Liberation and Its Path Choice (zhong guo nong cun fu nv jie fang kun jing ji qi lu jing xuan ze). *Theory Research*, (34), 114–115.

Sung, S. (2003). Women Reconciling Paid and Unpaid Work in a Confucian Welfare State: The Case of South Korea. *Social Policy and Administration*, 37(4), 342–360.

Tang, W. and Yang, Q. (2008). The Chinese Urban Caste System in Transition. *The China Quarterly*, 196, 759–779.

Tao, T. and Li, D. (2015). Couples' Relative Occupational Position and Subjective Family Well-being (fu qi zhi ye xiang dui di wei yu jia ting xing fu gan guan xi yan jiu). *Population Research*, 39(3), 74–86.

Tessier, S. (2012). From Field Notes, to Transcripts, to Tape Recordings: Evolution or Combination. *International Journal of Qualitative Methods.* 11(4), 446–460.

Tian, X., Yu, X. and Klasen, S. (2018). Gender Discrimination in China Revisited: A Perspective from Family Welfare. *Journal of Chinese Economic and Business Studies*, 16(1), 95–115.

To, S., Lam, C. and So, Y. (2020). A Qualitative Study of Rural-To-Urban Migrant Chinese Mothers' Experiences in Mother-Child Interactions and Self-Evaluation. *Applied Research in Quality of Life*, 15(3), 813–833.

Tong, X. (2011) *Introduction to the Gender Studies,* 2nd, Peking University Press, 1–19.

Tong, Y., Shu, B. and Piotrowski, M. (2019). Migration, Livelihood Strategies, and Agricultural Outcomes: A Gender Study in Rural China. *Rural Sociology*, 84(3), 591–621.

Tsui, M. and Rich, L. (2002). 'The Only Child and Educational Opportunity for Girls in Urban China', *Gender & Society*, 16(1), 74–92.

Vantieghem, W., Vermeersch, H. and Van Houtte, M. (2014). Why 'Gender' Disappeared from the Gender Gap: (re-)introducing Gender Identity Theory to Educational Gender Gap Research. *Social Psychology of Education*, 17(3), 357–381.

Wan, J. and Wei, D. (2009). Gender Analysis of Rural Women's Family Status in the West of Fujian Province. *Journal of China Women's University*, 21(1), 76–80.

Wang, C. and Wu, H. (2020). Left-behind Women in Dilemma in the Perspective of Rural Victimization Strategy (xiang cun zhen xing shi ye xia de kun jing liu shou fu nv). *Journal of China Agricultural University (Social Sciences)*, 4(37), 93–100.

Wang, C. and Ye, J. (2020). New Characteristics and Outstanding Issues for Left-Behind Women in Rural China: From the Perspective of Rural

Vitalization (xiang cun zhen xing shi ye xia nong cun liu shou fu nv de xin te dian yu tu chu wen ti). *Journal of Chinese Women's Studies*, 157(1), 17–25; 55.

Wang, C., Sheng, Y., Li, C., Zhang, T. and Liu, Y. (2021). *Rural Women's Economic Empowerment Scan Research Report (nong cun fu nv jing ji fu neng sao miao yan jiu bao gao)*. Philanthropy and NGO Support Center, 1–11.

Wang, G. (2013). The Basic Theory of Urbanization and Problems and Countermeasures of China's Urbanization. *Population Research*, 37(6), 43–51.

Wang, H. (2015). *Ministry of Civil Affairs: China's Rural Hollowing Out Is Becoming More and More Significant. The Total Number of Left-behind People Exceeds 150 Million*. [online] People.cn. Available at: http://politics.people.com.cn/n/2015/0602/c70731-27093835.html [Accessed 20 Oct. 2018].

Wang, H., Ma, A. and Guo, T. (2020). Gender Concept, Work Pressure, and Work–Family Conflict. *American Journal of Men's Health*, 14(5), 155798832095752.

Wang, T. and Zeng, R. (2015). Addressing Inequalities in China's Health Service. *The Lancet*, 386(10002), 1441.

Wang, W. (2006). Citizens and Villagers: Double Structure of Identity Definition (gong min yu cun min: shen fen ding yi de shuang chong jie gou). In Zhang, J (Eds.) *Status Identity—Idea, Attitude, Justification (shen fen ren tong yan jiu)*. 1st ed. Shanghai: Shanghai People's Publishing House, pp.147–196.

Wang, W. (2013). Comparison of Urban and Rural Neighbourhoods and the Construction of A Harmonious Community in the New Countryside (cheng xiang lin li guan xi dui bi ji xin nong cun he xie she qu gou jian). *Journal of Henan Business College*, 26(2), 87–89.

Wang, X. (2012). Thoughts on Moral Standards in Social Investigation (dui she hui diao cha dao de gui fan de si kao). *Journal of Zhejiang University of Science and Technology*, 24(2), 126–131.

Wang, Y. (2009a). Face Competition in the Daily Lives of Peasants (nong min ri chang sheng huo zhong de mian zi jing zheng). *Journal of Zhoukou Normal University*, 26(6), 26–29.

Wang, Y. (2009b). Face As an Instrument of Control in Rural Society: Meaning, Characteristics, Operating Mechanism (zuo wei xiang cun she hui kong zhi shou duan de mian zi: han yi, te zheng, yun xing ji zhi). *Journal of Tianjin Administration Institute*, 11(4), 56–60.

Wang, Y. (2009c). Mechanisms for the Operation of the Face of Rural Society (xiang cun she hui mian zi de yun xing ji zhi). *Jiangxi Social Sciences*, 180–184.

Warren, T. (2011). Researching the Gender Division of Unpaid Domestic Work: Practices, Relationships, Negotiations, and Meanings. *The Sociological Review*, 59(1), 129–148.

Weng, T. and Li, H. (2019). Seized Power after Marriage?—the Gender Practice and Power Reconstruction of Rural Young Women (hun hou duo quan—nong cun qing nian nv xing de xing bie shi jian li cheng yu quan li chong jian). *Henan Social Science*, 27(10), 113–118.

Wheeler, S. C. and Petty, R. E. (2001). The Effects of Stereotype Activation on Behavior: A Review of Possible Mechanisms. *Psychological Bulletin,* 127(6), 797–826.

Wolfinger, N. (2002). On Writing Fieldnotes: Collection Strategies and Background Expectancies. *Qualitative Research*, 2(1), 85–93.

Wu, H. and Ye, J. (2016). Hollow Lives: Women Left-Behind in Rural China. *Journal of Agrarian Change*, 16(1), 50–69.

Wu, H. and Ye, J. (2010). Analysis of the Psychological Influence of Husband Out-migrating for Work on Rural Left-behind Women (zhang fu wai chu wu gong dui nong cun liu shou fu nv de xin li ying xiang fen xi). *Journal of Zhejiang University (Humanities and Social Sciences)*, 40(3), 138–147.

Wu, H. (2011). The Phenomenon of Left-behind Women and the Changing Gender Relations in Rural Society (liu shou fu nv xian xiang yu nong cun she hui xing bie guan xi de bian qian). *China Agricultural University Journal of Social Sciences Edition*, 28(3), 104–111.

Wu, H. (2017). The Impact of Social Support on the Willingness of Elderly People in Urban and Rural Areas to Be Aadmitted to Nursing Homes—Findings Based on Survey Data from Seven Provinces and Districts (she hui zhi chi dui cheng xiang lao nian ren ru zhu yang lao yuan yi yuan de ying xiang). *Journal of Hangzhou Dianzi University(Social Sciences)*, 3, 16–21.

Wu, L., Chen, X. and Gu, L. (2013). Land Protection and Food Security in the Accelerated Urbanization Progress of China. *Issues in Agricultural Economy,* (1), 57–62.

Wu, Q., Tsang, B. and Ming, H. (2014). Social Capital, Family Support, Resilience and Educational Outcomes of Chinese Migrant Children. *British Journal of Social Work*, 44(3), 636–656.

Wu, X. (2019a). Inequality and Social Stratification in Post Socialist China. *Annual Review of Sociology*, 45(1), 363–382.

Wu, Y. (2019b). Becoming New Urbanites: Residents' Self-identification and Sense of Community in 'Village-turned-community'. *The Journal of Chinese Sociology*, 6(1), 1–19.

Wu, Z., Yang, Z. and Wang, M. (1980). Experimenting with the Reproduction of Our Population (shi lun wo guo ren kou zai sheng chan). *Population Research*, (01), 25–31.

Xie, G., Zhang, Y. and Li, X. (2017). Women and Family in Transitional China: Family Structure and Elderly Support. *Kazoku syakaigaku kenkyu*, 29(2), 165–179.

Xie, X., Xia, Y. & Zhou, Z. (2004). Strengths and Stress in Chinese Immigrant Families: A Qualitative Study. *Great Plains Research*, *14*, 203–218.

Xie, Z. and Peng, Y. (2008). Study on the Improvement of the Status of Rural Women from the Right of Discourse (cong hua yu quan shi yu yan jiu dang qian nong cun fu nv di wei de ti gao). *The South of China Today*, (100), 224–225.

Xinhua News. (2019). *Anxiety! Anxiety! The Countryside Here Is Not Silent (xin bing! xin bing!zhe li de nong cun bing fei jing qiao qiao)*. [online] Available at: <http://www.xinhuanet.com/politics/2019-02/11/c_1124097331.htm> [Accessed 17 June 2022].

Xinhua Website. (2006). *Xinhua Survey: Who Cares for Rural 'Left-behind Women' (xin hua diao cha: shei lai guan xin nong cun liu shou fu nv).* [online] Available at: <http://news.sohu.com/20061107/n246236556.shtml> [Accessed 8 April 2022].

Xinhua. (2021). *Decision of the State Council of the Central Committee of the Communist Party of China on Optimising Fertility Policy for Long-term Balanced Population Development (zhong gong zhong yang guan yu you hua sheng yu zheng ce cu jin ren kou chang qi jun heng fa zhan de jue ding).* [online] gov.cn. Available at: <http://www.gov.cn/zhengce/2021-07/20/content_5626190.htm> [Accessed 13 July 2022].

Xiong, X., Cheng, Y. and Hu, Y. (2020). Research on the Influencing Factors of the Chinese Elderly's Preference of Patrilineal Inheritance (zhong guo lao nian ren nan xing dan xi ji cheng pian hao de ying xiang yin su yan jiu). *POPULATION ANF DEVELOPMENT*, 26(1), 2–11.

Xu, A., Xie, X., Liu, W., Xia, Y. and Liu, D. (2007). Chinese Family Strengths and Resiliency. *Marriage & Family Review*, 41(1–2), 143–164.

Xu, C. (2010). Study on the Marital Stability of Left-behind Women in Western Rural Areas and Its Influencing Factors (xi bu nong cun liu shou fu nv hun yin wen ding xing ji qi ying xiang yin su fen xi). *Journal of China Agricultural University (Social Sciences Edition)*, 27(1), 97–106.

Xu, C. (2020). Tackling Rural-urban Inequalities Through Educational Mobilities: Rural-origin Chinese Academics from Impoverished Backgrounds Navigating Higher Education. *Policy Reviews in Higher Education*, 4(2), 179–202.

Xu, L. (2016). Cultural Differences Between Chinese and Western 'face' and Cross-cultural Communication (zhong xi fang "mian zi"wen hua cha yi yu kua wen hua jiao ji tan xi). *Journal of Hubei University of Economics (Humanities and Social Sciences)*, 13(1), 138–139.

Xu, R. (2012). On the Employment Discrimination of Women in China from the Perspective of Urbanization (cheng shi hua shi jiao xia wo guo nv xing jiu ye qi shi wen ti tan jiu). *Fujian Tribune*, (S1) 199–120.

Xu, Z., Shen, J., Gao, X. and Zhen, M. (2022). Migration and Household Arrangements of Rural Families in China: Evidence from A Survey in Anhui Province. *Habitat International*, 119, 102475.

Yan, B., Lin, Z., Deng, S. and Zhang, Y. (2014). A Study on the Relationship of Work-Family Facilitation and Subjective Well-being Among Professional Women: An Analysis Based on the Sample of China (gong zuo—jia ting cu jin dui zhi ye nv xing zhu guan xing fu gan de ying xiang—ji yu zhong guo yang ben de fen xi). *JOURNAL OF SOUTH CHINA NORMAL UNIVERSITY (NATURAL SCIENCE EDITION)*, 46(6), 121–127.

Yan, J. (2002). Interviews in the Internet Age Still Need to Be Face-to-face (wang luo shi dai cai fang reng xu mian dui mian). *Military Reporter*, (5).

Yan, Y. (2003). *Private life under socialism*. Stanford: Stanford University Press.

Yang, C. and Yang, M. (2018). A Study of the Changes in Rural Social Relations in the Process of Urbanization—An Example of Marriage Changes in H Village (cheng zhen hua jin cheng zhong nong cun she hui guan xi bian qian yan jiu—ji yu dui wu wei ying shang yi H cun hun jia bian qian wei li). *Modern Communication*, 6, 84–85.

Yang, D., Yang, M. and Huang. (2018). *Education Blue Book: China Education Development Report (2018)*. 1st ed. Beijing: Social Sciences Academic Press (CHINA).

Yang, F. (2016). The Influence of Modernisation of Family Relationships on Women's Preference for Sons. *Collection of Women's Studies*, 135(3), 101–108.

Yang, J. (2012). A Study On Building of the Harmonious Society in China's Rural Area During the Process of Urbanization. [Online]. University of Electronic Science and Technology of China. Available at: http://kns.cnki.net/KCMS/detail/detail.aspx?dbcode=CDFD&dbname=CDFD1214&filename=1013149639.nh&uid=WEEvREcwSlJHSldRa1FhcEE0RVZyS3ora1NOVXZoZ2RveGlYMXVrUXdGVT0=$9A4hF_YAuvQ5obgVAqNKPCYcEjKensW4ggI8Fm4gTkoUKaID8j8gFw!!&v=MjU0OTlOVkYyNkhiSzhGOWZQcHBFYlBJUjhlWDFMdXhZUzdEaDFUM3FUcldNMUZyQ1VSTEtmWStSc0Z5bm5XNnzM= [accessed 18 October 2021].

Yang, J. (2018). New Issues Facing Families in the New Era and Future Research Directions (xin shi dai jia ting mian lin de xin wen ti ji wei lai yan jiu fang xiang). *Journal of Chinese Women Studies*, (06), 9–12.

Ye, J. (2017). Stayers in China's 'Hollowed-out' Villages: A Counter Narrative on Massive Rural–urban Migration. *Population, Space and Place*, 24(e2128), 1–10.

Ye, J. and Wu, H. (2008). *Dancing Solo: Women Left-Behind in Rural China (qian mo du wu: zhong guo nong cun liu shou fu nv)*. Beijing: Social Sciences Academic Press, 1–20.

Ye, J. and Wu, H. (2009). The Influence of the Husband's Migrant Work on the Marriage Relationship of Left-behind Women (zhang fu wai chu wu gong dui liu shou fu nv hun yin guan xi de ying xiang). *Academic Journal of Zhongzhou*, 171(3), 130–134.

Ye, J., Pan, L. and He, C. (2014). *Double Coercion: Gender Exclusion and Inequality in Rural Left-behind Population* (*shuang chong qiang zhi:xiang cun liu shou zhong de xing bie pai chi yu bu ping deng*). Beijing: Social Sciences Academic Press, pp.35–40.

Ye, J., Wu, H., Rao, J., Ding, B. and Zhang, K. (2016). Left-behind women: Gender Exclusion and Inequality in Rural-urban Migration in China. *The Journal of Peasant Studies,* 43(4), 910–941.

Yi, Z., George, L., Sereny, M., Gu, D. and Vaupel, J. (2016). Older Parents Enjoy Better Filial Piety and Care From Daughters Than Sons in China. *American Journal of Medical Research*, 3(1),244–272.

Yin, H., Wu, Y., Wang, S., Wang, Y. and Wang, H. (2018). The Effects of Child Gender on Women's Family Decision-making Power in Poverty-stricken Rural Areas (mu ping zi gui:zi nv xing bie dui pin kun di qu nong cun fu nv jia ting jue ce quan de ying xiang). *Chinese Rural Economy*, (1), 1–16.

York.ac.uk. (2004). *ESRC Research Ethics Framework Working paper—for discussion only*. [online] Available at: <https://www.york.ac.uk/res/ref/docs/REFpaper3_v2.pdf> [Accessed 28 August 2022].

Yu, J. (2014). Gender Ideology, Modernization, and Women's Housework Time in China. *Chinese Journal of Sociology*, 34(2), 166–192.

Yu, S. and Chau, R. (1997). The Sexual Division of Care in Mainland China and Hong Kong. *International Journal of Urban and Regional Research,* 21(4), 607–619.

Yu, X. (2014). Is Environment 'A City Thing' in China? Rural–urban Differences in Environmental Attitudes. *Journal of Environmental Psychology*, 38(6), 39–48.

Yuan, F. and Shi, Q. (2019). From Returning Home to Starting a Business: An Empirical Analysis of Impacts of the Internet Access on the Decision of Migrant Workers (cong fan xiang dao chuang ye—hu lian wang jie ru dui nong min gong jue ce ying xiang de shi zheng fen xi). *South China Journal of Economics*, 38(10), 61–77.

Yuan, S. (2009). Culture of consumerism, Face Competition and the Decline of Filial Norm in Contemporary Rural China(xiao fei wen hua\mian zi jing zheng yu nong cun de xiao dao shuai luo). *Northwest Population Journal*, 30(4), 38–42.

Zhai, X. (2004). The Reproduction of Favours, Face and Power-social Exchange in an Affective Society (ren qing, mian zi yu quan li de zai sheng chan—qing li she hui zhong de she hui jiao huan fang shi ). *Sociological Study*, (5), 48–57.

Zhan, H. and Montgomery, R. (2003). Gender And Elder Care In China: The Influence of Filial Piety and Structural Constraints. *Gender & Society*, 17(2), 209–229.

Zhang and Wildemuth (2017). Unstructured interviews. In Wildemuth, B. (Eds.) Applications of Social Research Methods to Questions in Information and Library Science. 2nd. *California: Libraries Unlimited*, pp.239–247.

Zhang, B. and He, P. (2015). An Empirical Study on the Impact of Urbanization on Rural Residents' Consumption (cheng shi hua dui nong cun ju min xiao fei ying xiang de shi zheng yan jiu). *Rural Economy and Science-Technology*, 357(01), 98–99,192.

Zhang, G.S.(2007). A Study on the Urban Integration Mechanism for the Citizenship of Migrant Workers (nong min gong shi min hua de cheng shi rong ru ji zhi yan jiu). *Journal of Jiangxi University of Finance and Economics*, 50(2), 42–46.

Zhang, G., Wang, R. and Cheng, M. (2020). Peer-to-peer Accommodation Experience: A Chinese Cultural Perspective. *Tourism Management Perspectives*, 33, 100621.

Zhang, H. and Tsang, S. (2012). Relative Income and Marital Happiness Among Urban Chinese Women: The Moderating Role of Personal Commitment. *Journal of Happiness Studies*, 14(5), 575–1584.

Zhang, J. (2017). The Evolution of China's One-Child Policy and Its Effects on Family Outcomes. *Journal of Economic Perspectives*, 31(1), 141–160.

Zhang, J. and Zhang, Q. (2006). Survey on Abnormal survival among 50000 Thousand 'rural female stayers' (5000 wan 'liu shou cun fu' fei zheng chang sheng cun diao cha). *China Economy Weekly*, 373(40), 14–19.

Zhang, J., (2008). On Intergenerational Conflict and Communication in the Family (lun jia ting zhong de dai ji chong tu yu gou tong). *KAOSHI ZHOUKAN*, (16), 239–240.

Zhang, L., Zhang, Y. and Zhang, H. (2018). Investigation on Sleep Quality of Rural Left-behind Women and Study on the Correlations Between Sleep Quality and Depression, Social Support in Shaanxi (shan xi sheng nong cun liu shou fu nv shui mian zhi liang de diao cha yi ji shui mian zhi liang he yi yu, she hui zhi chi de xiang guan xing yan jiu). *Maternal and Child Health Care of China*, 33(6), 1374–1376.

Zhang, N. (2013). Rural Women Migrant Returnees in Contemporary China. *Journal of Peasant Studies*, 40(1), 171–188.

Zhang, N. (2014). Performing Identities: Women in Rural-urban Migration in Contemporary China. *Geoforum*, 54(4), 17–27.

Zhang, Q. and Chen, H. (2018). Human Exchange and Rural Civilization in Rural Areas Under the Ideology of Face (mian zi si xiang xia de nong cun ren qing jiao huan yu xiang feng wen ming jian she). *Modern Business*, 160–161.

Zhang, Q. and Pan, Z. (2012). Women's Entry into Self-employment in Urban China: The Role of Family in Creating Gendered Mobility Patterns. *World Development*, 40(6), 1201–1212.

Zhang, W. (2020). A Study of Gender Perception Differences in Megacities (te da cheng shi zhong xing bie guan nian cha yi yan jiu). *Social Science Journal*, 250(5), 126–135.

Zhang, Y. (2011). Labor Supply Pattern and Family Welfare Effect of Left-Behind Women in Rural China (zhong guo nong cun liu shou fu nv de lao dong gong ji mo shi ji qi jia ting fu li xiao ying. *Rural Economic Problems*, (5), 39–47.

Zhang, Y., Hannum, E. and Wang, M. (2008). Gender-Based Employment and Income Differences in Urban China: Considering the Contributions of Marriage and Parenthood. *Social Forces*, 86(4), 1529–1560.

Zheng, C. (2019). On face perception and basic-level consultative democracy in rural society. *Journal of Jiangsu University of Science and Technology (Social Science Edition )*, 19(4), 58–65.

Zhou, L. and Zhang, S. (2017). How Face As a System of Value-constructs Operates Through the Interplay of *Mianzi* and Lian in Chinese: A Corpus Based Study. *Language Sciences*, 64, 152–166.

Zhou, X. (2016). Practical Kinship: Anthropological Study on Niangjia (Natal Family) and Pojia (Married-in Family) (Continued) (shi jian de qin shu guan xi—guan yu "niang jia" yu "po jia" de ren lei xue yan jiu xia). *N.W. Journal of Ethnology*, 88(1), 104–117.

Zhou, Y. (1998). A Critique and Preliminary Exploration of the Conceptual and Theoretical Values of Patriarchy In Jin, Y and Liu, B (eds.) *Women and Development in China at the Turn of the Century.* Nanjing University Press.

Zhu, G., Wu, J. and Zhao, G. (2007). Analysis and Reflection on the Basic Situation of Returning Migrant Workers in Anhui Province—Based on Interviews with 66 Returning Migrant Workers in Wuwei, Yingshang and Other Places (Anhui fan xiang nong min gong ji ben qing kuang diao cha fen xi yu si kao—ji yu dui wu wei, ying shang deng di 66 wei fan xiang nong min gong de fang tan). *East China Economic Management*, (8), 25–28.

Zhu, K. and Wu, L. (2007). A Literature Review on the Urban Integration of

Migrant Workers (nong min gong cheng shi rong ru wen ti wen xian zong shu). *Journal of Eastern Liaodong University*, 9(3), 29–32.

Zuo, J. and Bian, Y. (2001). Gendered Resources, Division of Housework, and Perceived Fairness—A Case in Urban China. *Journal of Marriage and Family*, 63(4), 1122–1133.